On the Fly

On the Fly

A Hockey Fan's View from the 'Peg

by Wayne Tefs

TURNSTONE PRESS

On the Fly:
A Hockey Fan's View from the 'Peg
copyright © Wayne Tefs 2012

Turnstone Press
Artspace Building
206-100 Arthur Street
Winnipeg, MB
R3B 1H3 Canada
www.TurnstonePress.com

Turnstone Press gratefully acknowledges the assistance of the Canada Council for the Arts, the Manitoba Arts Council, the Government of Canada through the Canada Book Fund, and the Province of Manitoba through the Book Publishing Tax Credit and the Book Publisher Marketing Assistance Program.

Acknowledgements photo on page 287 from Wayne Tefs' private collection.

Printed and bound in Canada by Friesens for Turnstone Press.

Library and Archives Canada Cataloguing in Publication

Tefs, Wayne, 1947–

On the fly : a hockey fan's view from the 'Peg / Wayne Tefs.

ISBN 978-0-88801-402-3

1. Winnipeg Jets (Hockey team). 2. Hockey—Manitoba—Winnipeg—History. 3. Tefs, Wayne, 1947–. 4. Hockey fans—Manitoba—Winnipeg—Biography. I. Title.

GV848.W56T43 2012   796.962'6409712743   C2012-904933-6

for Kristen and Andrew

A novelist is someone who remembers nothing yet records and manipulates different versions of what he doesn't remember.

—Julian Barnes

ON THE FLY

SNAPSHOT: Teemu Selanne

April 1993: the NHL Jets are stumbling to the finish of the season, just into the playoffs, a not unfamiliar position. Despite the mediocre season, the Winnipeg arena is crowded for the contest between the Jets and Quebec Nordiques, the air thick with anticipation. Whenever number 13 is on the ice, quivers of excitement run through the crowd, conversations cease, all eyes are riveted on jersey number 13, Teemu Selanne. Toward the middle of the third period a pass flashes up from inside the Jets end and Selanne cuts through centre; gathering it up in one twist of the wrists, he slides the puck through the Quebec defenceman's feet, then flicks it past the stick of the goaltender, outstretched as he lunges forward to intercept it, his only chance to prevent a goal. The puck flutters, and then bounces into the open net.

Bedlam. Fans leap to their feet, Selanne himself makes a quick pivot in the corner of the rink and comes back out, throwing one glove into the air and imitating with his upraised stick the pumping and shooting action of a shotgun, as the glove drops to the ice. He's just scored his seventy-sixth goal as a rookie, surpassing the record set by the great Mike Bossy. It's an amazing feat. For most players, fifty goals is beyond imagining, for a rookie to beat that by twenty-six puts him among the greats of the game. An icon.

Our Jet. The Finnish Flash.

Everyone in the arena is standing and clapping and shouting and whistling. The noise does not die out when the announcement is made.

If anything it grows louder. Girls are weeping, fans are bouncing up and down, the cry of "Teemu, Teemu," reverberates around the arena, Selanne's teammates are on the ice with him, there are tears in the eyes of the older man standing beside me. My heart rate must be 150. It's going to explode out of my chest from joy.

SNAPSHOT: BABY BULLIES

Spring 1977. It's the era of Hedberg, Nilsson, and Hull, the unstoppable WHA threesome, Hull with the power of a bull, Nilsson slick as oil, Hedberg who can dash from one end of the rink with the puck and score in eight seconds. I've timed him. The play has come to a halt. A forward from the Birmingham Bulls, Boileau, call him, a beefy Bluto-like thug with a bushy black mustache, mediocre talent, and the temperament of a psychotic, has one of the young, European Jets down on the ice, punching him in the head. Within seconds all the players on the ice have paired off, throwing punches, and within only a few seconds more both benches have cleared, players tearing at opponents' sweaters and locked in tussles, faces grim with fury. Gloves litter the ice, sticks, at least half the players are down to their equipment, elbow and shoulder pads on view.

If you look closely you can see blood running out of noses, blood smeared on the ice, red and blotchy faces where punches have been taken, where black eyes will develop. Everyone in the arena is on their feet, screaming, booing, screeching at the refs and the Birmingham players. My voice is part of the chorus of boos. The man beside me, my friend Garin, a mild-mannered professor of history, is screaming, "Kill Boileau, kill Boileau!" His face is flame red, his teeth are bared like a dog's. He's throwing one arm up rhythmically, punching the air and screaming, "Kill Boileau!" I feel my cheeks are red, too, my heart rate must be 150, it feels like it's going to explode in my chest from horror.

My friend Garin will tell me a week later that he will no longer attend hockey games. He is appalled by what he saw in himself that night—and disappointed in himself. He tells me he now understands what it must have felt like to be in those mobs in Germany during the thirties, roaring at every sentence shouted by *der Führer*, pumping arms in the air and screaming "*Sieg Heil!*"

I understand what he's getting at. He was out of control that night.

I'm a season ticket holder. I renew. Something draws me back, despite the horror of the incident. It's not the violence of the donnybrook in 1977, though some armchair psychologists will want to claim that; it's the feeling of being utterly in the moment, being so completely absorbed by the events unfolding in front of you that you are no longer part of the mundane world of career, family, the clock controlling your every moment, your every thought, your every action, that's what draws us back. Intensity. We seek intensity. And when we find it, we return to it. It's a drug: your being so utterly in the moment that *you*, your ordinary workaday self ceases to exist.

Whether it's the Thrill or the Horror, being in the stands spells heightened emotion, emotions that, despite their seeming contradiction, have more in common with each other than with everyday excitement or disappointment, the pulse of physiological and psychic electricity that pounds the message: This is Life!

For me that intensity has always been associated with the game of hockey. I grew up playing on organized teams, but more important, playing shinny on outdoor rinks every hour of every day that it was possible to get out onto the ice. We wore mitts and we wore hockey socks on our heads to fend off the cold, the thigh-end fit perfectly over our skulls, the foot end trailed behind with a certain majesty when we sped down the ice. We scraped snow off the ice—the rink attendant was a neighbour, he left the shovels out so we could scrape the ice in the early hours before he arrived to flood the surface. We played and we played and we played. If we weren't skating we stood three or four feet away from the boards and practised slapshots. From time to time the puck would go over the boards, you had to leap over and scuffle about in the thigh-deep snow to find it. Sometimes it was gone. But maybe not for good. In the spring when the snow was melting, we went puck-hunting, building up a cache for the next hockey season.

It starts, then, with a boy who learned to skate by pushing a painted wooden chair up and down the icy driveway and then graduated to inching along the length of the local rink with one hand gripping the boards for balance. That lasted little more than an hour. Then came the freedom of skating. Then came the game.

SNAPSHOT: THE GAME

The game is always with me.

I wake in the night and see Dale Hawerchuk moving across the other team's blue line, sliding down the zone toward the faceoff dot and then shifting the puck through a defenceman's feet and coming out behind him, laying a perfect pancake pass to Paul MacLean, who snaps it into the net. Hawerchuk. As nifty a stickhandler as any who has ever played the game, equal to Gretzky, who he resembles in a number of ways. Not a great skater, slow, a little awkward, seeming off-balance some of the time, hence his nickname, "Ducky." I submit that in the hundreds of games I saw Hawerchuk play he always did at least one thing with the puck I'd never seen done before, or made at least one move worth the price of admission.

The game is always there. A dream, a memory, a trancelike moment that breaks in on my everyday life.

An old clip of a game between the Oilers and the Jets is shown on a highlight package and Don Wittman's voice takes me back to Morris Lukowich speeding down the wing and hammering a shot at goal. From the stands comes the cry *Ran-ford, Ran-ford, Ran-ford,* a derisive, rhythmic jeer, a hex that's supposed to throw the Oilers goaltender off his concentration. It rarely worked.

The game is always there, it comes back like a song you knew the words to that you hear on the weather channel and can't shake for two days. "Hotel California." An empty popcorn box, thrown from the higher seats sails past my head and tumbles into the bench of the Vancouver Canucks, just missing the head of Harry Neale, the Canucks coach. He turns and looks over his shoulder at us. I smile and wave and shrug my shoulders. Harry's a good guy, he recognizes us, we've engaged in some banter over the years. He smiles, he wags his finger at us.

I dream. I'm on the ice with the Manitoba Bisons, I'm a professor at the University of Manitoba but somehow I've qualified for the team. I have amazing skills, my skates don't touch the ice, I can swoop down the rink effortlessly and with dazzling speed, I stickhandle like Henri Richard and shoot like Bobby Hull. I score, once, twice, I'm a god. There's a voice-over explaining that, yes, I'm not a student technically but I still qualify to play, I'm part of the U of M, words that seem to be coming from inside my head and over a loudspeaker, both at the same time.

The game shimmers like a mirage on tarmac on a blistering hot prairie day, an evanescence, elusive, haunting as the girl you went skating with on a crisp December evening in 1964, you were in grade eleven and she was in grade ten and as you circled the rink you held mittened hands and kissed at her back door. What was her name? Deanna?

I wake from the dream and get up and make coffee and sit outside with a chunk of baguette alongside Kristen, and the feelings I had scoring the goal in the dream are alive inside me, they're as real as the throbbing blister on my toe, as real as the devotion I feel for my wife, the affection I feel for my son, Andrew. Alive, they tingle through me. It's late November but I'm sitting outside on a plastic chair with a book on my lap in Tucson where I spend chunks of time every winter; the sun is warm on my face, my body is in Arizona but my mind is on a sheet of ice in Winnipeg.

I'm at Dutton Arena on Sunday morning, breaking across centre ice, saying to myself *chop chop chop*, these five strides at speed will take me into the opposition end. I will pay for the effort later. I cross the blue line. Luds is carrying the puck, he glances at me on the right wing but then visibly moves the line of his vision to the left, where Brady hugs the boards; Luds looks as if it's Brady he intends to pass to. For a second my insides sag, but I say, Keep going, stick on the ice. At the last second Luds slides the puck between the defender's outstretched stick and skates, right onto my stick, I hack at it crazily, I'm an old fart, there's no finesse in my hands any longer, with these guys, men twenty and more years my junior, I score twice, maybe five times a season. The puck goes in, high over the goaltender's stick, under the bar. Jesus.

Is there any better feeling?

The game is always with me. A visual earworm that runs over and over in my brain, Guy Lafleur dashing down the ice, his hair streaming off his neck, a stick I took in the mouth in Ste. Agathe, blood pouring down my

Silver Bullets jersey, leaning on the boards with Al W during a break in a junior practice.

I do not bid these images to haunt my dreams, I do not call them up from the "vasty deep," as Shakespeare puts it, they are simply there, they have a life of their own, they arise, are with me, an electric current that runs along my nerves for three or five minutes. The dark-haired girl in college that I dated once and who kissed me long and hard before she got out of the car. Nancy? I lie looking at the bedroom ceiling, savouring the goal, or sit in the desert sun seeing Hawerchuk kick the puck back between his feet as if he's lost control of it, enticing the defenceman to lunge for it, and at that precise second he kicks it back up onto his stick and sidesteps so slickly it makes fifteen thousand spectators gasp.

Kristen breaks in on my reverie. "What were you thinking about?"

How do you say to your wife of twenty years that you were thinking about a girl you kissed forty years ago? Goals you scored in a dream? "I was wondering," I say, "how Andrew's making out with all that snow that fell at home last week."

I wasn't thinking of Andrew and the snow, but then I wasn't thinking at all in the way usually meant by that, as you might be if you said: *I was thinking of the best way to invest the funds that came out of Mom's estate.* The exercise of conscious faculties on an issue or problem. I was in reverie, a trancelike state I fall into perhaps more often than is good for me. When I was a boy my father once told me somewhat frowningly, "You're a dreamer." Someone else once said to me, "Too much imagination is a bad thing." Well, the hell with them.

I'm not obsessive about hockey. But then again that's what an obsessive is likely to say, isn't it? I am obsessive about riding my road bike, going out several hundred days a year and trying to average more than fifty kilometres per ride at an average velocity of twenty-five kilometres per hour. So I know what it means to be obsessed. I've been down the road of obsession with the bike. But then a little voice asks, Is this blather about cycling a justification for the hockey thing?

You tell me.

SNAPSHOT: Deep Past

A spring afternoon in 1959, the indoor arena in Fort William, Ontario. My Pee Wee team, just called "Atikokan," is contesting the championship. It's late in the game, the score tied, when a pass comes out of our end to my stick on the left wing. I'm a big kid for my age, I did not learn to skate until I was eleven, but I power down the ice, past the opposition. Some few feet above the faceoff dot in the other team's end I take a shot, a wrist shot. I do not know if it took off like a beam, a dart of a projectile, or if it wobbled as it made its way toward the goalie, or if it went up and then dropped. I might have had my head down, I probably had my head down. What I do know is that this shot, fired with all my pre-puberty power, went into the net. A red light went on above the goal and behind the screen netting.

Elation. Teammates rushing over to slap me on the shoulders, smack my butt with their sticks. I glance into the crowd. My parents are there, my father smoking his pipe, my mother daring a wave. Did they ever once miss a game? Other mothers and fathers, their friends, and parents of my teammates, Rolland C, Johnny Z, are cheering and waving. Can there be anything better than this?

The game is not over. There are shifts left to play. One more and then one more after that. We hold off our opponents through the next few minutes. We win the Northwestern Ontario Pee Wee Championship.

I've netted the winning goal.

Hockey, I have discovered, is not just a game; hockey is truth, hockey is life, the measure of what makes a man: its give and take between you and others, its demand that you always give your best. The puck wants to slip off your stick at the critical moment in front of the goal, it says to you, *Come on then, show us what you're made of;* you must control it behind your goal, in front of the other team's net. It says to you, *Are you a man, then, can you prevail over these others with your strength and willpower?* Hockey is a test of character, the books say, a test that has pushed me right to the edge, a test I have passed.

On the drive back to Atikokan, my father says, "It was a good game, you played well," hiding in that second-person plural whatever pride and delight he feels that his boy, on this day at least, has been a little bit of a hero.

Who were we playing? I cannot recall, this is reverie, this is remembrance that slides over you like fog when you're lying in bed at four in the morning, staring at the ceiling, this is velvet reminiscence as you sit on the porch nursing a glass of port on a late August evening, warm prairie air drifting around in smoky whorls like recollected moments themselves. Glorious.

It starts with a boy who skates every day in winter, hour after hour, no matter the cold, no matter the wind. It starts with a boy on a team who cannot get enough of the ice, who swaps bubble-gum cards of hockey heroes with his pals, who watches the Leafs and the Habs on a snowy black-and-white TV every Saturday night with his father. It starts with a passion for a game before he even knows what *passion* means.

SNAPSHOT: Our Jets

For many Winnipeggers, that passion and energy found a focus in the city's pro hockey team, the Jets, who arrived in Winnipeg to much fanfare in 1972: the organization's frontman and titular owner, Ben Hatskin, presenting the legendary Bobby Hull with a cheque for one million dollars at the corner of Portage and Main—an unheard-of signing bonus for a pro athlete in 1970s. Hull's signing set in motion an era of unprecedented hockey enthusiasm in the city: the Jets became the cornerstone franchise of the WHA, the rival pro league to the NHL during its seven-year existence. The Jets were not just the cornerstone franchise of the new league, they were its most successful team, its "poster-boy": the team had flare on the ice that matched the best the NHL had to offer; and stars equivalent to those of the older circuit.

Winnipeggers were in hockey heaven. Hull, Hedberg, and Nilsson, the so-called "Hot Line," dazzled us with their skill and finesse. In the early years this team was as worthy of hockey enthusiasts' notice as the magnetic Habs of the NHL. Winnipeggers were enchanted and delighted. The city had a team worthy of its great hockey history and an outfit that could stand alongside the best in the world. The Jets contended for the league's premier prize annually—the AVCO Cup—and won it more often than any other team. We were enthralled by the players; and agog at the team's success; and delirious about its future.

We bought season tickets; we cheered until our throats ached; we purchased jerseys with our favourite players' names on the back; we wore white shirts to playoff games, initiating a trend that continues in pro hockey to the present day. We were, in short, fanatics, fans; if we were students of the ancient tongues, we knew the word derived from *fanaticus* (*fanatici*), Latin for *devotee*. Attending and cheering on the Jets assumed a religious dimension—they were our team, we cared about them in a way the community has never cared about anything before or since. (With the possible exception of kielbasa, rye bread, and Bothwell cheese at wedding socials.)

But through the '70s the WHA was a floundering organization. Not enough of its teams had sound financial backing; not enough of its franchises were supported by the cadre of fans required to keep a multimillion-dollar operation in black ink. In 1979 the league folded and four teams were absorbed into the NHL (Hartford, Edmonton, Quebec, and Winnipeg), but only after agreeing to give up to NHL teams all but three of the players on their current rosters. Their squads of twenty-some were much more than literally "decimated."

They struggled on in the NHL, despite their rosters of second-rate players. But the big brothers in established NHL cities—many of whom still smarted from wounded pride over the WHA's impudent challenge to their lucrative monopoly in the pro game—saw to it that financial arrangements and related fiduciary matters in the old league undermined the former WHA upstarts: to the degree that first Quebec City and then Winnipeg ceased operations in the '90s—and their teams were "re-franchised" to Denver and Phoenix, respectively. The Jets were moved out of Winnipeg in 1996—and with them went the hearts of their fans—and a piece of the city's soul.

Some cried bitter tears; some swore to never watch another NHL game; some accepted the loss with despairing resignation; some pursued other entertainments—the opera, the symphony, the theatre; some simply moped. All were devastated. An era of the city's history, an era of Winnipride had come to an end.

And for fifteen years things remained that way. There were rumours of a team returning to Winnipeg, of the city returning to the big league. But we were wounded cats—guarded, wary. We were not getting excited about the NHL. Winnipeggers had been down that road. We were not taking an emotional plunge until it was clear just what kind of water awaited us. Our roots are in the prairie and we take our lead from laconic farmers who gaze out on promising spring crops with a *wait-and-see* bearing.

That doesn't mean the city didn't go half mad when the announce-ment came that, indeed, a new franchise was coming to Winnipeg. It did. Within days—hours—of the official revelation, the city was a-buzz with enthusiasm. Fifteen years had elapsed since the Jets were "transitioned" out of the city. Jets jerseys that had been mouldering in closets suddenly came out of closets, and with them the passions of the team's thousands of devotees. Hurrah! Back in the bigs! Call-in shows couldn't keep up to the thirst for information, discussion, and debate. The city had a focus for its sport energies. Long-dormant civic pride blossomed overnight; a communal obsession had been re-ignited, and with it came an enliv-ened sense of community: Go Jets, Yay Winnipeg! Books appeared in bookstores. TV camera crews were sent to work on documentaries about the return of the Jets. Thousands rushed out—stood in line—to purchase season tickets. Eight thousand more fans than could be accommodated put their names down on a waiting list.

It wasn't just the return of a team to a city; it was an hysterical love affair.

And in sober moments it made many of us think: what the hell is going on?

With my wife, Kristen, and my son, Andrew, I numbered myself among that lot. And being a writer, I've attempted to answer that ques-tion. What is behind our city's passion for our team, what motivates com-munal obsession, what energies are stirred in the breasts of ordinary folks that makes them follow with devotion and zeal the exploits and antics of twenty-some young men on a sheet of ice, that turns them (us) into compulsives screaming Go Jets Go!, into enraptured fans that cannot get enough of an—after all, in the sober business of life—unimportant sports team?

It's the final pre-season match leading up to the regular season.

The game is scheduled to begin at 7:30, but the crowd is beginning to gather in the concourse before 7:00, guys in retro Jets jerseys, their girlfriends studying their phones or giggling together near the hot dog kiosks. They're excited, wanting to get into the arena proper to see the pre-game warm-up, check out the team as it goes through skating and shooting drills. There's a lot you can learn taking in these drills—who's on the limp, who's going well. Or just watching your favourite players: gritty Captain Andrew Ladd, smooth defenceman Tobias Enström, big winger Blake Wheeler.

SEC: XX ROW: XX SEAT:XX

PRE-SEASON HOME GAME

JETS VS PREDATORS

SEPTEMBER 30, 2011

SEC: XX
ROW: XX
SEAT: XX

By 7:20 the concourses are crowded. Cheers of Go Jets! People signalling over heads to their friends, slurping beer in plastic cups. The noise level is high, the crowd excited. Electricity running this way and that. This is what you come for.

We make our way to our seats. Anticipation fills the arena, already there are scattered chants of Go Jets Go! The game is a sellout, even though it's an exhibition match, the game means nothing. But not to big-league-hockey-starved Winnipeg. Oh, no. Here, in the year the city returns to the big league, every game is an important event

We gawk around. The MTS Centre is plush, with padded seats, newly painted railings. And it's intimate, capacity only 15,000, so the crowd is scrunched in, the sight lines superior to those of the old arena. And the fans have changed. Overall louder than in the '80s and '90s, enthusiastic to the point of frenzy now that the city has returned to the league that turned its back on us in 1996.

Suddenly the teams are coming onto the ice. Noise fills the building. About half of the crowd is on their feet. I expect hoopla. NHL games these days begin with loud rock music, smoke, flashing strobes—in San Jose the mouth of a shark for the players to skate through as they come onto the ice. Maybe Jets management is saving all that nonsense for the regular season, maybe they know that in blue-collar Winnipeg what matters is the performance of the team on the ice, not pre-game razzmatazz.

To one side of us a guy in a retro jersey is trying to start up the Mexican wave, below us kids are waving a banner: THANKS TRUE NORTH. Behind us, two old guys are muttering about the team's defence. One offers guttural opinions—they're not heavy enough, they lack speed, opinions that are not contradictory to him, it seems.

Go Jets Go! Banners flap: BACK IN THE BIGS reads one. Fans cheer and shout.

The game starts slowly. Nashville is playing the trap. The Jets bring the puck out of their end but are checked at the Nashville blue line. They seem confused, they can't get the puck into the opponents' zone, they have no speed. When the puck is turned over, Nashville rush into the Jets' end, firing shots on goal. By mid-period the shots are two-to-one in their favour. Then they score.

The energy drains out of the building like air from a balloon. Behind us the old guy grumbles, "They got no speed, they gotta get off their butts."

Winnipeg fans claim all they want from their team is a good effort. Yeah, sure. It's not for lack of trying that the Jets cannot break through Nashville's defence.

The trap. Perfected by the New Jersey Devils, honed by the Minnesota Wild. Utterly stupefying. But successful. Stop the other guys from doing anything. Then pounce on a mistake or a powerplay opportunity and win by a single goal.

The period ends 1-0 in favour of the visitors, the shots on goal a telling 11 to 5.

The old guys behind mutter and grumble through the period break. Team needs more speed, Wheeler's a bum. Why is it that sports fans do so much grumbling? Why do they feel it's their right? Do they switch off crappy action films with a curt "Do something, Bruce Willis"; do they slam novels shut saying, "Not enough colour, not enough crisp dialogue"?

It's grumble about this, pick away at that. Even when the team puts in a good effort, even when they win, what you hear on the way out of the arena is, "Yeah, but the powerplay stunk," and "Wait until the Flyers are in town." I'm not exempt, I've been a grumbler in the day, too.

The Jets are a transformed team in the second period, countering the trap with dump-and-chase. Their speedy forwards chase the puck into the corners, fire shots at the goal from all angles. The crowd is re-ignited. In a lull in the play, a guy over to the left shouts out, "Nashville you're terrible!"

Soon the shots are in the Jets' favour. Now Nashville look like they're skating in sand. The Jets' puck pursuit is electrifying. Fittingly it's team captain Ladd who scores. A mighty roar. Continuous chants of Go Jets Go! The team feeds off the energy of the crowd. By period end the shots are 15 to 13 in favour of the Jets.

That's more like it. This is the team of WHA Jets Hedberg and Nilsson, and NHL stars Hawerchuk and Lukowich, Labraaten and Steen. Speed, finesse. The Jets have never employed the trap, last ploy of desperate coaches and mediocre skaters: block the centre of the ice with a forward who hangs near the blue line when the team is attacking in order to be a third defenceman when the puck changes hands. Terrible.

In the third period the Jets continue the attack, buzzing the opponents' goal. Shots pile up. The fans are on their feet *ooh*ing and *ahh*ing with near misses. But it's Nashville that score. This time it does not deflate the team or the fans. The guy over to the left still cannot get the wave to catch on. But the Jets score near mid-period, the new sensation in town, rookie Mark Scheifele. I say to Kristen, "The kid's got the stuff."

She agrees. "He's the real deal."

The Jets apply more pressure, now Nashville are just hanging on. The shots pile up, but Lindback, the Nashville goaltender, turns them back time and again. In a lull the guy over to the left shouts, "Nashville, you're still terrible!"

Right at game end there's a flurry of shots in the Nashville end. But no result. "What'd I tell you," the old guy behind grumbles. "They got no finish."

The game ends in a tie, with no result in overtime. Nashville win the shootout.

On the way out of the arena, I ask Kristen, "What'd you think?"

"It was good."

"It was entertaining. They've got promise. Could be .500."

She's the daughter of a famous broadcaster, she's been around sports and sports talk all her life. "We'll see," she says.

"We'll see."

SNAPSHOT: PUNDITS

Every year before the season starts, the TV sports guys gather to make their guesstimates about the upcoming eight months of play. The guys on the Toronto Sports Network sit around a studio table in Toronto. Most of the talk is about teams from the East; the Loafs get more than their share of attention.

What do they think? They believe only two Canadian teams will qualify for the playoffs, the Canucks and one other team—the Canadiens? They give a thumbs-up to Winnipeg, management and fans, they want the team to do well and think the season will be a great success just because the city is again hockey mad. They reckon the Jets' travel schedule will be their doing-in. Fair enough.

When it comes to the top fifty players in the league, not a Jet is mentioned. Only one Flame makes the list, Jarome Iginla; only one Canadien, goaltender Carey Price; no Leaf, no Oiler, no Jet. Four Canucks make the grade: the Sedins, Kesler, Luongo. At least no Leaf has been touted. Maybe these guys are learning something.

They conduct a fantasy draft: three forwards, two defence, one goaltender, one rookie. The predictable names come out: Crosby and Ovechkin, the Sedins, Stamkos, Perry, St Louis; on defence: Weber, Visnofsky, Chara, Keith. A few long-shot picks—Giroux, Couture. Debate about goaltenders is more lively: Luongo or Price, Thomas or Miller? No one knows quite what to do about rookies, such a crap-shoot; they're on entry-level contracts, any of them might be sent back to junior or the AHL. The panel pick Nugent-Hopkins, Larsson, Hodgson. No mention of Jets rookie Scheifele.

Fair enough.

What do I think? I'm a Winnipeg fan, used to the underperforming

Bombers, used to seeing the old Jets scrape into the playoffs every second or third year and go out in the first round. It's a blue-collar town. Our expectations are perennially low, as those in flashy Toronto are always high. I think the team might win as many games as they lose, depending on injuries, and intangibles such as someone having an off year, or a career year. They could squeak out a playoff berth. What more could we ask? It's a blue-collar town. We expect only that the team work hard. At least that's what we say. Everything beyond that is gravy.

There's a buzz in the city, there's a buzz on the street, there's a buzz in the concourse of the arena.

The Habs are in town. The iconic Montreal Canadiens, winners of more Stanley Cups than any other team in history. The Habs are in town. And not just for any game, for the first game of the regular season for the Winnipeg Jets 2.0.

In the concourse forty-five minutes before game time hawkers are selling commemorative programs, $20 apiece; there is not a great demand. Winnipeg is a blue-collar town. We pass three guys decked out in white tuxedos. Horns blat, cheers from the arena, where the teams are going through pre-game warm-ups. Every second person is wearing a Jets jersey from a bygone era. Hawerchuk, Essensa, Selanne. Don Cherry is in town to do a bit for *Hockey Night in Canada*.

Inside the arena there's an electricity. Go Jets Go!

All over the city, we will learn later, crowds are watching on TVs in bars, a mob mentality developing at gathering holes and places like The Forks, where fans jammed together to see Winnipeg's reinvented team. Our city at the junction of two rivers going crazy.

When the pre-game ceremonies end—a tribute to a player who passed away in the off-season, a military band, the national anthem—the team is introduced. The biggest cheers are for Andrew Ladd and Dustin Byfuglien and Mark Scheifele. Strobe lights, some smoke, much less hoopla than I anticipate.

Game on!

Less than four minutes in the Jets give the puck away in their own zone and a Habs forward pounces and scores. "Same old Jets," Grumbler behind says.

They do not fold, though Montreal carry the play. By mid-period the shots on goal are 5-1 for the visitors. This new version of the Jets, it seems, starts slow. By period end the game has settled into a truly professional contest: bursts of attack punctuating long intervals of tight checking and efficient positional play. Both teams are playing a good "road game": no one giving anything away. At the end of the period the shots are even at eight apiece.

"They gotta shoot more," someone behind says.

"Terrible passing," his pal adds.

Grumbler concurs. "Playing too fancy."

But it's the template of the game. These are both finesse teams, so there's a lot of speedy attacking but not a lot of bone-crunching checking. Penalties abound, though. The referees seem whistle-happy. They send player after player to the sin bin. It ruins the flow of the game, it sucks the energy out of the crowd. In this first game that matters, there's nowhere near as much chanting or cheering as in the pre-season games.

This contest counts for something, this game is the business of pro hockey.

Then the visitors pounce on another mistake by the same Jets defence-man who coughed up the puck on the first goal, Johnny Oduya. He looks jittery tonight. So do others. It's no surprise the team might be experiencing a kind of stage fright in front of their new home crowd. The air goes out of the arena.

The Canadiens goaltender, Carey Price, last year won more games by a single-goal margin than any other in the league. Scoring two will be a mighty task, three seems beyond the pale. The period ends 2-0 with the shots 17-17.

In the intermission I say to an older man behind me, "Can they come back?"

"Yes," he says, "I'll come back." He's in his late seventies or early eighties, maybe, wearing a business suit and white shirt with tie.

It's noisy in the building. Just below our seats *Hockey Night in Canada* host Ron McLean is interviewing former Jets star Dale Hawerchuk. A crowd gathered around them is chanting at a frenzied pitch, "Go Jets, Go!"

I repeat in a louder voice, "Can the Jets come back in the third period?"

"Oh," the old fellow says, waving one hand, "Easy, it's just two goals."

At the bar below our seats we order two beers that come in plastic cups. Twenty dollars. I say to Kristen, "That used to be the price of admission. Twenty bucks for two beer!"

Winnipeg is a blue-collar town. We expect our team to work hard, we expect value for a dollar.

Back at our seats we watch a guy "caped" in a Jets flag stumble up the stairs to his seat. Throughout the two periods of play he's been going down to the bar frequently. In fact, the whole crowd seems on the move while play is in progress. This did not happen in past times. Fans sat in their seats during the periods and only got up in the intermissions to visit the concession kiosks and toilets. Is there more money around, do people care less about the actual game than before, is this a generational thing, a hangover from the AHL set-up, minor professional behaviour?

In the crowd a guy holds up a placard: THE PRICE IS WRONG.

When the puck is dropped, an anxious silence hangs over the arena. Tension has replaced excitement. The Jets press but with no result. Soon the shots favour the home team by five. We've seen this before. Outplaying the opponents, outshooting them, but behind on the scoreboard. Plenty of bustle but no finish.

Then a breakthrough. Following a scramble in front of the Montreal net, the puck slides in. Everyone is on their feet. The first goal for Jets 2.0 has been scored by the giant forward, Nik Antropov, jamming away at the puck, outmuscling the Montreal defence. It's a worthy Winnipeg goal—high on hard work, low on finesse.

The old fellow behind taps me on the shoulder. I turn to face him. "That's one," he says, a big smile wrinkling his cheeks.

The Jets press. For the next few minutes the puck stays in the Montreal end, shots buzz their net. The Jets' forwards cycle in the corners, their defence launch laser beams from the points. The Jets are coming back, they will pull this out of the fire, it's Nilsson and Hedberg all over. Then amid a flurry of shots, the Jets' bulky defenceman, Byfuglien, is given a questionable penalty. Fans boo and shake fists.

There's nothing worse in sport than having the referees influence the outcome, sometimes determine the outcome by a bad—or series of bad—calls. Montreal score on the powerplay. When the Jets press, Montreal counterattack and score again. And then again. Final: 5-1. Shots on goal 31-22, favour of the Jets. We've been down this road before. The Jets have always been a high-energy outfit, speedy, feeding off the juice of the crowd, an exciting, attacking team but a team prone to get burned by counterattack.

"Geez," Kristen mutters, "that shouldn't happen."

But the crowd is on its feet. Standing ovation.

How often does a hockey team get a standing ovation for a 5-1 loss?

As we're leaving the arena, I say, "Well?"

We're walking with one of Kristen's colleagues. "There's going to be eighty-one more of those," he offers stoically.

Someone behind us mutters, "It's gonna be a long season."

SNAPSHOT: Sports Fever 1

We come back.

We wave banners, we blow horns, we cheer until hoarse. Go Jets Go!

Kane wheels at the top of the circle, takes a quick snapshot, the net bulges. Yay, team; yay, Kane! Bogosian steps up at the blue line and lays a crunching hit on an opponent. Well done! Ladd outmuscles a defenceman in the corner and throws it out front where it's jammed into the net. Yay, team!

We are beside ourselves with joy, we sense the same ecstasy throbbing through the other fans around us, the same shared resolve, the same feeling that we are part of something bigger than ourselves, an engine with a collective will. We're the sixth skater on the ice, our will is the extra man on the team.

For once we are not anonymous cogs in the corporate machine, no identity, grinding away at mundane jobs, nobodies. Here, among ten or twenty thousand of the like-minded, we are one entity, cheering on our team, feeling their deflation when things go bad, sharing their delight when they go well.

We shriek: Go Jets Go! We scream, "Kill Durocco!" We punch the air along with thousands of others in an ecstasy of encouragement, drawing on our collective energy for an impact; we could well throw our arms up and shout "*Sieg Heil!*"

It's the mob mentality.

In a church in the southern USA, a hundred believers are gathered singing and praising the Lord, shrieking, losing control of their limbs, calling out, "Oh Jesus!" singing lustily and beautifully. This is benign mob mentality. On the far end of the spectrum lie the crowds of Nürnberg, cheering every word out of the mouth of *der Führer*. *"Sieg Heil!"* But both are part of the same urge in us, the urge to belong to a greater thing than our isolate egos, something that absorbs us in common meaning, intent, and joy, that frees us from the burden of thinking, of making responsible decisions, of personal accountability. That's the story.

We yearn to be part of something bigger than ourselves, something more important, more powerful, something that makes an impression on the world. No more sucking up to the foreman, the boss, the bank, heinous Americans / capitalists / socialists. And extremism offers excitement.

Into the cauldron of compulsions, then.

We go back. Hit 'em, Bogosian! Go Jets Go! YES!

SNAPSHOT: The Fan

She's middle-aged, she's a mother, she's a Jets fan.

Her name is Mary or Margaret. She's built a shrine to the Jets in her house, mostly a shrine to Teemu Selanne, it seems, there's a blue away jersey with number 13 on it hanging behind her. She owns two red bleacher seats, rescued from the old Winnipeg Arena when it was torn down. She sits in one of them to tell her story.

It's a story about how her father took her to Jets games as a child, how she loved the game, the team. Wore her Teemu shirt to school the day after he netted goal 76. Tears well up in her eyes as she recounts the last days of the team in the city, the tearing down of the old arena. As she talks, she wrings her hands together.

She's being featured on a TV documentary, *The Return of the Winnipeg Jets.* Behind her, the camera catches glimpses of memorabilia, some tacked to the walls of the shrine, others on tables: posters, pompoms, caps, pins.

Her story is about taking part in the Save the Jets campaign in 1996 in the last months when the team was in the city. Two hundred million dollars was needed to rescue the team. Supporters took to the streets to encourage politicians to come up with the money. They waved banners at Portage and Main. The camera shows a collection box dating from that time: clear plastic, with money donated to the cause: dollar bills, quarters, dimes, and pennies.

They did not impress Gary Bettman and the NHL's board of governors. They wanted local businessmen to step up and take over the team. None materialized.

The Fan's story is about elation when it's announced the Atlanta franchise has been sold to True North Sports. Mark Chipman, his partner David Thomson. Fifteen years later, a local businessman *has* stepped forward. Visible delight. Jubilation when the team is once again named the Jets. When she hears that season tickets will be sold online on a given day, the Fan calls together a handful of friends, who each sits at a computer at the designated time and, through good luck and clever timing, they acquire tickets. The Fan leaps up from her computer, her blonde hair flying, arms thrown over her head.

This is a FAN!

I myself was a season ticket holder of the Jets for all the years they were in the city, WHA and NHL, I attended hundreds of games, I cheered when the team won, groaned when they lost. About equal parts. I count myself as a fan and I am pleased the team is returning. I have acquired season tickets to Jets 2.0. In the pantheon of fans, I'm not a Casual, the few-games-a-year crowd; nor am I a Fan, the brigade who buy team jerseys and wear their hearts on their sleeves. I'm in a middle grouping, who follow the standings, watch games on TV, ponder how the team can be improved. Moreover, I'm a writer: one who observes, who notes, who tells the story—half in it myself—and half outside it. I did not cry when the team went under, nor, when the new team put tickets on sale did I sit at a computer with friends or throw my arms up in elation.

What does it take to care this much? Who is Teemu Selanne to her; who is the Fan to Teemu Selanne? How can an ordinary person be so passionate about two dozen young men who chase a hockey puck around a sheet of ice? She is not one of them, no husband / brother / son / nephew of hers is on the team; she does not know them in any way other than as a fan. And yet, there she is. As ecstatic as those girls who used to scream whenever the Beatles appeared on stage.

Her story is about her son, a boy of maybe six or eight. The camera shows her helping him pull on a Jets T-shirt. The story is about how her father will never be able to take his grandson to a game. She chokes up and trembles, tears well up in her eyes. The camera cuts away.

We turn on the TV in the family room, or tune in the Jets hockey broadcast, or gather at the sports bar with the big screens. The team is in Chicago, first road game for our newly revitalized Jets. Everywhere there's apprehension. The team looked out of its water against the Canadiens, and that was on home ice. And this is the Blackhawks, two years ago the Stanley Cup Champions.

After the 5-1 thrashing at the hands of Montreal on home ice, there's now a palpable degree of trepidation in the city, a sense that we'll be lucky to put in a good showing. Maybe, we hope, the team will not embarrass themselves. The puck has not dropped but the evidence is already there in the patrons of the sports bar: a tight smile on most faces, no chants of "Go Jets Go!" A loss by a goal or two will be okay; more than that will be another humiliation. A tie, a win are almost beyond hoping for.

It's Winnipeg, our expectations are low.

So when the puck drops, we take in a deep breath, blow out our cheeks and prepare for a long night.

The Chicago arena is buzzing, and so, to begin with, are the Blackhawks. They know they're getting a team on the back heel, a team with not a lot of confidence to begin with. The Atlanta version of the team finished thirteen points out of the playoffs last season. There were deep flaws in the squad, especially on defence. There's a lot of work to do before the Jets resemble a contender.

Surprisingly, the play is even right from the start, the puck moving up and down the ice freely, the players playing a professional game, not too many chances—staid defence first, flashy attack after. The Jets look more comfortable than they did at home to Montreal. Their nervousness that night could be put down to the occasion, maybe: the first game of the newly-minted team, the arena a madhouse, the players eager to put in a good showing—and as a result, trying too hard and "overplaying."

Just get through the first ten minutes without being scored on, I say to myself. That's when the visiting team is most vulnerable, leg-weary, maybe, the home team feeding off the energy of their crowd. More games are given away in the opening ten minutes of road games than in any other ten-minute segment of contests.

So it's a surprise when in the fifth minute the Jets score, Jim Slater tipping in a shot from the point by Oduya, the goat in the home-opener. Hope flutters about like a butterfly. I sip at a beer. It doesn't change the overall feeling of foreboding. *Get through the first ten minutes.* Only minutes later, the Jets score again, on a very similar play: a shot tipped in by Slater, one of the team's checkers and energy guys, a gritty performer. Ahead 2-0 before the ten-minute mark. Hurrah.

This is more like it, fans of other teams might think. But Jets fans? Jets fans can be forgiven for being cautious. We've been watching guys wearing these sweaters for more than thirty years. They often fall behind 3-0, then scratch their way back to a 3-2 loss. Just as often they go ahead by a couple of goals early and slowly give the game away, losing 5-4.

Just get through the first ten minutes.

But they don't. Chicago score at 9:45, fifteen seconds before the magic mark of ten minutes. The Jets are still ahead but this mini-collapse is ominous.

I turn to my son, Andrew. "They didn't get past the ten minutes."

He grunts. "Just about, though."

"It's gonna be a just-about season."

"Yep. Likely."

He's more a rugby than a hockey fan but he understands the passion that goes with caring for one team more than the game itself. He pats my shoulder. Hockey is something we share in the TV room, as rugby is something we share there too. He's learned my game; I've learned his. Though neither of us is as passionate as was my father, watching the Leafs and the Habs in the days of the old six-team NHL, jumping up for a smoke when things were going bad, pouring a whiskey when they were going good. My father, who never laced on a pair of skates in his life, but knew the joy and the anguish of being a fan.

The puck goes up and down the ice, the shots are even, both teams look comfortable and competent. But there are a lot of turnovers in the Winnipeg zone. You can sense what's going to happen in the rise and fall of the TV announcer's voice.

The fifteen-minute mark passes. A lot of time is being spent in the Jets end.

Just get through the first period still ahead on the scoreboard.

But they don't. With three minutes to play, Chicago tie the score. The period ends even. Shots on goal favour Chicago 11-9.

On the road you try to scratch out wins. The home team wants to put on a show in front of their fans; the home team skates with verve and presses; the home team has the energy of the crowd with them, sometimes gets calls from officials on the strength of the crowd's cheering or jeering. If you get ahead on the road, you play defence first and offence second. If you get ahead by two goals, you try to shut the other team down by fierce forechecking and backchecking and defensive zone coverage. You do not cough up a goal three minutes after you score. You do not let a lead of 2-0 slip away in ten minutes.

You do not cough up yet a third goal in the opening minute of the next period.

It's déjà vu the old Jets.

It's at this point that you work on the Zen of fandom. Keep the emotions flat and steady. Breathe in, breathe out. The game has not been lost and there are two periods yet to play, a lot can happen in two periods, the team can come back. But fans of the Winnipeg Jets are not glass-half-full types; they're not even glass-half-empty types; they're glass-empty types.

So we groan when an apparent goal is taken away from the Jets at the three-minute mark, a goal-mouth scramble, and then a similar goal is awarded to Chicago only minutes later.

4-2 Chicago.

I miss the Grumbler. I need to hear his gravelly voice saying the refs are bums, I need to share this disappointment, this despair, he's my shadow self and I need him to mutter, "The refs are against us."

"Us." It has not taken long for me to subsume my identity in that of the team, to think my fate is theirs, it's *us* versus *them.* There are fans who feel this so strongly that they actually feel they are Hawerchuk gliding down the ice, it's their hips that dipsy-doodle at the top of the circle, their hands that take the snapshot that bulges the twine, their arms flung into the air to celebrate the goal. Well, their arms are flung into the air. With his deft moves, his uncanny timing, Hawerchuk gives shape to their desires, which their own bodies cannot articulate. But it's more than that; he's not just the embodiment of their desires, he's their alter ego, in some supernatural way their yearning to transcend life's humdrum reality is so great that they come to believe that they are the instrument of his feats, they are not just puny nobodies in a crowd roaring their need, they are also Hawerchuk hearing that roar, hearing their own petty lives achieving the fame we all so deeply crave. This is what it means to be a Fan.

In the midst of these thoughts the Jets' Kyle Wellwood jumps out of the penalty box and the puck bounces onto his stick as he comes to the Chicago blue line. Breakaway! But right at the line he stumbles and the puck flutters into the corner. Beside me, Andrew groans. "Wellwood," he mutters in the tones of a true Winnipeg fan. It's not easy to describe the exact combination of exasperation and misery that goes into the muttering by the disappointed fan at an inept play.

I laugh and so does Kristen. "I need another beer," I say.

But Wellwood redeems himself only seconds later, tucking a backhand into the Chicago net. "Well," I say to Andrew, "Wellwood's one and one now."

"You forgot about the empty net in the first period," he states flatly.

I laugh again. He punches me in the shoulder.

Still 4-3. At the beginning of the game this would have seemed an okay result. Now it's an ominous indication of how things are likely to end up.

In the third period both teams settle into a road game, playing tight defence punctuated by occasional offensive flurries of shots. The Hawks get more chances but the Jets are kept close by their goalie Ondrej Pavelec, and have a couple chances to tie the game. The final shots are 32-30. First loss on the road to complement the first loss at home.

It's all too familiar. Jets 2.0 are a facsimile of Jets 1.0. JETS 4 EVER screamed the banner hanging from the rafters of the old arena. Jets forever bums. This is the way it feels in Winnipeg. Maybe it's the way it feels in all cities.

SNAPSHOT: RIVER CITY

Is there anyone more self-satisfied than the Winnipegger strolling down Selkirk Avenue of an afternoon, having just come out of a Thai restaurant with a loaf of rye bread from a Jewish bakery tucked under the arm? To the south lie the rail yards of the country's two railways, the scree and scraw of trains intoning an industrial dirge over the streets. This is what Winnipeg prizes, the ethnic mix, the broken-nosed and hard-headed attitude of the working man who grinds out a living on Machine Street, far from the commercial niceness of Stock Market Muse and Boutique Boulevard.

Sure, we like to think, we're a metropolis on the upswing. We are soon to boast a stunning human rights museum; we enjoy a social-democratic government, and a symphony, an opera, and we've had a gay mayor. And we have a state-of-the-art international airport and a new, if smallish, arena. We're cosmopolitan.

But what we're proud of is our working-class heritage, our perseverance, our heritage of sticking it to the Man. This is where the great General Strike of 1919 took place. And this was the cornerstone franchise of the WHA, rebel league to the NHL. Talk about sticking it to the Man. Take that, Toronto, with your precious (but inept) Maple Leafs, take that, Montreal, with your storied (but overly swank) Canadiens.

We're smug about not being smug.

We're a big small city but we prefer to think of ourselves as a small big city.

Hockey, with its pug-nosed attitudes, its give 110% attitude, its beat 'em in the alley if not on the ice, is the perfect sport for this town.

The city was founded by Brits and Francophones (there's a city within the city, Saint Boniface, where primarily French is spoken). In the late nineteenth and early twentieth centuries, large populations of Germans, Ukrainians, Poles, Icelanders, and other Europeans flooded in, creating a multicultural mix that makes for tolerance, if not always ethnic harmony. In the past two decades immigration has continued apace, but now it's "visible minorities" that are coming: Filipinos, Indians, Japanese, and Chinese. Maybe we never knew, but certainly in the new millennium we're not quite sure who we are anymore; yet the wealth of restaurants serving up delicious—and inexpensive—foods from around the globe compensates for any cultural confusion and angst we might feel about our collective identity.

Every year we welcome tens of thousands of newcomers to a province of one million, an increase of about 5% to 7%, the largest in the country. Almost all of these newcomers settle in to jobs at the lower end of the socio-economic pyramid, but they settle in happily, determined to improve the lot of their children, if not their own. Like so many who have arrived here for the past two centuries, their values are lower-middle class and working class. They value education and Medicare highly and are supporters of the welfare state, in all its splendour and ungainliness.

On the street you see men wearing turbans, Hutterite women in black dresses, Hasidic Jews, girls with hair so blonde they might have been flown in from Stockholm. We're the Global City. A dazzling mix of skin colours, a breathtaking array of beliefs.

The one thing we agree on is that the loss of the Jets in 1996 tore the heart out of the city. *Boo*, Gary Bettman, *boo* NHL. The one thing we glory in is their return. *Yay*, Mark Chipman, *yay*, David Thomson. About that, Jews stand arm-in-arm with Sikhs, the Irish with the Welsh. This has been so since the early '70s, when Bobby Hull stood at the corner of Portage and Main and received that million-dollar cheque. It was so when thousands flocked downtown in 1996 to support the Save the Jets campaign—and failed utterly. *Boo*, Gary Bettman, *boo*, NHL. We've loved our team.

But not uncritically. Because the roots of hockey go deep in the city. Every fan in the stands has either played the game or has a brother / sister / son who did, and knows what effort is required to make a championship team—or even a respectable one. This is not a fancy-Dan town and it doesn't much care for fancy-Dan sports—tennis, golf, dressage.

More important, the city's roots are in working-class jobs—the two railways, CNR and CPR, the stockyards, feed mills, tractor and heavy equipment manufacturers. There's no Bay Street in Winnipeg, no Wall Street or Silicon Valley. People who earn respect in Winnipeg get their hands dirty. It's a sweat-of-the-brow and power-of-your-back kind of place. People work hard for their livelihoods, and they expect their pro athletes to demonstrate the same ethic, the lunch-bucket ethic, however slickly they play, however many millions they are paid. When Winnipeg fans cheer forechecking or a solid hit, they're cheering, we like to think, the same effort the guys at the rail yards put in, rain, sleet or snow; when they boo it's because we sense the team is just going through the motions. We take our working-class roots seriously and affect more than a little reverse snobbery about fey Toronto and dopey Vancouver.

In one way, you can't blame us. We languish in the shadow of oil-rich Calgary and Edmonton, with nothing to compare to Vancouver's beauty or style. We were once the biggest city in the country west of Toronto, the Chicago of the North, hog-butcher, rail centre, all that Carl Sandburg stuff. We're proud of our city in a broad-shouldered, don't-mess-with-us kind of way.

The two most common shouts you'll hear at the arena are "Go Jets Go!" and "Get off your butts, you bums."

SNAPSHOT: OLD GLORY

Winnipeg has a long and neon hockey history.

In 1896 and then again in 1901 and 1902 the Winnipeg Victorias won the Stanley Cup. This was in the days when the trophy was given to "the champion hockey team in the Dominion of Canada," before the swindlers of the NHL hijacked it for their league, composed of primarily USA-based teams having little or no connection with the Dominion of Canada. Which goes to prove that the NHL has always been run by weasels, much before current charlatans like Clarence Campbell and Gary Bettman took charge.

The list of Allan Cup winners, symbolic of senior hockey supremacy in Canada, is representative: Winnipeg Monarchs, Winnipeg 61st Battalion, University of Manitoba, Winnipeg Maroons. In 1922 the Winnipeg Falcons won the Allan Cup—in those days next below the Stanley Cup in importance—and then went on to represent Canada at the Olympics where they won the country's first Olympic gold medal in hockey.

During the late '60s and early '70s Father David Bauer's National Team played many games in Winnipeg, where it flourished, challenging the great hockey machine of the USSR. Long before the NHL was aware of the skill, power, and organization of "The Bear," Winnipeg fans were treated to dozens of games in the arena. Electric stuff. Names such as Dineen, Lefley, Huck, Mott, Bourbonnais, and Johnston were household coin.

The glory years of pro hockey in Winnipeg were witnessed in the mid and late '70s with the WHA Jets, perennial challengers for the AVCO World Cup and three-time winners. When the league was disbanded in 1979, the trophy found a home in the city.

No line has electrified a city in the way that the "Hot Line" of Hull, Nilsson, and Hedberg did Winnipeg in those years.

So it was with enormous sadness that the city saw the WHA fold in 1979 and the team they had grown devoted to pillaged by the NHL, as the price for being allowed to join that league. Hedberg and Nilsson were grabbed off by the New York Rangers and never appreciated in that city. Hull, "The Golden Jet," *retired*, eventually returning to play a couple dozen games with the Jets and the Hartford Whalers. The team was left to protect only three players from its AVCO Trophy–winning roster, one goaltender, and two skaters. Perhaps the greater disaster for the team was the naming of John Ferguson as its manager; he promptly replaced the brilliant threesome with plodding thug Jimmy Mann (a player in Ferguson's own mould), and such glittering stars as Ryan Stewart and the Pooley twins, who managed to play fewer than thirty games in the NHL among them.

No wonder Winnipeg fans chafe at the mention of the NHL. No wonder Gary Bettman, Gary "Bête Noire," is roundly booed when he appears in the city. "Go Gary Go"—far away!

Phoenix, desert home of Jets 1.0, Gary Bettman's chosen destination for the 1996 "transitioned" team. The Coyotes are a solid outfit now, made the playoffs last year, play a disciplined if uninspired game.

In their arena on this night half the fans are wearing Jets jerseys, the new "air force" style as well as the old style with the commercial jet and the hockey stick. There are placards, too: Jet Fuel, Defeat Desert Dogs. The *home* Coyotes fans look a bit bewildered; the Jets fans are more vocal than they are, more animated.

"What d'ya think?" I ask Kristen.

"Could win."

"Could." I'm a longtime fan, I have low expectations. "I suspect the Jets will lose 3 to 1."

"We'll see."

"If only," I say, "they can get through the opening ten minutes."

But they don't. Less than a minute in, Phoenix score. Does the brain groan? I don't think either of us actually utters a sound, but it seems as if we groan in unison.

Before ten minutes have passed, Phoenix score again. The Jets have had only two shots on goal to the eight by the Coyotes.

Then the game settles down. Both teams carry the play at times, both buzz the opposition net, both have good scoring chances. As the period closes, I say, "This team is good at falling behind 2-0 and then playing a solid game."

And they are. The second period is played evenly. Rushes go from one end to the other. The Jets are prone to giveaways in their own end but they block numerous shots and the goaltender bails them out with good saves. Though Phoenix score to make it 3-0, the Jets manage a goal in the final minute. By the end of the period the game is a real contest, the shots 21 to 13, a typical differential in favour of the home side. Both teams still have a chance to win.

"If they can just get the next one," Andrew says.

But Phoenix score early in the third period and the game is over.

The Jets keep trying. They work hard and put in an all-out effort, dashing into the Coyotes' corners after free pucks, flailing in front of both nets. In Atlanta they were aptly named the "thrashers": there's a lot of effort with little result. The defence seem not strong enough to hold opponents off in front of their own goal, the forwards flounder to make an impression in the opposition end. No Hull and Hedberg here, no Hawerchuk, no Steen or Nilsson.

Only the beefy Byfuglien has *presence*, the ability to take the game in hand. At least once every game he wheels from behind his own goal and carries the puck the length of the ice, brushing aside checkers, moving across his own blue line and then the centre red line. He wheels past his own teammates, who slow for him, knowing he is not going to pass to them, and charges bull-like into the opposition end. Sometimes he dishes the puck off to a teammate, sometimes he gets away a stinging shot, often the puck dribbles harmlessly into a corner.

That's the cost. Byfuglien's rushes often come to nothing at the opposition's blue line, trapping him up ice, forcing one of the Jets forwards to improvise defence in his place, a forward who is not familiar with the nuances of checking while skating backwards. For a moment, though, the Jets fans have risen with him, swept up in his daring dashes—a great thing might happen, a goal could be scored, the game could be turned around. He has force, awe-inspiring power. He intimidates opponents.

I've played against a man like this.

Twice a week in a North End arena a dozen guys of my ilk, guys who played junior or college hockey (or just about) are joined by a handful of ex-pros who live in the area: Ray Neufeld, Wayne Babych, Thomas Steen. Sometimes, too, there's Dave Pitcher, who was a running back in the pros; in his mid-forties he's still a fit and strong athlete whose strides take him down the ice in powerful chops before he unleashes a heavy shot. If you're skating backwards, defending, he's a force to be reckoned with. But moreso is Babych. At 265 pounds, Babych outweighs me by 90 pounds, maybe 40 or 45 of which represent a few too many plates of perogies. So his body is slightly out of control, some of that weight has a mind of its own. He's not mean but he's dangerous. If he hits me, he'll knock me into another time zone, clear through the roof of the arena, where my body will no doubt orbit the earth until doomsday, a pulverized mass of flesh and bone.

I have some idea what's it like to look Dustin Byfuglien in the eye.

Opponents must have felt this way facing Bobby Hull. Remember those end-to-end rushes? Hull would gather the puck in his own end, circle behind the goal and power down the length of the ice. By the time he hit centre ice, the crowd was on its feet, defenders were pointlessly reaching out sticks, hoping to dislodge the puck, but not daring to step into his path. Somewhere near the top of the opposition's faceoff dot Hull would unleash one of his slapshots. No one saw the puck: the crowd, the defenders, the goaltender, maybe even Hull himself. The net would bulge behind the goaltender, the red light would go on, we'd spot the puck then, spinning on the ice behind the goal line.

Hull was inspiring, Hull was iconic. Watching Bobby Hull in these moments was akin to seeing Jim Brown breaking through the defenders' line and rumbling down the gridiron for a touchdown; equivalent to seeing Babe Ruth at home plate swinging his massive body, swatting a big fly into the far bleachers. Witnessing Hull in full flight was one of the grand moments in all of sport. It took your breath away.

Byfuglien promises to do this. Maybe his much younger teammates on the Jets will mature into agile and valuable pros, maybe they will "gel" into a team. In two or three years—months?—the defence may play a disciplined game that yields results, the forwards may develop an effective attack that wins games. All of that is *maybe, if, hopefully*; all that possibility hovers elusively in Tomorrow Country. Right now they're "thrashers";

right now what Winnipeg has to be truly inspired by is the erratic but stirring Byfuglien.

On the Sunday morning *Sports Reporters* program the pundits are reviewing the opening week of the new NHL season. The Leafs are unbeaten, the Jets winless. Which is more likely to occur first, the host asks, Jets post a win or the Leafs lose a game? Unfortunately, the panel concludes, it's the Leafs losing: "These Jets don't look like they're going to win any time soon."

Groan, mutter, grumble.

In the sitcom *Corner Gas* there was an old codger, Oscar, who found fault with everything. He had no time for new-fangled mobile phones, satellite TV, or Blackberries. A real Grumbler. "Two bucks for a cup of coffee? Why I remember…"

So I know it's hopelessly Oscarish to conclude after only three games that the Jets season is already lost, that the six points they've given away will be their undoing in March and April when the struggle for every point will be a dogfight.

I know that, but it doesn't stop me from festering and mumbling.

There's a Grumbler in me too.

It's equally Oscarish to think, two hundred and eighty-five bucks for a pair of tickets! The face value on the ticket from the last game the old Jets played was less than $50, about $96 for a pair. Well, everything goes up. And in order to purchase season tickets at $10,000 a pair, many folks have had to pool together, split the full freight into quarter shares. Even then, the tickets are pricey, beyond the reach of many. Where the north-end bleachers once were home to a robust working-class element (ironically situated below a gigantic portrait of the Queen), the new arena does not really accommodate these types. But those who are there are committed, in the way cash commits. That commitment comes with its own price: this is not the crowd that will put up with the fumbling ineptitude of a team twenty points out of contention at Christmas or 4-1 losses to teams from Florida and Arizona. So new Jets: it's no more sixteen-game losing streaks, no missing the playoffs year after year, or the record-breaking streak of futility in 1980–81 when the team went winless for 30 games (23 losses, 7 ties). The guys sitting beneath the Queen were prepared to put up with that, but this new crowd …

This new crowd is up for the Penguins, one of the marquee teams of the past decade. Crosby, Malkin, Fleury in goal. A recent Stanley Cup. But for nine months now Crosby has suffered symptoms of concussion and will not play; ditto Malkin, out with a knee injury. You can almost hear sighs of relief rippling through Winnipeg. With Pittsburgh's two big guns out, the Jets may have a chance. But good grief, how did we arrive here, when it's more important that two of the game's greatest stars be out of the lineup when they play the Jets than on the ice for the match? We'd rather lose the quotient of entertainment they bring to the game than lose another game.

Would you go to the theatre knowing the lead actor was laid up that night?

It's the Garrison Mentality: batten the hatches, bar the doors, hold the fort.

Get through the first ten minutes.

It's more important that the game grind along in close checking, semi-paralytic inertia and that the Jets have a chance to win (okay, we'll settle for a tie) than that we be treated to thrilling end-to-end rushes and brilliant stickhandling by Crosby and Malkin. The hell with that. We need points! Bring on the trap.

The chant of Go Jets Go! has hardly begun after the drop of the puck when the Jets score on a Pittsburgh miscue. Eight seconds ties the record for the fastest goal in franchise history. The fans in the arena cheer lustily. But I'm still silently intoning to the Jets: *get through the first ten minutes.*

They do, though it's a hair-raising ten minutes, both teams dashing up the ice recklessly, pucks flying around both goals. Can the players maintain this pace for a full game? Fire-wagon hockey. Great stuff from the entertainment point of view, but the stuff that turns coaches' hair grey. And diehard fans'. With just over a minute left in the period, the Jets net one again.

Another two-goal lead, ripe to be blown. At least that's how we die-hard fans think as the teams go into the second period. Glass half-empty.

The crowd remains enthusiastic. Go Jets Go! And they hang on. At the game's halfway point it's still 2-0, an uneasy 2-0, with Pittsburgh pressing and blasting shots at the Jets goal, but the lead holds up until the dying minutes of the second period. It's 2-1 heading into the third. We've seen this movie before: get ahead early by two goals but lose 3-2 by the final whistle.

At the intermission I say to Andrew, "You can play this game to stop the other guys from scoring, you know?"

"I know." His voice resounds with resignation.

"You can play defensive hockey when you're up 2-0."

"I know, Dad."

"There's no embarrassment in defence."

"I know."

There's no sign of the trap in the third period either. That's not how these Jets are going to play, it seems. They play to score and they play to entertain, which is not always what fans like me want. Entertainment, that's for the circus. This is the real cleft stick for me and thousands of fans like me. Do we want high-wire games, played at a fast pace with buckets of shots on goal, or do we want results, which sometimes only come if a team hangs onto a lead with tight checking? Half of the crowd wants the former, half the latter; and even those of us who occupy one position or the other swing between them in a given game, urging the Jets to go for it at the game's start, but forty minutes later groaning when they cannot hold a lead by playing lockdown.

But they do. Despite Pittsburgh's best efforts in the third period, scrambling around the Jets goal on a half-dozen occasions, when the final whistle blows it's 2-1 for the home team, first victory of the season, a wild crowd shouting and dancing in the stands as the game's three stars are announced.

The Toronto pundits, it turns out, were only half right. The Leafs go down to Colorado 3-2 the same night the Jets garner their first win of the season.

Is there a city that Winnipeggers enjoy beating more than Toronto? The Great Grey City, smog-shrouded, sitting beside its fetid lake, is the big brother to all other Canadian cities, lording it over the country with its TSN sportscasts, its TSX. It's the Imperial Centre: its taste, its *Globe and Mail*, its CBC 1 and 2 radio programs cast shadows from coast to coast. The culture of the country emanates from there, and, frankly, it rankles.

May as well state it straight, then: when it comes to Toronto, there's a chip on our shoulders.

Oddly, we love their Blue Jays; we snicker at their Argonauts. We even, at times, feel sorry that their Maple Leafs have performed so poorly for so long, sad really, in light of the city's wealth, power, and hockey history. The athletes play hard. It's not so much the sports teams of Toronto that we dislike as the sleekly coiffed and suavely-suited presenters on their sport channels, who purport to make their commentary of national interest, but who, at the slightest opportunity, slither into Toronto-babble like oiled pigs on duckboards.

So when our Jets travel to Toronto to play their Leafs, we have no interest in seeing an entertaining game, we want our guys to thrash theirs.

Watching on TV, the first thing that's notable is how many empty seats there are in the Air Canada Centre. This is corporate sponsorship, the buying of blocks of tickets by big companies who have to find someone to take them for every game. So the call goes out from the office manager: four tickets are available for tonight's Leafs game, anyone interested? Early in the season, against Winnipeg? No thanks. So there are four seats empty here, a block of eight there. This wouldn't have happened in another era, when there were standing-room tickets for the working stiff, and seats in the end blues went for a couple of bucks.

In the scattered crowd there are almost as many Jets jerseys as Leafs. One guy has a poster: WELCOME BACK WINNERPEG. And the Jets fans are vocal. They out-shout their hosts: Go Jets Go! And they do. Both teams begin with high energy, but it's the Jets that score first, on a powerplay right at the halfway mark of the period. It's the Jets' first such goal.

The period continues apace, a good game from the entertainment perspective, dashes up and down the ice, hard but clean bodychecks, blocked shots. One thing that's noticeable about the play in the NHL after a sixteen-year absence is that every player skates very speedily now, and with the altered rules about obstruction, the game is much more wide open and fast-paced. The Leafs tie the score, the Toronto crowd become involved. The period ends at 1-1, shots 9-6 favouring the Jets.

At the intermission the colour guy says the Jets put in a "blue-collar effort," using dump-and-chase to put pressure on the Leafs defence. Like most Jets fans, I'm pleased to hear this. And delighted when the Jets jump into the lead again early in the period and extend it near the midway mark, when the rookie Scheifele scores his first NHL goal. The camera shows four guys in the stands wearing Jets jerseys giving each other high-fives.

Though the action is furious for the rest of the frame, hair-raising rushes up and down the ice, shots hitting goalposts, pucks loose in both creases, the score at the intermission is 3-1. From a neutral's point of view, it's been a good game, highly entertaining.

Still, I can't help thinking as the teams come back on the ice, *Get through the first ten minutes without giving up a goal, get through those first ten minutes.*

But they don't. Before the halfway mark, the Leafs score on a power-play, and then a few seconds later on another. The cry of Go Leafs Go is thunderous. I wring my hands. Were we stiffed on that first penalty, as on the penalty against Byfuglien in the Montreal game? No point in thinking that way. I say to Kristen, "This is getting hard on the nerves, I'm going to have to pour a Scotch."

The minutes wind down. The Leafs press, the Jets try to counterattack.

Another two-goal lead blown. "Same old Jets," I mutter.

"No," says Kristen, "these guys are fighting back. In the old days, even when we had the Young Guns (Selanne, Tkachuk, Zahmnov, Davydov), the Jets would have folded. These guys are fighting back."

As if to prove her point, the play goes up and down, Toronto's Kessel missing a close one, and Jets' Wheeler having a good chance at the other end. "There always seems to be this impression that Wheeler's got more," the colour guy says, "that he's just scratching the surface of what he can be." But neither team can put one in. Nor does that happen in overtime, the Jets' first in their new incarnation. The shootout goes to Toronto.

"A point," I say to Kristen with a sigh. "Would have been nice to get two."

"Would have."

Andrew chimes in: "But would we have taken one point before they dropped the puck?"

"Absolutely would have."

Another two-goal lead blown, a game the Jets should have won, having outshot Toronto 29-23. Five games played: three losses, one win, one tie. I don't think the coach will be exactly happy with that.

SNAPSHOT: COACH

Spring 1964, Carman Arena. Our team is in the provincial play-downs. I'm on the bench watching Smitty make a move at the Carman blue line that takes him into their zone to the top of the faceoff dot. Smitty is deceptive, one of those guys who seems to be moving slow but somehow slips past by going sideways, sliding the puck through your feet, then past your outstretched stick. The Carman defenceman looks confused when Smitty slips past him and rips a wrist shot at the net, bulging the twine over the goalie's shoulder. Beside me Johnny G lets out a yelp.

Johnny is a farm boy with hands like hams. A mesomorph, who though not tall, is solidly built and dishes out crushing bodychecks. He's used to throwing hay bales and shovelling grain into silos. He has the shoulders, arms, and wrists of a man. He's hit me in practice and I've felt it. Though he's neither as good a skater as me nor as slick a stickhandler as Smitty, it's Johnny that the scouts from the Brandon Wheat Kings have come to look at.

Coach taps me on the back. He's a veteran of the Korean War, a hard-nosed, take-no-prisoners kind of guy and an RCMP constable. On the ice he barks at us: *Full stop at the red line, no gliding!* He's a mesomorph too. He went at me in front of the net once and knocked me on my butt. "You gotta get position, Tefs, you gotta stick your ass out." Another time he cross-checked me in the crease; the bruise on my ribs throbbed for three days. At practice before this game he said to me, "You've gotta take position in front of the net, Tefs, you gotta make it yours. You got size. I'm counting on you." Coach is not a man you say no to.

I hop over the boards for a faceoff in our end. Check the scoreboard. We're up 3-1. My eyes roam to the stands. To one side of our net my father is standing with my uncle Bill. They're brothers but with totally different builds. My father stands five-foot-nine and is wiry and intense; my uncle stands six feet and is big-boned and slow-moving. Of the two of them, I resemble my uncle more than my father. Though we all have the Buechler schnozz. I take my spot and get ready for the drop of the puck. The Carman centre is messing with a scrap of tape on the blade of his stick. I glance at my father and uncle again. My uncle is a farmer in the Carman area; he's more successful than my father, but my father has one thing my uncle never will: a son. But he's standing tall on this day. He knows what's being said in the stands behind him. *See that number 6, that's Bill Tefs's nephew.*

The puck goes into the corner but I go to the front of our net. Gregorash is scrapping in the corner for possession. I'm jostling with Carman's big winger, number 12, a farm boy, too, he has a giant butt and he's sticking it in my side. I give him a cross-check to the back to move him. More jostling. The thought occurs to me that Coach has made sure I'm on the ice against this guy, their big scorer. I dig in harder. *Make it yours.* The puck is still being contested in the corner. Number 12 has spread his legs, bent at the knees, and is shoving me sideways, but I've got my stick on his back, pushing at him, so we're both rotating, and in a moment we're facing each other. I give him a shot to the jaw. He lashes back. We've both got our sticks up in each other's face. The whistle blows. My lip stings. The referee points us both off the ice. As I skate to the penalty box I touch my mouth with my glove. Blood. Loose tooth. It's then I notice stinging in my eyes, headache in my temples.

Number 12 has got me pretty good. And I've drawn the extra penalty. We kill it off.

When I come back to the bench, I plunk down beside Smitty. He taps me on the shin pad with the blade of his stick. Coach touches me on the shoulder and leaves his hand there for an extra heartbeat. There are boys you take up a hill in Korea with you and boys you do not. He knows and I know.

SEC: XX ROW: XX SEAT:XX

AWAY GAME 06

JETS VS SENATORS

OCTOBER 20, 2011

SEC: XX
ROW: XX
SEAT: XX

Should have won that game in Toronto. That lost point will come back to haunt the Jets in the drive to the play-off. And now it's the second of back-to-back games in Ottawa. The Senators do not have a strong team and it should be relatively easy to pinch two points from them, but then the Jets are not a strong team either, and they will be leg-weary in the third period. The signs are not good.

But they start well and count the first goal. The Senators look a bit lost and their home fans are not very forgiving. The boo-birds come out. This is a city used to getting its own way, baby of the family to Toronto's big brother role: spoiled, soft, a city of transient bureaucrats feeding off the fat of the land, a city of "objectives for a new millennium," "sustainable policies," and "forward thinking," a city at the other end of the *grit* spectrum to Winnipeg. Once a promising squad, the Senators have for years been stumbling and staggering; their fans have been nurturing frustrations and resentments for quite some time. They want results, but their team is aging and look to be stuck near the bottom of the league for years to come.

By the end of the first period Ottawa has tied things up on a power-play. Now a second pattern is emerging: Jets get the early lead, then give it away on a powerplay.

"This is a must game for the Jets," the colour guy says at the break, "the kind of game that gets you into the playoffs or spells your demise."

A woman in the crowd has a placard with a huge gavel on it placed above the words: Senators Rule.

Ottawa score before the five-minute mark of the second frame. There's still hope, the play is even and so are the shots on goal. But then Ottawa score again near the fifteen-minute mark. 2-1. There's still hope, but it's looking now like winning the lottery, long odds. In the third period Ottawa score near the ten-minute mark. In desperation the Jets coach pulls the goaltender with more than two minutes to play, and the Sens get an empty-netter, so the final is 4-1. Six games played, 21 goals surrendered. Not just a mediocre team; a feeble one.

The template for the new Jets: get the early lead, blow it by the end of the first period; fall behind in the second; collapse in the third. Do stats lie? Of the 11 they've tallied thus far, the Jets have scored 6 in period one; on the other hand, they have been out-scored in the third 8-1.

It's painful, and going to be worse. It's also ridiculous after only six games to be reading into the team's performance a whole year's futility. And yet. Despite what you want to hope, you know that when a team starts out a season at the bottom of the table, it's unlikely to rise much above that. The Grumbler knows it; anyone who was around the old Jets also knows it.

Was it Samuel Johnson who once quipped that marriage was "the triumph of Hope over Reason"? Fans hope, but they can also reason. And experience tells them that a mediocre team that cannot beat another mediocre team is doomed to play a sub-.500 season, miss the playoffs, be mired at the bottom of the table. It's a good thing the NHL does not follow the "relegation" system of the European football leagues: after only a half dozen games the Jets would already be in the dogfight to avoid that painful humiliation.

I'm being an old codger here. Doomsayer. Glass-empty Grumbler-type of fan.

What impresses me about fans, real fans—not the ones who show up and treat games as social occasions, an opportunity to drink, swap stories in the concourse, miss halves of periods yakking and swilling beer—real fans are at least part of the time sour about their team. "Bergman, you bum," "these guys suck," "a hundred bucks for a ticket, they should be paying me a hundred bucks to watch these clowns." It's in the nature of being a fan to arrive annoyed, see that annoyance turn to rancour and then morph into sullen silence. It's a struggle not to fall into bitterness about your home team, plummeting into a dark resentment that only heavy drinking or disengagement from the team's fortunes can transcend. It's no good saying, *It's just a game,* because it's not just a game to the players—it's their livelihood; they have to succeed or give their place up to someone younger, stronger, more talented. And it's not just a game to fans, it's something to do with who we are and how we see ourselves and how we want the world to see us, our very identity.

SNAPSHOT: SPORTS FEVER 2

We return.

Loss after loss. Our heads slump forward, we breathe out heavily and bang the railing in disbelief. We mumble and grumble.

Enstrom is trapped against the boards in his own end. The puck comes loose. He makes a desperate lunge to retrieve it but the opponent throws it out front of the net and the other team's sniper snaps it home. Burmistrov scoots into the other team's zone, does a nifty 180 pirouette at the top of the circle, takes two strides back toward the blue line, then pirouettes again, losing the puck to a bigger, stronger opponent.

The chants go out like a candle flame. We drop our heads. Behind us the guy moans, "Oh, Enstrom." Grumbler says, "See, like I said, too fancy."

There's a knot in our gut and we think, This doesn't happen at the opera. Not so much is at stake, somehow. And it's so much easier on the system, enjoyable, but not gut-wracking. Or the symphony. Sane, adult entertainments. Sensible pastimes.

I think from time to time about the relation between sports and theatre. Both offer burning drama about essentially unimportant matters in our actual lives. Too, we become deeply engaged in the theatre, horrified Juliet will actually tip the vial of poison to her lips. But it's not heart-in-throat intense, like the game. We know, although we have willingly suspended disbelief, as the poet put it, that Juliet will kill herself, and that Romeo will follow suit. But in the game the outcome is unknown, and that makes all the difference: the result hangs in the balance.

Though the team is playing poorly, there may be a sea change. The game and the players are not locked into roles that lead to proscribed conclusions.

And so it is.

Byfuglien wheels at the top of the circle, takes a quick snapshot, the net bulges. Yay, team, yay, Big Buff! Bogosian steps up at the blue line and lays a crunching hit on an opponent. Well done! Antropov outmuscles a defenceman in the corner and throws it out front where it's jammed into the net. Yay, team!

We are beside ourselves with joy, this is how life should be lived.

The rink is a limited arena, confined to 200 feet by 60, six players on a side, referees to curtail cheating, a time frame of minutes and seconds in which the result is decided. Our own lives have an amorphous framework; the job may carry on for weeks; weaselly co-workers undermine us and scheme for the promotion we should rightly get; the work goes on year after year; no one says thanks or well done; no one cares how many tax forms we read through, how many pots of pasta are cooked on the stove, how many shingles banged into roofs or history papers marked.

Our lives have few distinct edges, are filled with minor setbacks and defeats and humiliations and disappointments. How much for the children's orthodontist? Good god, have to work another year before retiring. Your ailing mother is coming to live in the guest room? How many months will that be, years? Rumours of layoffs, cutbacks, a new tax—to pay for what? Our lives are a tangle of obligations and frets and endless responsibilities over which we can exercise no control.

Life wears us down. We're dishrags of worry and turmoil.

But these young men. They fly up and down the ice, they score, they celebrate goals with teammates, they bash into each other. Oh, to be able to hit the boss that hard, to leap from the car and administer a thrashing to the jerk who cut you off in traffic with the grim satisfaction evident on these players' faces as they head to the penalty box. To feel the elation of the tying goal, the game-winning save. By the end of an hour (and maybe a bit) of play, a conclusion has been reached. It's all black and white, it's all good and bad, it's all *us* and *them*.

A simple, defined, delimited world. And no consequences. Not for us fans, at least. Just the unmixed pleasure of throwing our own desires and fears out there with the boys and letting them work things out.

Projection, psychologists call it. Parents at a game lustily cheering on their child, reliving their own youth, hoping that their offspring will today be the hero they never quite could be, the star fawned over by the madding crowds. Reliving their own past moments of glory in seeing a bit of yourself excel.

Yay, Burmistrov! Go Jets Go! YES!

———————

Despite the Jets' stumbling start to the season, their fans are wholly behind their team. Before the opening faceoff they're chanting Go Jets Go! The arena is packed, another sellout. On the CBC, the TV commentator notes, "Hockey is back in Winnipeg, another boisterous crowd tonight. And I love it."

Get through the first ten minutes.

The buzz in the stands rises and falls. The Jets get their first shot. The crowd is already working their *psyche* on Boucher, the goaltender: *Boo-shay, Boo-shay.* They do this standing, making a tomahawk motion, directed at the opposition goal, while chanting the goaltender's name, drawn out in a mocking way, as would be done on the schoolyard. And it does echo of schoolyard bullying, though mostly it resonates prankish juvenile buffoonery.

"It's a young team," the commentator says, "you have to be patient. They're fast and learning to play together, but they will deliver, the question is just how long it will take."

The play is even, the crowd noisy. Carolina score just before the five-minute mark, from a scramble in front of the net, the puck jammed in, an ugly goal. For a few minutes the crowd is deflated, but it's not long before the cheering starts again: Go Jets Go! Then Carolina score again just past the halfway point of the period. The Jets coach changes goaltenders.

Here we go again.

I'm sitting in a bar in Kenora with a writer pal, Dennis. We share a love

SEC: XX ROW: XX SEAT:XX

HOME GAME 07

JETS VS HURRICANES

OCTOBER 22, 2011

SEC: XX
ROW: XX
SEAT: XX

of sports: baseball, hockey, CFL football. "They don't look very good," he says.

"Terrible," I say. "All over the place."

"So many young players."

"They're up and down, violent swings. Whole periods when they look awful, followed by whole periods when they look unbeatable."

The words are hardly out of our mouths when the Jets score, and then begins a flurry around the Carolina net, the Jets pressing, pucks zinging at the Carolina net, the Hurricanes back on their heels. They're at the end of a long road trip and playing the second of back-to-back games. But they're ahead.

Against Carolina the Jets are playing chameleon. One sign of a young team—or a team that hasn't found its identity, which often amounts to the same thing—is that it takes its cue on how it plays on a given night from its opponent. If the Flyers are playing a grind-it-out, hard-checking physical game, complete with fisticuffs—the Jets do that too. They let the other guys dictate the style of play. If Carolina plays fire-wagon hockey, dashes up and down the ice, wild scrambles around the nets, the Jets follow suit. There doesn't yet appear to be a Jets "style" of play. Like a younger brother, they follow the lead of older bro. And it means fans are never quite sure what they're going to get on a given night—a 5-4 hair-on-fire tilt, or a 2-1 close checking contest.

At least in their home buildings, where the fans, where the last line change influence the pace of the game and nature of the checking, most teams play an established brand: Montreal is going to feature end-to-end hockey in the tradition of the great Canadiens—Rocket Richard, Guy Lafleur. And Boston is going to use its big bashers to choke off such wide-open play and try to win by fierce checking and "shut-down" tactics.

The two previous incarnations of the Jets—WHA and NHL both—played "river" hockey, because Hull, Hedberg, and Nilsson could carry the game with speed and finesse, and Hawerchuk, Lindstrom, and Steen were shifty and nifty, brilliant in the opponent's end and dazzlingly enter-taining. The "new" Jets could fit this mould—they're young, fast, skilled. They could gel as a dynamic force in the NHL. But it will take time. And in the meantime, they're likely to take their cue on any given night, cha-meleon-like, from their opponents.

The Jets score again right at the buzzer marking the end of the first period. It's been a wild twenty minutes, first Carolina carrying the play for ten minutes, then the Jets. But the crowd senses the momentum has shifted. As the teams leave the ice the chants of Go Jets Go can still be heard. And they start up again before the teams are back on the ice for the second. For the young Jets, who played in front of 8500 indolent fans in Atlanta the past few years, this gung-ho support must be buoyant.

They score early in the second period to make it 3-2, and then rattle in two more goals within a matter of minutes, the second by young Evander Kane, one of the team's up-and-comers, a snapshot he gets away from the top of the circle with lightning speed, a goal instantly imprinted in the brain to remain forever: a different kind of snapshot. By the halfway mark of the period it's 5-2 and the shots favour the Jets by a margin. The turnaround has occurred. This how it is with young teams: dreadful for ten minutes at a time, unbeatable for twenty minutes running.

Still, there's that third period, where they've been outscored 8-1. Can they hang on? Their record is not heartening. But Carolina already look leg-weary.

They hang in there, though, pressing at times in the third period, at times holding steady against Jets forays into their end. The crowd keeps chanting: Go Jets Go! Carolina press, hit the post. On a power play, the puck dribbles through the crease; Mason, the goaltender, makes a great save, then three more in a flurry. Then they score: 5-3. The Canes, buoyed by the goal, keep skating, and the Jets take first one penalty, then another. Shots whistle past their goal, hit the post again; Carolina jam the crease, the puck flutters along the goal line behind Mason, but is swept away at the last second. Hair-raising stuff. Carolina has a 7-2 advantage in shots. The Jets take another penalty, then another; Carolina has a five-on-three advantage and lift their goaltender, attacking with fury. Somehow the puck stays out of the Jets goal. They gasp to the final buzzer. The game ends 5-3.

"They didn't make it easy," Dennis says.

"Nothing's going to be easy with these guys."

On the positive side, they netted five goals, where in the previous half-dozen together they had managed only eleven.

There's that third-period, though. They've been outscored 9-1 in seven games. We fans are wholly behind the team but are we ever satisfied?

SNAPSHOT: JETS 4 EVER

From the upper deck at the last home game the Jets played in 1996 hung a banner that read WE WILL LOVE OUR JETS 4 EVER. It was a vertical banner of maybe twenty feet in length and there was one word on each "step" downwards, bright red letters against a white background, possibly a bedsheet.

The banner was a testament to a team that had emerged in the city in 1972, and which, through the WHA era, specialized in delight and success for seven years. A team that excelled at the kind of hockey the city loved: open play, end-to-end dashes, players with pizzazz and finesse. And they were winners: in the WHA they had won 302 games out of the 555 they played. They had been in five WHA finals and won the Cup three times, the last in the league's closing year of operation.

The WHA Jets passed that legacy on to their NHL club—though there was a painful interregnum immediately following the transition, when the NHL effectively dismantled the team. Overall, still, the team did well.

But that banner was about more than the team's success. It was equally—if not more—about the fans. Look at those opening words again: "We Will Love Our Jets." The banner is about the fans, how the fans felt (and feel) about the team, the way they care, come hell or high water. They love the team the way a mother loves her child: always and deeply—even if it's wayward or difficult, even if it's a pain in the ass. In many respects a pro team is its fans, more than it is its players. Players, for all their endearing play, move on, sometimes signing better contracts with other clubs, often traded, sometimes just leaving the game as younger, better players surpass them—or out of exhaustion. The same is true of coaches. They come and go. Intensely involved in the club during their tenure, coaches are fired or take a better position with another club. In their seven-year history the WHA Jets had six coaches. Managers fare better, but they too come and go. It's the fans who are the continuous presence in the club, and though some of them come and go, the core of fans remains constant, the real centre of the team.

They fall into three rough categories. Casual fans attend two or three games a year, read the sport pages, watch games on TV, and are interested in the game in a global sense—they're fans of the game rather than supporters of the home team. More committed are the Regulars, attenders who have season tickets and go to half the home games or more. They know the roster, who is injured, and what prospects the club has in the minors. They rail against bad trades and applaud the club's courage to stick with promising players and coaches that have a system which may take time to produce results. They cheer when the team win and are deflated when they lose, but it's not life-and-death. Then there are the fans, who deck themselves out in team jerseys for every game, attend as many home games as possible, travel to see games in other cities a few times a year, flock to rallies, visit blog sites, broadcast their views on Facebook, phone call-in shows, feel their lives are intertwined with the team's.

Real Fans are obsessives. Families and friends know that if they hold a child's christening on a home date or schedule a party, the Fan will not attend, offering a weak excuse; they're at the game. They make things difficult on their families and make ridiculous demands—that Gran's eigtieth birthday party be rescheduled to not conflict with home games. They drive their work colleagues crazy with constant talk about the team, and with absurd analogies about wider events: how the stock market collapse is just like the home club's current losing streak; how the US involvement in Iraq is like parachuting in free agents to a team trying to make it into the playoffs; how the team's current difficulties in the locker room are like the unravelling of a marriage. They know they're a nuisance to everyone around (except other Fans), but they can't do anything about it; they're obsessives—the gamblers, collectors of dolls, watchers of "their program" on soap TV. But they are the club and the club is them—in most important respects. Without them, there would be, very possibly, no club as an entity at all. They come to feel that after a decade or so, they *are* the team, they're its continuity and its history. They are the core of the club; in the non-financial sense, they "own" the team, and the team owns them—their fears, wishes, anxieties, dreams, everything, goal-line to goal-line.

So, yes, "Our Jets 4 Ever."

SEC: XX ROW: XX SEAT:XX

HOME GAME 08
JETS VS
RANGERS
OCTOBER 24, 2011

SEC: XX
ROW: XX
SEAT: XX

There's an expectation in the arena. The Jets have won two home games in succession, tied the Leafs on the road. That's five points in the past four games, a better than .500 record, things seem to be looking up. But don't hold your breath. It's the Jets. Disappointment waits around the next corner, desperate as a mugger.

Just get through the next ten minutes.

That's my mantra.

The crowd marches to the beat of a different drummer. Go Jets Go! They're not holding their breath. They're expending huge gasps of exultation. And the Jets are playing the Rangers, an Original Six club. Go Jets Go! Stamping and waving banners five minutes before the drop of the opening faceoff. The arena is throbbing.

Go Jets Go! This is the three-word refrain of the fans. Each word comes out separately and with increasing emphasis, the opening "Go" starting at a low register that builds into the word "Jets," stamped with guttural authority and followed by the repeated "Go," now loud and at a higher pitch and greater intensity, becoming at its climax a fierce shout. Almost never do the fans chant the phrase just once. A second triad follows the first, and a third the second, so that a virtual verbal assault occurs—three triads built one on top of the other in rapid succession, a ninefold cry at higher and more urgent pitch that fills the arena with sound and vibrates its plexiglass: Go Jets Go! Go Jets Go! Go Jets Go!

The game begins at high tempo, both teams defending their ends well, both pressing the forecheck, both attacking with poise. There aren't many shots and yet the play is engaging, exciting. This is real pro hockey. I shift in my seat, interested, one hand stroking my jaw as I lean forward.

In the stands the crowd picks up the chant from time to time: Go Jets Go!

The Jets take a penalty. The Jets coach, Claude Noel, has said, "We're taking too many penalties." He's right, it's been the team's Achilles' heel; they're taking a lot of careless, unnecessary fouls and killing them at only

13%, 22nd in the league. A good percentage would be around 20%, average in the NHL.

In the current NHL, rule changes have made penalties abound. A lot more obstruction is called, and hooking and holding too. Any time a player reaches in with his stick from behind toward an opponent carrying the puck and unbalances him or tangles up his hands, or impedes his speed, there's a chance one or the other will be called. Players have to position themselves beside opponents now to avoid such calls, and that means catching up to speedy skaters, not always easy to do. And any contact along the boards is open to various calls, from boarding to unsportsmanlike conduct. So the Jets are not so much playing dirty, knocking opponents over in the crease with cross-checks and the like, as they're showing their inexperience in the greyer areas of foul play.

Whatever, they're taking penalties at an alarming rate—and giving up a lot of goals.

Still, the first period ends 0-0, a solidly played first frame, if not blazingly exciting. Shots 8-3 favouring Jets. We'll take it.

The Rangers continue playing a very good game: organized in the Jets end, disciplined in the neutral zone, holding their positions in their own. As with any team, there are flurries when the opposition gets them running around, and the Jets are good at that—but then so are the Rangers in the Jets' end. It's an enjoyable game to watch, both teams energetic and looking like they could win.

At the five-minute mark of the second period, the Jets take a penalty, and a minute later the Rangers score a powerplay goal on only their sixth shot of the game. The Grumbler behind says of the Jets, "They're not strong enough in front of net."

But the Jets press on. They're playing a good game too, a professional-looking game: clearing their zone cleanly, forechecking well, not taking too many chances. I'm enjoying it. This is the best the Jets have looked this season.

And they score. In the fifteenth minute, big Antropov again. At the end of a fairly slow but well-played period the score stands even and the shots are 15-10, Jets.

In the intermission, I'm standing near the bar near our seats and feel a hand on my elbow. "Here he is," a voice says, and when I turn I encounter my old high-school friend, Smitty, who led our juvenile team to the finals of the provincial play-downs two years running, yogs and yogs ago.

"How about that," I say, "I was just thinking of you today, those games in Pilot Mound and Cartwright. And La Broquerie."

"Right, great games, good times." He runs one hand through his silver-grey hair.

"We lost."

"I know that. Hoo-boy, I know that."

"Even though in both cases we were ahead coming home."

"We remember this stuff," he says to Kristen, standing beside me. "Forty-some years ago and we remember this stuff, every detail, the score was 6-5." He runs his hand through wavy hair again and shakes his head. "Hoo-boy, do we remember."

"I coughed up the puck in our end."

"Hah. It wasn't you who lost us that game."

"It was, you know. I was the goat."

"You were not to blame."

"Well," I say, "and what do you say about this game?"

"A little slow in spots. But good. They have a chance to win."

I ask him, "You got an old Royals jacket kicking around?"

"Maybe not a jacket, maybe a crest from a jacket."

"Even better, that's what I actually want."

He raises his eyebrows. But he's a lawyer by training, he knows not to ask. "I'll look around," he adds. "In the clutter. I might just have one."

The third period goes on as the two previous. The crowd comes to life when one of the Rangers is levelled by Byfuglien near centre ice. Go Jets Go! rings through the arena. Near the four-minute mark the Jets put on sustained and great pressure in the Rangers' end, zinging shots on goal, pinging one off the post, it goes on for almost three minutes; they have to score. But they don't. And then the Jets take another penalty and the Rangers score. The crowd goes silent.

Though the Jets press, coming close several times, the Rangers check hard in the Jets zone, limiting their chances, and the game ends 2-1, shots in favour of the home team 28-17. A groan goes through the crowd.

"Should have won that one," I say to Kristen.

"Good game though."

"Their best, their most professional."

"Entertaining," she concludes, "but yeah, too bad."

As we leave, I locate Smitty in the crowd, still sitting, one hand slowly stroking his jaw. He knows too.

SNAPSHOT: Years Ago

Late spring 1964, the arena, La Broquerie, Manitoba. It's late in the third period of the juvenile play-downs. The puck flutters into our end, shot by a forward from Pilot Mound. I wheel and dash into the corner, the Pilot Mound centre hot on my tail. I feel his warm breath on my neck, hear him grunt as we get to the puck, which slowly tumbles along the boards in the direction of the net. I'm in panic mode.

The puck cannot come out of the corner. We're ahead by one goal in a home-and-home set that will take either them or us to the finals. We've gone into their arena and beat them 4-3. Though we're actually the Royals from Steinbach, the La Broquerie Arena is our home ice.

I jam one skate against the puck. The Pilot Mound guy is shorter than me but has a fire-hydrant build, when we come together on the boards he uses his weight to try to leverage me off the puck. I shove back. He gets his stick between my feet and hacks at the puck. I push back. I hear other skaters throwing up ice near our goal, my teammates arriving to help. Do I relax in that knowledge? Whatever, the Pilot Mound guy forces the puck free, it dribbles past my feet. I stretch my leg to trap it again, my stick goes out on my extended arm to retrieve it but he's already pounced, and in one motion whips it out front. In a moment it's in our net.

Goat. Our parents and fans sigh and groan. Pilot Mound's few supporters, who have travelled from the far corner of the province, cheer lustily. Smitty taps my shin pads with his stick. Tough luck.

There are still five minutes to play. From the bench I watch our guys move into the opposition end and fight mightily to score. I put my head down. Gary L punches my knee with his gloved fist. We'll get them. I feel sick enough to puke. The period ends.

Overtime. The puck goes up and down the ice. Smitty makes a dash into the opposition end and takes a wrist shot high to the stick side; the goaltender fends it off. On the bench I take a deep breath. I can feel Gary L breathing hard to my side. If we win, it's the finals against Cartwright, a team we beat last year. Smitty comes to the bench. I tap his knee pads. Tough luck.

One shift follows another. Both teams are tiring, I sense it in my legs. Ten minutes in, I fumble the puck near centre ice. A Pilot Mound forward jumps on it. He's between me and the boards and can't get past me with the puck so we end up trundling against each other in the corner. I jam my skate against the puck. It can't come out. His breath is hot on my neck; with his free hand he shoves the middle of my back. He's another short guy who levers me off the puck. It springs loose and he pounces on it and in one motion wheels to the front of our net and jams it in.

Silence chokes the arena.

In the dressing room, we sit with our gear on, heads down. Coach tells us we played a great game, a couple of bad breaks. I can barely swallow. I look across at Smitty. His mouth forms a bitten smile. Tough luck. I look away. He's my pal and my hero, a slicker player than me, more savvy. I've let him down.

The coach says we'll come back next year.

I look at Smitty and he smiles another tight smile. Next year we'll be in college in the city. We've missed our chance. Is there any worse feeling?

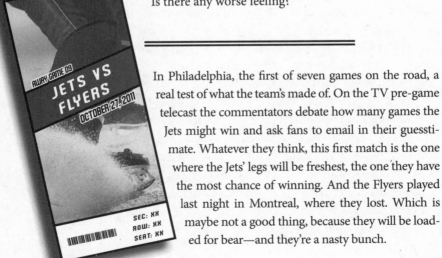

In Philadelphia, the first of seven games on the road, a real test of what the team's made of. On the TV pre-game telecast the commentators debate how many games the Jets might win and ask fans to email in their guesstimate. Whatever they think, this first match is the one where the Jets' legs will be freshest, the one they have the most chance of winning. And the Flyers played last night in Montreal, where they lost. Which is maybe not a good thing, because they will be loaded for bear—and they're a nasty bunch.

They score first—despite Jets pressure and at the four-minute mark, not the most encouraging sign. But the Jets don't fold, they tally three goals before period end in what will become one of the most bizarre games ever seen. By the middle of the second period the Jets are ahead 5-1, then 6-2, though the Flyers are outshooting them by a wide margin; by period end when the score has become a remarkable 6-4, the shots are 32-19 in favour of the Flyers. Their crowd is on a roller-coaster ride, first seeing their team close the gap, then seeing it widen again.

The commentators are beside themselves. So is the Flyers coach. His squad is a tight-checking outfit, the Jets are known as a team that has difficulty scoring. The third period opens with the Flyers scoring three unanswered goals, taking the lead 7-6. But they give it up and the Jets go ahead early in the period 8-7. Only to see the Flyers tie the score with less than four minutes remaining. Jets fans' hearts sink. Here we go again, the Jets will be lucky to salvage one point from what looked like an easy victory. But then with less than two minutes left, the Jets score again, making the score 9-8, and though the Flyers press through the remaining time—goaltender lifted, nasty tactics in front of the Jets goal—they cannot tie the score and it ends 9-8.

In the post-game interview the Jets coach, scratching his head, can only say he's never seen anything like it. "We'll take the two points," he says, "but there's a lot of work to be done." Two points, though, against a division rival, 7 of the last 12.

SEC: XX ROW: XX SEAT: XX

AWAY GAME 10

JETS VS LIGHTNING

OCTOBER 29, 2011

SEC: XX
ROW: XX
SEAT: XX

Coming into Tampa Bay the Jets coach has one more thing to say: his team is taking too many penalties, averaging seven a game; he'd like to see that down to four.

Tampa Bay is a team loaded with talent. Lecavalier, St. Louis, and Stamkos all boast dazzling scoring statistics in the NHL. Their powerplay is potent. Yet the Jets play even with them through the first period, a good professional game, disciplined but with chances at both ends. But no scoring. The pattern continues in the second, the team's trading scoring chances, and it isn't until very late in the frame that Tampa tally, on a powerplay. In the third, the Jets press, but without losing their form; yet, despite their efforts, the game ends 1-0 for Tampa, an exciting game despite the low score. (And only four penalties.)

A certain irony is beginning to develop about this version of the Jets: when they play a solid and professional game, they lose by a low score: 2-1, 1-0. In their more wide open games—the match against the Flyers tells the tale—they seem to have better luck, though they haven't won many of those games either. It's early in the season, they're a young and inexperienced team, they're learning to play with each other, they're developing a style. Clichés? Rash hope of the desperate fan?

Their record after ten games is three wins, six losses, and one tie, seven out of twenty points. A lot of work to be done.

29 October 2011

Team	GP	PTS
Pittsburgh	13	18
Toronto	10	15
Washington	9	14
Philadelphia	11	13
Buffalo	10	12
Florida	10	12
Tampa Bay	11	12
Ottawa	11	12
Carolina	11	11
Montreal	11	10
New York R	9	9
New Jersey	9	9
New York I	9	8
Winnipeg	10	7
Boston	10	6

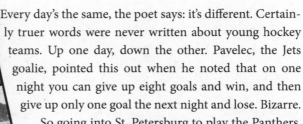

Every day's the same, the poet says: it's different. Certainly truer words were never written about young hockey teams. Up one day, down the other. Pavelec, the Jets goalie, pointed this out when he noted that on one night you can give up eight goals and win, and then give up only one goal the next night and lose. Bizarre.

So going into St. Petersburg to play the Panthers, no one is quite sure what to expect. The Jets score early. And then before the ten-minute mark, again. Florida is a speedy team, so it's a bit of a surprise that the Jets outplay them throughout the first period, though the Panthers score with less than three minutes remaining in the period. And the Jets have been outshot 20-7.

There's really little to choose between the teams, both relying on speed to carry the play, tempo, pace. But the Jets are beginning to show a weakness—when the other team presses around their goal, there are furious scrambles that the Jets seem unable to clear. And the other teams are catching on. There's a lot of play in close, right in the blue paint. And goals are being coughed up: Enstrom doesn't have the body weight to be effective there; Jones seems a little lost. If they're not scored against, the Jets are taking penalties that too often lead to powerplay goals. Yes, work to do.

Still, the second period is scoreless, so the Jets go into the final frame ahead by a goal. Can they hang on? They can't. They give up an early goal and then with less than three minutes remaining, Florida go ahead. 3-2. Another heart-sickening loss, it appears, same old Jets, but in the dying seconds they score to tie the game, and then win in the shootout. It seems a miracle, a nearly perfect comeback.

Three games into the road trip, they've won two and lost one. And the two most recent games have been played with discipline and patience.

Can they continue that against the Islanders?

In New York the Jets are without their puck-moving defenceman, Enstrom, whose collarbone was broken in the Florida game, and their most consistent blue-liner, Hainsey, still out with his injury. They're thin on defence and have called up players from the minors. Road trips take their toll, and this is a team that struggles in its own end. Things do not look good.

But they come out playing hard and score before the five-minute mark. Can they hang on? Past evidence says *no*, but that's why the games are played, and this one is an even contest from the outset. Evander Kane, who scored the first goal, hits the post on a penalty shot. *Could have used that little cushion.* The first period ends 1-0 for the Jets, and in the second they hang on, though the Islanders pour on the pressure and the Jets take penalties and fling their bodies in front of fourteen shots that don't even get to the net (nineteen do), and it's déjà vu all over again. It seems like just a matter of time before the collapse begins. But at period end the score stands 1-0.

Can they possibly hang on like this? Another defenceman has gone down with an injury. *Get through the first ten minutes.* They do, and then score on a lucky bounce with less than five minutes remaining and pot an empty-net goal—3-0. With 34 shots taken at their goal and 19 blocked in addition to that.

A wild ride that has brought the team close to a .500 record. 5-6-1.

And feisty Kane has tallied a "Gordie Howe hat trick": goal, assist, fight.

But the team is beat up—beat up, injured, and tired. The seven-game road trip has brought the team to the point of exhaustion. You can see it toward the ends of periods in every game now: skaters are leg-weary, there's a lot of stretching to make poke checks where a jumping step is what's required to truly challenge for the puck.

Extended road trips are a crime, really, they cheat fans, because a team playing on the fifth of eight days inevitably becomes leg-weary past the halfway point in the game. But that's the price fans pay for the greed of the owners and players, both wanting to maximize ticket sales—at the expense of the quality of the game. So teams play 82 games in a period of about 180 days, a game every 2.2 days. That's hardly a day for rest and recovery between each and every game. With the air travel and shuttling between hotels and arenas, trying to squeeze in "morning skates," and the occasional practices, the players are constantly on the move, "flus" rage through locker rooms, further exhausting them, minor injuries pile up, every season becomes a marathon.

Getting through the schedule is a campaign of attrition, and winning teams are those that survive, as much as play brilliant hockey. It's the life. From the outside it might seem glamorous—television exposure, fat salaries, the adulation of fans—but the life of the pro hockey player is a grind. By their late thirties—only rare athletes manage to play past forty—when these guys retire, they're worn out. Beat up from years of travel and dozens of major and minor bone breaks, tendon tears and the like, they look at forty-five to be ten years older, and many hobble through the remainder of their years, barely able to play a round of golf every week or so.

Pro athletes make a lot of money in their brief careers but they're modern-day gladiators, sacrificing their bodies on the altar of our entertainment whims and the lust for more revenues that drives team owners and Gary Bettman.

SNAPSHOT: Bête noire

What is it with Gary Bettman?

We despise him in Winnipeg, he took our original Jets away. But the man is widely and profoundly disliked across the NHL, booed loudly when he shows up to make official presentations in other cities. So this odium is not confined to our city.

He's arrogant, sure. He represents New York and all that self-important town stands for. But there's something else. Some people just come across as slippery.

Then, too, he's the epitome of the current CEO, driven by the business ethic of the bottom line. He spouts words like "transitioning teams" and "rebranding." We know what he really means; but it's the pretence turns our stomachs.

We suspect he cares nothing about hockey; he may know little about the game, and he cares little for its fans, its players, or the cities that they play in. He probably has never put on a pair of skates in his life. Diamond-box defences, near-post passes are foreign words to him. But he can zip through double-entry bookkeeping at the speed of Jeff Skinner, he can maneuver through a financial spreadsheet with the skill of Pavel Datsyuk.

He was probably surprised, maybe even shocked, at the outpouring of emotion when teams were pulled out of Quebec City and Winnipeg. Save the Jets campaigns, women weeping in the street. He has no emotional attachment to the game of hockey, how could these people be so upset? How could they say he'd ripped the heart out of their city?

Sports is not hearts, it's product.

It's the Monopoly mentality. Teams are "franchises," tokens on a board. Things aren't working out on Tennessee Avenue, move to Marvin Gardens, maybe things will go better there.

In England there are fans who follow football teams passionately. They stand in the rain and sleet and snow of autumn and winter, cheering their home team. They attend every home and many away games. These are not the fans of Queen's Park Rangers or Manchester United, these are the fans of Leyton Orient and Banstead Athletic, lower divisions of the Football League, standing in bleachers in arenas that hold no more than 10,000 spectators. They may attend a Premier League game every now and then—they can easily afford to do that, cost is not the issue—but their real love is the home team. Because it's theirs, because lads from the neighbourhood play on it, because it has a past and history stretching back over a hundred years, because it's a cornerstone of the community, their granddad cheered for this team, their dad, it's *theirs*. Their hearts are in it.

Would Gary Bettman understand this?

He's the opposite of the woman in tears because her father will never get to go to a Jets game with her son.

Gary Bettman wants his league, the NHL, to be a big-time league. For that to happen, it must be located in major US cities, "keystone" cities:

Chicago, New York, Miami, Atlanta, Dallas, Los Angeles, Phoenix. Only then will it be equivalent to other leagues, the NFL, the NBA, Major League Baseball. It can afford a small market team here and there—Edmonton, the NHL's Milwaukee—but for the NHL to be big-league, it must be in major US cities, where it can acquire "maximum exposure," and the giant TV contract that supposedly goes with it.

This is what Gary Bettman cares about: bottom lines, franchises, branding. In our hearts we know this guy and we fear him: he's a dangerous man because he has no commitment. Tomorrow he could be the commissioner of the newly formed World Jai Alai League.

SEC: XX ROW: XX SEAT:XX

AWAY GAME 13
JETS VS DEVILS
NOVEMBER 05, 2011

SEC: XX
ROW: XX
SEAT: XX

"I suppose," Kristen says before the beginning of the game in New Jersey, "we should not hold out much hope for the remaining three games."

We shouldn't. The Jets have performed admirably in the opening four: three wins and one loss. Almost too much to have hoped for. To play evenly against their opponents in the final three games will require discipline and good luck.

It's clear from the outset that the Devils know the Jets have injury difficulties; they start with a full-court press, hemming in the depleted Jets defence, focusing their bodychecks on key Jets forwards Kane and Ladd. Can the Jets hang on? They can. By mid-period the Devils have dropped the intensity of their attack and the game is played at a slower pace, fast and focused, but not frenzied. The period ends with no scoring and the shots close to equal.

The Jets are not as lucky in the second period. The Devils score early and then again just past the halfway mark of the frame. 2-0. It's going to be a long way back. And the Devils are in control, both through the remainder of the second period and the early part of the third.

"Not much chance," Kristen says, sighing.

"Never know," Andrew says. "If they can get one…"

I agree. "These guys have been resilient on this trip, more resilient than I thought they could be." But I'm also thinking, *not likely.* After five hard games, the tank is near empty; it must be easy for the Jets to think, *oh well, fold up the tents.*

But they don't, scoring near the seven-minute mark, and then pressing onto the attack, taking the game away from the Devils. This is what it means to be young; self-belief matched by seeming boundless reserves of energy. By mid-period the game is up for grabs, and the Jets score with less than three minutes left to tie it up, rumbustious Jim Slater showing once again tenacity and vim.

It's amazing, really. The Devils are a strong squad. And among the best in the league at holding onto a lead.

"I'm impressed," I say in the break before the overtime. "Not just by the salvaged point but by the never-give-up attitude. These guys have got sand."

Andrew raises one eyebrow. "How's that now?"

"Sand, you know, grit, stick-to-itiveness."

And even though they give up a goal in the overtime, that impression remains at game-end. These guys don't give up.

But the schedule does not relent, either. Less than twenty-four hours later, the Jets face off in Madison Square Garden against the Rangers.

What does this night hold?

Another good game, it turns out. The Rangers are a well-coached team and they play a solid professional game, especially between the blue lines, where they are organized and check the opponent, waiting for breaks to occur, from which they forge speedy, forceful attacks. But the Jets play well, too, dumping the puck deep, cycling and pressing the net, and the first period ends a scoreless draw, both teams working hard, both teams playing disciplined hockey.

SEC: XX ROW: XX SEAT:XX

AWAY GAME 14

JETS VS RANGERS

NOVEMBER 06, 2011

SEC: XX
ROW: XX
SEAT: XX

One noticeable difference between NHL hockey in 2011 and that of 1996 is the preparedness of teams at the beginning of the season. In 1996, teams kind of worked themselves into the season through October and November, and then started to play seriously in December. This is not the players themselves we're talking about; by the 1990s players were arriving in training camp in top shape, having spent the summer working out in the gym and playing "shinny" with buddies. Everyone was arriving in mid-season form.

Back in the day, in the 1960s, players "played themselves into condition" in the pre-season games and the early matches of the schedule. The New York Rangers held their training camp in Fort Frances, Ontario, when I was a teen, a rink rat who helped out at the local arena, got to do a little skating in off-hours, and saw guys like Andy Bathgate come to camp huffing and puffing through skating drills and sweating on the bench between shifts of intra-squad games. All that changed through the '80s and '90s. Players showed up ready to go near top speed.

But the teams themselves were not as prepared. They began the season in a sort of experimental phase, juggling lines, feeling out opponents, viewing the opening twenty or so games as a run-up to the real playing, which began around Christmas. Now that has changed. Every game, from game one onward, is contested as if it was game eighty. The play is intense, the skating full-out. Every point counts. Everyone is aware that points lost or gained in October are as important as those in March. On the night the Jets came back against the Devils to salvage a point with a 2-2 tie, there were eleven other games played, seven of which were won by one goal or went into overtimes and shootouts to determine who got the extra point on the night. Nothing is being given away.

At Madison Square Garden against the Rangers, surprisingly, the Jets, playing game seven in ten days, do not look tired. They do, though, start to take penalties in the second period, and one of these costs them a goal just past the halfway mark of the game. It proves to be the winner. For the Rangers check fiercely afterward, and well into the third period, and from a badly-timed *pinch* by Byfuglien at the Rangers blue line, add the marker that seals the deal. Final score: 3-0.

One more game on the road trip.

It's in Buffalo and the Jets start fast, taking a 2-0 lead but through blundering play and a lashing of penalties by a pair of Jesuitical referees, they lose in overtime. A very frustrating game, a game determined—and ruined— by the officials.

These are the kinds of games that got my father's goat, as he would have said. In his day there were only six teams in the NHL. The '50s and '60s. The CBC brought us one game a week, on Saturday, always the Leafs or Canadiens. You were forced in effect to become a fan of one or the other. My father would not cheer for the Canadiens, he hated John Ferguson, a bully in his opinion, and cheering them was like pulling for God, since they won often. So, a farm boy, an underdog, a Winnipegger used to being oppressed by fat cats in the East, by default he was a Leafs fan. (One who possibly didn't recognize the paradox of his position.) And when Leafs gave up bad goals or leads late in games, or suffered a series of bad calls, he rose from the sofa in the living room, went into the kitchen and poured a hefty whiskey. A way of dealing with stress. When you watch games on TV, it's a different experience than in person. At arenas you're part of a crowd, you can scream aloud, jump to your feet, stamp cement flooring, scream more. But at home that release is not on offer. You're tempted to punch the wall, throw furniture. But mostly you don't. You internalize this stuff, pour a strong drink, and feel a hard knot in your gut. This meme has been passed down in the Tefs family.

Still, a close game, 5-4, which concludes the seven-game road trip 3-2-2, eight of fourteen points. Leaving the ice in Buffalo, the Jets look exhausted; but they should not be demoralized: over the ten-day road trip they've played well and shown composure, resilience, and determination.

Several things, though, have become clear through the opening fifteen or so games.

First, two of the team's supposed leaders, Ladd and Byfuglien, guys who should be showing the way to their younger teammates, are becoming liabilities. Both are showing bad judgement on the ice—pinching at inopportune moments, coughing up the puck in their own end—and taking bad penalties, infractions borne of frustration.

Second, Claude Noel, the coach, is making mistakes. Through the season's opening games he has had two solid lines, and on the night of the Buffalo game he breaks one of them up, his "fourth" line, his checkers, presumably to gain offence, but instead he sacrifices the line's dogged skating and fierce checking, which often turn around the momentum in games, and this move gains nothing in return on the offensive side.

Finally, it's clear that the NHL is still dogged by incompetent officiating. The two doufuses in charge of this game, Dean Morton and Ian Walsh, make a total hash out of things. They manage to give Buffalo three 5-on-3 odd-man advantages, and call thirteen penalties against the Jets to five for the Sabres. It may sound like home-team sour grapes, but very, very few games are that one-sided, and these two effectively determined the outcome of the game by doing their job ineptly.

It raises a question we sometimes ask of players in the NHL but never, it seems to me, about its referees: *who are these guys?* We're aware the players come up through the ranks, often from straightened circumstances, often from small towns, pro hockey being their one ticket out of Nowheresville. Paperback heroes, in the words of the songster. It's not entirely the case; more kids are going to US colleges on scholarship and more are seeking similar avenues on the Canadian scene. But junior hockey—and its promise of a pro career—remains an escape for what in the cycling world are known as *ploucs*: farm boys and working-class kids with few other prospects in life who would otherwise be looking at little more in their lifetimes than throwing bags at the airport or washing windows.

It's the long-established story of pro sport being an avenue out of poverty and limited opportunity for boys from backgrounds of hard work and hard knocks. This is true about the players but it's equally true of the referees, who are guys who could not make it past junior hockey, pro wannabes, who can skate and know the game from having played it, but these may not be the premier credentials for a career in officiating, which requires sober judgment, level character, and personal poise.

SNAPSHOT: SPORTS FEVER 3

We go back.

We're angry at the two doufuses who wrecked the game in Buffalo with their incompetent officiating, we're sore that neither the team nor its coaches have the strength of character to speak out on the issue publicly, and we're bitter that the NHL, despite its many claims to have "the best officials in the world" still allows such ineptitude to go on uncorrected—though it zealously goes after players and coaches who cross the lines of decorum and nails them with suspensions and fines. Typical hypocrisy from Gary Bettman & Co. Boo, NHL.

Despite all that, we come back.

The team returns from the road trip. They're exhausted but they have performed admirably, not only garnering eight points of the available fourteen, but playing well: attacking with zest, bouncing back from adversity, hanging on to slim leads late in games, not losing composure in the face of dodgy officiating.

We see the contradictions, we may even be conflicted by them, but we return.

Twenty minutes before game time against Florida the arena is packed with noisy fans. Go Jets Go! When the team comes on the ice they're greeted as if they've just won something. They have. Our hearts. Banners wave, chants begin, there's clapping and blatting of horns. We rise as one for the anthems and roar *True North* when the phrase comes up in the singing of "O Canada."

This isn't just a game. This about justice and fairness.

But for now, we'll put that all behind us. Yay, Burmistrov, yay, Wellwood!

SNAPSHOT: JUST A GAME

It's no good saying, *It's just a game,* because it's not just a game to the players—and it's not just a game to fans, it's something to do with who we are and how we see ourselves and how we want the world to see us, our very identity.

It's an accepted notion that we fans are partaking in vicarious pleasure when we go to games, but I can tell you as a longtime occupier of seats above ice level that what we're experiencing in the stands is not a second-hand feeling, the joy of the players in scoring a goal or winning a game washing up from them in a wave that dilutes as it flows up from the ice to where we stand cheering. It's not what they feel experienced in diminished form. What we feel is in some extraordinary way what they feel, "along the blood," as the poet puts it, even though they're the ones who score the goal and make the little circle on the ice at the game's end to acknowledge selection as one of the Three Stars. The ecstasy of those three WHA championships was not just a celebration of the team's achievement but a celebration of our own success, and when the Jets were moved to Phoenix we didn't just feel a second-hand remorse; we felt as if our hearts had been ripped out, and many of us dropped into a pit of self-pity from which we only arose when the Thrashers were bought by Mark Chipman and David Thomson and were restored to us as the Winnipeg Jets—that's why it was so important that the name be Jets, not Polar Bears or Falcons or any number of the other worthy names proposed. The team was part of us and we were a part of the team, in many ways more so than the players themselves, who were subsequently traded, or moved on, or retired. We were still here, and though it may strike some as misplaced enthusiasm to put it this way, those of us waving banners and screaming our heads off in the stands worked as hard for those championships in the WHA days as the players did, and it's arguable that the fans of the Jets appreciate the team's return to the city more than its owners or the players on the team, because we have been the one continuous element in the club's history over all those years since 1972, where players have come and gone, coaches, managers, even owners.

SEC: XX ROW: XX SEAT:XX

HOME GAME 16
JETS VS
PANTHERS
NOVEMBER 10, 2011

SEC: XX
ROW: XX
SEAT: XX

It's a well-accepted saw in the world of professional hockey that teams coming off of extended road trips suffer a lapse. *Whew, that's over!* The air travel, the back-to-back games, the shuttling from hotel to arena is behind them. Returned to their wives, families, friends, girlfriends, back in their own beds, they can finally relax. A physical sigh of relief runs through their bodies and it's accompanied by a psychological one that is not always in the best interest of pro athletes. Legs seem to lack jump, minds seem distracted. An overall fatigue settles in. In short, teams that come off of long road trips have difficulty playing well in the first game back home.

Will this be the fate of the Jets against the Florida Panthers?

The crowd hopes not. Go Jets Go! The excitement is palpable. Go Jets!

They start well, pressing Florida's goal. Kane misses two terrific chances in close. And, of course, on their first real foray down the ice, their first shot, Florida score. The fans continue cheering: Go Jets Go! But an alarm bell has gone off.

Didn't get through the opening ten minutes.

The game settles down into a pro contest, tightly played, almost no chances at either end, controlled pace. Then just before the end of the period, on a powerplay, Florida score again. This time there's notable deflation in the crowd.

"They can come back from two down," Kristen says.

"But not three."

Is it always the fate of Jets fans to voice such feelings? We expect the worst. But we haven't yet turned on the team.

In the intermission a guy is waving a placard: MORE GST. We laugh at this joke about our goods and services tax, widely hated, where Glass, Slater, and Thorburn are widely loved.

The crowd is silent at the start of the second period, hoping for a change in momentum, fearing the worst, holding its collective breath. After Florida's first goal, the team seemed to lose its jump. They ended the first period with only four shots on goal and they looked tired and demoralized. Not much changes in the second. Florida is boxing off the centre of the ice and the Jets seem unable to mount anything in the way of threatening attacks. And the Jets are taking penalties. When they attempt to clear the zone, the puck doesn't quite come out; when they contest faceoffs, they lose; when the puck is free in corners, the one-on-one battles go to Florida.

The crowd is growing restless. For the first time, ripples of discontent can be heard running through the stands. No outright booing or jeering, but a collective groan, rumblings of dissatisfaction. *Come on, you bums.*

"They look awful," I say.

They surrender a third goal early and a second powerplay goal late. 4-0. Game over.

A classic fatigue collapse. Silence in the arena.

"They play better on the road."

Andrew asks, "Have they won at home?" He's joking, his tone is acerbic.

They have, against Pittsburgh and Carolina, but that seems yogs ago, and their record otherwise is an uninspiring 2-3-0. "Doesn't seem so," I say, "does it?"

"No," he mutters. "But then their road record…"

The score ends up 5-2, and the Jets have taken five penalties and surrendered two powerplay goals. Damn. It looked as if they'd turned things around on the road. The bitter taste of the loss in Buffalo has morphed into full-scale anguish. A real downer.

"Hmmmph," I sigh, "this is getting depressing."

Kristen sighs too. "Yeah."

"I'm struggling," I add, "between being a fan and being an observer."

"The book, you mean."

"I'm too emotionally engaged. And yet the book seems to require it. Well, not *require*, exactly, but that seems to be where I'm going. It matters too much. Part of me wants to be the objective observer, reporting the team's progress from above, so to speak, a spectator, but a bigger part of me…"

"Yeah, we've become entangled."

"It's turning into a great story, though, lots of ups and downs."

"Plot twists."

"And it matters too much. I'm becoming a fan. And right now it's getting me down."

This is not a new feeling. Or a unique one.

Bitterness seems to go along with being a fan of a pro sports team. The disappointing losses are only the most obvious thing: *shouldn't have given away that game to Toronto.* There's all the little stuff, even when the team is winning. *The powerplay sucks, the penalty killing is dismal, the coaches are making mistakes.* There's always the nagging feeling that the team isn't doing as well as it should be: *why can't they play a fundamentally sound game and win? Why can't they put together a winning streak?* We want the club to do well—desperately sometimes—but we fear that they won't, we fear they can't, and all the positive feelings that go with every single victory, with carrying the day and taking the prize—*we can do it, we can win just this one time*—turn in on themselves and become bitter. And there's really nothing can be done about that: it's the condition of the condition, like paying for tickets and perusing sports pages. It's what it means to be a fan.

SNAPSHOT: Sports Fever 4

We return, despite the team's mediocre performance, despite the horror of the donnybrook, despite the team being out of the playoff race. So it's not the violence, any more than it's the elegance of the beautiful goal; it's the feeling of being utterly in the moment, being so completely absorbed by the events unfolding in front of you—the frantic dash down the ice, the antics of the crowd, the scuffle in the corner (hey, that's our slick Russian being roughed up by a thug!), your being so utterly absorbed that you are no longer part of the mundane world of career, family, the clock controlling your every moment, your every thought, your every action, that's what draws us back. Intensity. We seek intensity. And when we find it, we return to it. It's a drug.

The endorphins race, the adrenaline shoots up, cheeks flush, hands tremble, hair stands up on the back of the neck, throats go dry.

The body develops a life of its own, the mind is somehow blank and yet totally absorbed, both at the same time. Your being so utterly in the moment that *you*, your ordinary workaday self, ceases to exist, *you*, the little bundle of ego, neuron flashes, programmed responses, whatever "you" now means in a world increasingly moving away from the notion of self as a neat little psychic package operating inside a bag of skin, that *you* disappears in throbbing electric intensity, a spasm of pure being.

No wonder fans who throw trash on the ice or get into scuffles with bouncers and players plead, "I wasn't myself." They weren't, not in the way ordinarily meant.

Yes. We go back. We need another hit. Yay, team!

SEC: XX ROW: XX SEAT:XX

AWAY GAME 17

JETS VS
BLUE JACKETS

NOVEMBER 12, 2011

SEC: XX
ROW: XX
SEAT: XX

Not impressed. The Jets in Columbus. They go down 2-1, but more importantly they look awful. The road-trip hangover continues; the team seems to be skating in cement, they lack energy, they have no evident game plan; they've got a fistful of frustration, but they got no finish, they got no nothing. Beat 2-1 by Columbus, the worst team in the entire league—well, not the worst after this night. That dubious distinction now belongs to the Jets.

They're on their way to relegation. No, wait, that might be a good thing for the Jets. They might win something in the AHL, they might be competitive, they might look competent. These are boys playing against men.

They don't have a single player that can carry the play, they flail around in their own end, they seem not to have a plan of attack, their coach is not only making mistakes, he's no inspiration on the bench, he has nothing to offer by way of energizing his team. Bring back John Ferguson, for God's sake, a man who got angry when his team played like crap and at least intimidated them into playing better. Where's Kirk Muller, who was second in the running for the head-coaching job, Firecracker Freddy, heart on his emotional sleeve, fired up, dynamic, involved, committed?

Hold on, now, hold on one minute!

Maybe it's the long road trip catching up with them, maybe this tepid play can be explained away that way, maybe I'm being too harsh. But the Jets now boast a worse record than the Atlanta Thrashers of last year at this point in the season; they are now the worst team in the league. They stink.

This is what has to be said. Poor performances can be rationalized away: the defence has been trashed by injuries; the forwards seem to have no luck around the opposition goal; the lengthy road trip has caught up with the legs—and the hearts. But these are rationalizations. Other teams suffer through long road trips and play a respectable game: the Rangers were on the fifth game of a five-game road trip when they came into Winnipeg and beat the Jets with superior positional play, with smarts, with good coaching, with a degree of professionalism the Jets have not yet shown.

We need to see that soon. A professional team that goes about its business—winning at home by riding the energy of the crowd, playing sensible games on the road, steady and solid play. Right now this team flails and "thrashes," hoping for results rather than designing a game plan and playing to it.

In the end, it's down to the coaches, and this coach has not shown much. He has some good players—a very fine goaltender in Ondrej Pavelec, for one—but he can neither design a game plan nor inspire his team to follow through on it.

After the horrid performance against the Panthers in Winnipeg he said, "The honeymoon with the Winnipeg fans is over" (he heard those rumbles of discontent, too; it wasn't just the sausages served up in the concourse). And, he went on to add, "It's a good thing; the team should hear when they're playing bad." Sensible talk: Winnipeg fans know their hockey, they know when the team lacks energy and focus: this ain't Atlanta, boys, where you could get away with sub-par performances because no one knows the game, and no one cares. You gotta pull up your socks. He was right about that.

What he neglected to say was, *And their coach is screwing up.* After these two back-to-back abysmal performances, there's plenty of blame to spread around, and the coaching staff need to take a long look in the mirror.

Here endeth the sermon.

Tomorrow's another day. This too will pass. The team has shown sparks of inspirational play, they can bounce back, they can make a blue-collar city proud of their effort, if not their results. We fans have to believe that. We need something to soothe our savage breasts.

SNAPSHOT: Addiction

Is there anything more pleasurable than skating on an empty rink? For me the answer has always been obvious. When I was growing up, we were at the local rink every winter day, skating—the rink with its often bumpy ice and wooden boards was situated about twenty feet past our property line, and our house looked down on it, so my parents and sisters could sit at a bedroom window and watch me play.

That was great fun, being on a team. I enjoyed learning to pass, to shoot, to play a position on the ice, to make efficient line changes, the skills that are required to be a good player. Being with other boys, united in common purpose, learning to get along and to fit in with a group.

Heady days.

But nothing compared with just being out on the rink, skating.

The swish of blades beneath the feet, the surge of adrenaline as the skates cornered behind the net, picking up speed on the long straight from goal line to goal line, the freedom of swooping along ice at break-neck pace. On skates you travel many times faster than running and you're rewarded with that sense of being right on the edge of losing control that comes with such speed, you're toying with disaster, in a way, defying death. Glorious.

When I was a teen we lived in Steinbach, a biggish community in rural Manitoba, close to Winnipeg and its urban sophistication but still a small town with conservative values. Our juvenile team, the Royals, competed every spring in the provincial play-downs and two years in succession we made a concerted run at the championship.

We practised frequently: line rushes, powerplay strategy. Our coach was a hard-nosed taskmaster. He liked to have forwards attack defence-men on three-on-two rushes, sharpening the skills of both sets of players in these critical real-game situations. At one of those practices I was skating backwards when a teammate took a slapshot directly in front of me and his stick broke, and the blade flew at my head, cutting my skull for eighteen stitches. I was a sensation the next day at school with my bandaged head, but my mother was not best pleased. The lumpy scar is still there, I bump across it every time I brush my hair.

On winter mornings I rose at 6:30, ate a small breakfast and went out into the twilight with my skates in one hand and stick in the other. In the pocket of my jacket I carried two pucks. The rink was several blocks away from our house, surrounded by a six-foot wooden fence, but I stood over six feet at seventeen and I climbed it with ease, laced on my skates, and spent an hour breezing around the ice, shooting at the goals, drifting the puck into the corners from the blue line and following it behind the goal, carrying it up the other side of the ice, repeating the same routine. On those frosty mornings I told myself I was working on stamina and shooting accuracy, and I was. But I was really out for the feel of legs pumping up and down the ice, crisp air on the cheeks, ghosts of breath floating out of my mouth. I aimed my shots at the goalposts and got good at hitting them.

Twenty years later I was teaching at a prep school that had its own Olympic-size indoor rink. I coached teams there, Pee Wee, Bantam, the High School squad. Between classes I would scoot down the halls and head for the rink, where I had a locker in a room reserved for teacher-coaches. My skates were there and my gloves and sticks and when I'd dispatched my tie and shirt, I went out on the ice, skating for the first fifteen minutes with stick in hand—but no puck. I made loop after loop of the ice, sprinting between blue lines, carving figure-eights through centre ice, skating laps backwards. Only after fifteen minutes did I introduce a puck into the routine, shooting at the nets at each end, counting how many times I hit the posts.

Unlike those of my childhood and youth, these sessions had no ulterior motive; I was not practising to develop skills, or keeping in shape for upcoming play-downs. We had an old-timers' team at the school, a pretty good one, and we played other old-fart teams in the city; it was fun; we occasionally made road trips to towns in the country and to Minneapolis. But no one took any of that seriously. And I certainly wasn't out on the ice practising to play with our team of fat old guys.

No, I went out and skated on my own for forty minutes or so just because I loved doing it, feeling my lungs open with the exertion, enjoying putting stress on my legs, revelling in the ping of the post when my shots succeeded. That routine was a type of addiction, an addiction I've been proud to have had for more than fifty years now. Skating, I achieved a kind of Zen-like state, beyond the cares of everyday life, into a zone where all that mattered was going up and down the ice, feeling blades beneath my feet, hearing the whistle of steel on ice. For me there has never been anything to compare to skating for this sense of freedom and "lightness," that place beyond care and fret that we seek in the sheer physicality of muscle movement.

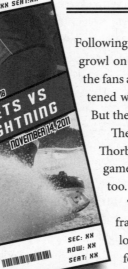

Following the disappointment in Columbus, there's a growl on in the city, the honeymoon definitely is over, the fans are asking questions. The team itself seem chastened when it comes on the ice to face the Lightning. But the crowd is still bright with cheers: Go Jets Go!

The coach starts the GST line, Glass and Slater and Thorburn, his "checking" line that he split up several games ago, to the team's detriment. He's learning, too.

The Lightning know the Jets' confidence is fragile, and they themselves are on a two-game losing streak, so they start strong, pressing the forecheck. They hit the post, the puck slides through the open cage behind Pavelec, but it stays out. Gasps from the crowd, followed by a huge collective sigh of relief.

Though the GST line is together, the coach is experimenting with the others. Wheeler has been dropped from the supposed number one line; in addition, the coach has broken up the team's most productive group, Antropov, Burmistrov, Kane. To him, the team is a work-in-progress, clearly, and it's a bit unsettling. Why break up the most productive line? Does he know what he's doing?

This is only the most obvious question. Where is Ron Hainsey, the steadiest defenceman in the pre-season? He's been out since the start of the season with an increasingly mysterious "lower body injury." There's no indication that his return is imminent.

Why can't the coaches find a regular spot for Wellwood, the team's most useful forward—he's been clever with the puck in the opposition end, never makes mistakes that cost goals, feeds his line mates, and is the top scorer on the team. He deserves better than to be shuffled from one line to another on a nightly basis, while lesser players (Little, Wheeler) remain on a line with Ladd, despite long-term mediocrity.

Queries, issues. We're all Grumblers. Queries, questions.

And the ever-present: Can the Jets get through the opening ten minutes?

They can. In fact, they score before the five-minute mark. Palpable relief.

That's more like it. Bustling Kane. This guy is good.

Then they tally again just past the ten-minute mark. The crowd is fully behind the team now, the chants have returned to raucous. It doesn't take much. Two goals and we're back on side. We fly up and down the emotional scale, screaming distress one day, adulation the next, whores to primeval passions.

Go Jets Go! Do something, you bums!

And so it goes. There are penalties to kill (two) but the period ends 2-0, and the second sees the lead extend to 3-0 (despite a four-minute penalty) before Tampa score just at the halfway mark of the game. 3-1. Maybe, just maybe.

But don't count on anything. This is the Jets. They take penalties, blow leads.

By the end of the second period Tampa is ahead on shots but the Jets have a comfortable 4-1 lead. They press in the third. Take over the game. How can a team that looked so outclassed in Columbus play so well only two nights later? It can't be the energy of the home-ice crowd, they looked shaky against Florida in Winnipeg on returning from the road trip. It must be that they're young, inexperienced, subject to radical swings in performance. (Other teams seem to be, too: Vancouver's Canucks, finalists for the Cup in spring, are all over the map in the opening dozen games of this season, winning big one night, falling apart the next. Is it the schedule? Parity in the league?) Whatever, the Jets score again at the period's halfway mark and ride out the victory, 5-2.

The crowd is ecstatic. This is what we come to see. This is how hope is built and faith in the team rebuilt.

I study the shots on goal: 39-32, in favour of the Jets; I study the penalty details: the Jets have scored on one of their two advantages, whereas Tampa did not score on any of their six chances, a good sign. Six penalties, though. Work to be done.

SNAPSHOT: Who Are These Guys?

After these opening twenty or so games, we're beginning to get a better picture of our somewhat faceless team—faceless because it's fair to say few Winnipeggers took any interest in the Atlanta Thrashers, and they were little more than ciphers to most. So, who are they?

The head coach is a work in progress. He lacks charisma, but counters that with a steady temperament that seems to calm the players and bring the best out of them. Most of the time. If he views his team as a work in progress, we fans view him in a similar way: let's see what he's got over the long haul.

The team is young and fast; and they're erratic. Prone to take penalties. But surprisingly resilient. The defencemen are unpredictable: Stuart is reliable, as are Enstrom, Hainsey, and Bogosian. Flood is something of a surprise: an offensive force, he takes few penalties and is rarely out of position. A find. But in the early going, Oduya coughs up the puck, and Jones looks a little over his head on occasion.

Of the forwards, some of them are gritty—Ladd, Slater, Thorburn, Antropov, Glass; a few are fast and nifty: Wellwood, Little, Burmistrov, Stapleton, Kane, who is also big and could be a power forward of considerable substance. Others fill in well: McCardle, Maxwell. Big Fehr could add some muscle. And then there's Wheeler.

SNAPSHOT: Whipping Boy

On every professional sports team in every city, there's one player the fans seem to turn on. He's not the worst player, he's not even a marginal player; often he's one of the best—or the most promising. A first-round draft pick, a European with flashy credentials, a star in junior who just hasn't lived up to his promise. He's the whipping boy. On the WHA Jets there was a defenceman named Thommie Bergman; big, rangy, with a heavy shot, Bergman out-muscled the opposition in front of the Jets goal and made breathtaking dashes up the ice. But at the crucial moment, with the game on the line, he had the habit—or so it was judged by the fans—of coughing up the puck. A great sigh went up from the crowd: "Oh, Thommie." And then began the jeers: "Do something, Bergman," and then: "Bergman, you bum."

On the Jets early in this season this is Blake Wheeler. He's big, he has a hard shot, he's not reluctant to go into corners—and he often comes up with the puck, using his big frame to push aside defenders. From time to time he gets a garbage goal in front of the net, every now and then he snaps one in from the top of the faceoff dot.

But not often enough. When he digs that puck out of the corner, he tries to pass out front but somehow it's deflected away by a defender; when he crosses the opposition blue line and lines up for a slapshot, it's knocked off his stick; when the puck comes to him at the faceoff dot it dribbles off his stick into the corner. "Do something, Wheeler," "Wheeler, you bum!"

He's not a bum. Consider this. In Canada there are about 350,000 kids over the age of twelve playing amateur hockey every year. A player like Blake Wheeler—he's an American, but bear with me here—a player like Wheeler has to be really good to make the all-star team for the city, say, even a better player to achieve that honour for the province. To be chosen for the actual provincial team he has to be very good indeed, and have the right attitude, to boot. Scouts comb these games and they will see him, but they're very selective in picking guys for the major junior teams. You have to have skill, determination, and preferably size. You have to be ready to hand out bodychecks—and to receive them. You have to be prepared to drop your gloves and scrap, if it comes to that.

Of those 350,000 kids only about 1000 play major junior hockey, another 1000 the next level of junior down. Of that number only the best 300 are picked in the draft every year by NHL teams. To even be picked you have to have remarkable talent, as well as that ever-touted quality, the right attitude—and not be injury-prone. These are the boys who play on Canada's Junior Team, which contests the Championship of the World every winter. That tournament was held in Winnipeg in 1999. We had a splendid team that just lost the gold medal—in overtime, to the Russians. These boys were the elite of the elite. From that team came a number of professionals: Roberto Luongo, Simon Gagne, Brad Stuart, Robyn Regehr. Maybe a few others. But of those twenty-odd boys, what happened to the rest? Blair Betts, who scored a crucial goal in the gold medal game, Tyler Bouck, Brad Leeb, Rico Fata?

A few are playing on American Hockey league teams, hoping for the call-up to the big club that becomes more elusive with each passing year. Some play in Europe; others have gone on to work for pro teams, as coaches, or in other minor capacities. Most of them are out of hockey altogether. And these were the *crème de la crème*.

Unless you're only a tough guy, to make it to the NHL, you have to be pretty good. To stay there, you have to be special. And Blake Wheeler has stayed there. With the Atlanta Thrashers in 2010–11 he scored 18 goals and tallied 44 points, fifth on the team. In most ways he's a very lucky man. He has chosen what he wants to do in this life, he is paid well to do it, he's garnered a bit of fame along the way, he has been single-mindedly committed to it. How many of us can say the same, how many of us have harboured a long-shot dream and pursued it to the point where we get the fame, the money, and, I have no doubt, the girl?

And yet, there he is in full view, fumbling for pucks in front of the opposition goal, missing passes, having shots dribble off the heel of his stick, proving ineffective time and again, to the annoyance and, finally, outrage, of the hometown fans. "Do something, Wheeler," "Wheeler, you bum."

"There always seems to be this impression that Wheeler's got more," the colour guy says, "that he's just scratching the surface of what he can be."

One of the great things about sport is its simplicity, a black-and-white-ness that leads often to cruel conclusions. A muffed shot is a muffed shot. You connected and scored—or you didn't. If you miss five out of six of these, it's clear you're not very good at this shooting business, you should seek another line of work. I spend most of my time in the world of the arts, where nothing is as clear as muffed shots or missed checks. In my world there are shades of grey, a pretty good article, a promising first book. You can get published in the country's best magazine if your father happens to be among the country's famous writers; you can have a column in a national paper if your husband owns the newspaper. It would be impossible for Wayne Gretzky to get his son on a pro hockey team if he lacked the talent, but it might not be so difficult for a great director to have one of his sons with only mediocre talent follow in his footsteps. In the world of sport there's no fifty-goal sniper languishing in a garret, but in the arts world there are mediocre writers and actors making a good living because they happen to know the right people, or were in the right place at the right time.

That's one of the things that brings us back to sport, despite the scandals about drugs, the ridiculous salaries, the labour disputes where two sets of millionaires argue about who gets the bigger share of the pie. You either have it, or you don't. And that clarity takes us back to a simpler world, a world that for me, anyway, feels as direct as honesty, free of slippery dealings, of favours, of inside contrivance, a world forgotten most of the time these days, a world where you're given a difficult job to do—in the sport of hockey often a brutally physical one—and you either do it or you mess it up. To me, at least, there's something invigorating about that, I want to go there.

What is going on?

The result against Tampa Bay was gratifying, particularly in light of the dismal performances against Florida and Columbus, two teams the Jets should beat. Tampa is a team they shouldn't beat. But what does *shouldn't* mean? At home? Away? After the Jets come off a road trip? While Tampa is on a road trip?

The Washington Capitals are one of the NHL's premier teams.

Hold your breath, Jets fans.

The crowd is hardly seated when Washington score.

Didn't get through the first ten minutes.

SEC: XX ROW: XX SEAT:XX

HOME GAME 19

JETS VS CAPITALS

NOVEMBER 17, 2011

SEC: XX
ROW: XX
SEAT: XX

Here we go again.

The cheering dies to an echo.

But the Jets do not fold. They press the play through centre ice and forecheck with intent. And they tie the score before the ten-minute mark. This is good. Part of the Jets' story this season is turning out to be their ability to bounce back.

Then both teams play fire-wagon hockey, electrifying dashes up and down the ice, shots whizzing at the nets. Breathtaking stuff, nail-biting stuff. The period ends with a total of 21 shots taken, fans exhilarated, and the score even.

But it's even. A creditable performance against a polished, high-quality team that has been touted for the Cup for about five years.

Can the Jets get through the opening ten minutes of the second period?

On past form ... Well, on past form, anything could happen, actually: they could collapse and lose 7-1, or they could roar and win 7-6. Most likely the score will end up 4-3 for somebody. Unlikely to be the Jets.

They score again, a nicely executed tally, the second by Kane on the night, and then on a powerplay Wheeler tucks the puck in after an impressive rush to make it 3-1 before the midway mark. (Finally, a goal from Wheeler, on the fourth line now.)

But both teams continue to play wide-open hockey.

I say to Kristen, "The Jets cannot survive this."

It's entertaining, top-flight excitement, and from a neutral's point of view, a fine game, the puck flying up and down the ice, buckets of shots at the goals—and on the net. With all their firepower—Ovechkin, Semin, Backstrom—Washington is sure to score again. The home team is living on borrowed time. But it's the Jets who put the puck in the net, wily Wellwood tallying, and the score stands 4-1 at the end of two periods. Shots: 25-24.

"They can't keep this up," I say, meaning if the teams continue to play fire-wagon hockey, Washington is likely to break through in the third period, that the Jets are living on a knife-edge.

Kristen makes the motion of an umpire signalling *safe*. Slow it down.

But they don't, at least not right away.

Washington presses, hoping for the early marker that will turn the tide. They don't get it, and by mid-period the Jets are playing a disciplined game between the blue lines and forechecking intelligently. Washington cannot break through, despite the efforts of Ovechkin and the slickness of Backstrom, and the final is 4-1.

Whew. Two wins back-to-back against superior opposition.

A cause for celebration?

Maybe more this: recognition that there really is parity in the league, that on a given night any team can beat any other. On this night, for instance, Nashville beats Toronto, Ottawa beats Edmonton, and Tampa Bay beats Pittsburgh, all not results that would have been predicted on the teams' past form. Conclusion? For even good teams, if you don't show up with your "A" game, you're likely to lose.

But that does not take away from the Jets' achievement on this night.

Once again they're knocking on the door of .500, once again we're hopeful.

What to expect? When these teams last met less than a month ago, a total of seventeen goals were scored in one of the oddest games ever witnessed in the NHL.

No one would claim to know what might happen. The Flyers are explosive; the Jets have shown they can score. And both teams have been scored against.

Anything could happen.

One thing for sure, the fans are up for it. In the crowd a woman waves a big yellow placard: CLAUDE RULES. Does this refer to Claude Giroux, top scorer on the Flyers, or the Winnipeg coach, Claude Noel?

The Jets have won two straight and have looked good winning them: organized in their own end, disciplined—for the most part.

Penalties are still an issue. Too many giveaways in their own end that lead to holding, tripping, and hooking penalties. Worse, too many penalties in the opposition end. Infractions in your own end might sometimes be tolerable, "good penalties" in hockey argot; two hundred feet away from your own net, they're unforgiveable.

In the stands a boy waves a placard: JETS SHOOT DOWN FLYERS.

Right from the start, the Flyers look a little out of it. The Jets attack from the drop of the puck and score before the five-minute mark—Brian Little, who has made the same kind of impression as Wheeler in the early going: promising play at times, but with no results. Then two minutes later, he scores again. A Little bit of spark.

The Flyers look confused. It's not easy to recover from two goals down, when you're on the road. That doesn't concern Jets fans, who are cheering lustily and have singled out Chris Pronger of the Flyers to jeer and boo whenever he touches the puck. Odd, since Pronger is a "local" boy, from Kenora, only two hours down the highway.

He's a whipping boy of a different kind: one of those players who is not well-liked around the league—except in the city where he's playing. Maybe it goes back to the way he left Edmonton and the Oilers, under a cloud because his wife, supposedly, didn't like the city; maybe it's his reputation as a chippy player. Did he say something unflattering about Winnipeg? That would not be unusual. Whatever, fans have a habit of turning against local boys. Do they expect too much of kids raised on their own turf? Envy them? Think they come off as big shots, too good for the place where they grew up? Is it evidence of our poor self-confidence—fear that promoting our own will seem brassy, too "Toronto"? It's the kind of reverse snobbery you witness in a city like Winnipeg, where the local opera star, the local writer / painter / running back cannot be recognized as equally good as others in their field simply because they *are* local. We're reluctant to applaud our own. Does this make us "provincial"?

It doesn't help when Pronger sets up a Flyers goal—on a powerplay. A chorus of boos when his name is announced on the assist list.

But the Jets get out of the first period ahead on the scoreboard.

They extend the lead in the second period, on a short-handed goal. There's been a bushel barrel of penalties in this game, too: at the halfway point of the game ten penalties have been called, seven against the Flyers. Too many; it ruins the flow of the game; it makes the game's result a matter of special teams' play—who has the better powerplay, who has the better penalty-killing unit.

The NHL has a distance to go before it reaches the point where its officials are as accomplished as its players, making the overall game competitive, well-balanced, and highly paced.

The third period opens 5-2 for the Jets.

Can they hang on? Can they play a tight-checking game that chokes off the high-scoring Flyers? Can they play defence?

They can't. By the midway point, it's 5-3, with the Flyers pressing and the Jets taking penalties. And with less than three minutes remaining, it's nail-biting time, a 5-1 lead having been whittled down to 5-4.

They hang on, scoring into an empty net. Final: 6-4.

But it shouldn't have been that close. To be a good team, the Jets must learn to play defence.

Still, the cheering is thunderous when the Jets skate to centre ice and salute the crowd by holding up their sticks.

Something to celebrate.

SNAPSHOT: Championship Game

St. James Civic Centre, spring 1990. I'm on a team with my nephew, Shane and his pals, twenty years my junior, the Silver Bullets. We're a pretty good beer-league team and we're playing for the championship of the Winnipeg Central League.

For a minute or so we've been applying pressure in the opponents' end, but when the puck is turned over, I'm caught against the boards at the top of the faceoff circle. I wheel at the blue line and take a couple of quick strides toward our end in an attempt to get back in the play. One of the other team's forwards, following the play, catches up to me, and as he does, he chops at my stick, trying to knock it out of my hands. He doesn't. But I've never had this happen to me before, a cheap move, I instantly hate this guy. He's quite a bit younger than me, maybe in his mid-twenties. As he passes me, he spits derisively above the hiss of skate blades on ice, "Keep up, old man!"

I say nothing, chopping as hard as I can back into our end. But I've taken his number. In my day that's what you did: took the guy's number, got him later. Now the protocol seems to be trash-talk back—or give him a two-hander on the calf.

My defence partner, Chewy, as reliable as they come, tireless skater, deft with the puck, has broken up the play at our blue line. I'm out of trouble. The puck comes up the boards in my direction. I corral it, wheel again and lay a pass onto Shane's stick, then boot it to the bench for a line change. Chewy is right behind.

"Thanks," I say on the bench. Meaning, for covering for me.

"You took it in there in the first place," he says. "Ate up a bunch of time." He punches my forearm. "Good work."

We glug back water from plastic bottles.

This is it, then, the game is looking me in the eye like a Gorgon once again, saying, *You may have met the test before but today brings a new test,* as it always must, probing for physical weakness, gnawing for emotional flaws, digging for cracks in character. What will it turn up today? Will I meet the test? Turn to stone?

We're ahead 4-3 in the decisive game. It's the third period, less than three minutes to play. We both study the ice. Shane and his line have come off with us and our most dodgy group is out there, Jerry and Geno and Skip, the former erratic and prone to cough up the puck, the latter two hot-headed, likely to get into something with the other team or the refs.

We watch intently, fearing the worst, sip from our bottles.

Get off the ice, I'm thinking, *let Zimmy's line take us to the final minute.*

The whistle blows. Faceoff in our end. I look at Chewy. He shakes his head. They're not coming off the ice; Skip is circling at the faceoff dot, tapping his stick belligerently on the ice, yapping at the other team. Chewy taps Alfred, team manager who organizes the team, though Chewy is the *de facto* captain.

Alfred yells, "Get off, come off!" And Geno and Jerry glance at the bench and begin, reluctantly to skate toward us. Skip is still circling—and yapping.

Chewy yells, "Off! Now!"

And Skip complies. When he gets to the bench, his face is a rictus of rage. "Fuck's sake!" he splutters, but not to Chewy. Not at anyone directly.

Zimmy's line takes the puck into the opposition's end and we change on the fly. Chewy and I jump over the boards. At forty-three I may be old, but I'm reliable, Garry Doak to Chewy's Bobby Orr, in my mind, at least. Shane and his line take the puck to the opposition corner, tie up the play, cycle and check, force a faceoff. The seconds tick by, furious stickwork near the opposition goal, then the horn blows, the championship is ours.

Chewy gives me a high-five. I give one to Shane.

Something to celebrate.

When was the last time I won anything?

As we're shaking hands with the other team, I pick out the guy who hacked at my stick. When we've tapped each other's gloves, I say just loud enough for him to hear, "Nice try, junior."

SNAPSHOT: The Jaundiced Eye

I'm watching the game between Tampa Bay and Toronto, November 22, 2011, on *NHL Center Ice*. They offer two transmissions, home and away, so you can choose between the broadcast from the Lightning's commentators or the Leafs'.

We're in the second period, towards the end, the Leafs leading 3-1. The puck is turned over in the Leafs end, then moved swiftly down the ice across the blue line into the Lightning end. A Leaf forward passes toward the front of the goal. Or does he attempt a shot that turns into a hard pass? In any case, it bounces free onto the stick of another Leaf forward who taps it into the open net. 4-1.

I'm listening to the Tampa broadcast. In the US it's common for the broadcast crew to be part of the home team. They don't have CBC, where commentators like Don Wittman and Jim Hughson maintain neutrality, delivering the play-by-play in an impartial manner. In the US, broadcasters are "homers," it's part of their tradition. Listen to a game on the Notre Dame network, the Red Sox channel, whatever. The broadcasters not only "pull" for the home team, they outright "cheer" for them; their voices give them away—exultant when the home team scores, deflated when the "bad guys" score. It can become irritating, if you're a neutral—or if you've grown up with different customs, conventions of neutrality.

But it's part of the American way, "us against them," it goes up the line, from Pop Warner football to foreign policy. If you're not in the Iraqi Alliance, you're with the bad guys, you're agin' democracy, God, and the good. They're Puritans, after all. In the political realm such biased report-age has been decried and the folks on the ground in Iraq and Afghanistan who have been feeding the American public one-sided news have been called "embedded reporters," not journalists in the strict sense but propagandists for the American military and US foreign policy, an arm of that foreign policy. CNBC, Fox, that crowd.

When the Leafs tally at the end of the second period to make the score 4-1, the Lightning announcers point out that the puck was deflected—by a turn of bad luck the puck landed on a Leaf's stick and went into the net. The goal was lucky, the Lightning have been cheated in some way. I switch channels. The Leafs commentators are reviewing the goal, first in real time, then in slow motion. They point out that much farther back in the play, in front of the Leafs net, a Leafs defenceman blocked a shot from a Tampa forward and then made a good pass up the ice to an attack-ing Leaf, who then made the pass that resulted in the goal. According to them, the goal was a result of good play by the Leafs.

So, this goal was: (a) a lucky fluke; or (b) the result of smart play. You can choose, depending on which team you favour, on which TV channel you choose to view. There's no impartial point of view, no neutral assess-ment. With us or against us.

Fan of the Leafs, or fan of the Lightning. There's no third option. Or fourth.

Does it matter? Should we expect more?

When the Leafs score early in the third period, making the score 5-1, the Leafs commentators concentrate on the brilliance of the Leaf player's shot, the Lightning guys focus on the lapse in defence that brought on the goal. Which is accurate? The answer is: both. The Lightning defenceman did flub the puck, the Leaf forward did snap it into the goal nicely.

It was like this too during the broadcasts of the first and great hockey play-by-play man, Foster Hewitt, who virtually "sang" when the Leafs played well, but also sounded like a curmudgeon when they played less well—and more important, lost. Hewitt was a bitter man, in some ways. From his perspective, the Leafs should always have played well at least—and won most of the time. If they didn't, he was prone to be a crank. Losing meant the Leafs had failed; little credit was given to the other team for prevailing.

So varieties of "homers," of "cheering" have been part of the game for a long time. It's not a new phenomenon.

But we've lost something in recent times. As teams in Canada have developed their own TV stations, their own broadcasters, the neutrality of Wittman and Hughson has almost disappeared in the hubbub of home-team cheerleading and bias. Play-by-play guys are increasingly part of the team, disposed in the American tradition to hometown boosterism, and the game has lost something of real importance: a sense of proportion, the end of the notion that broadcasting is journalism, and that what fans deserve is reporting by objective observers, not committed fans.

19 November 2011

Team	SP	PTS
Philadelphia	19	25
Pittsburgh	20	25
Buffalo	20	24
Toronto	20	24
New York R	17	23
Florida	19	23
Boston	18	22
Washington	18	21
New Jersey	18	21
Montreal	20	21
Ottawa	20	21
Tampa Bay	19	20
Winnipeg	20	19
Carolina	20	15
New York I	17	13

A three-game road trip following the home-stand of three wins includes games in Washington and Carolina over the American Thanksgiving week. Both are exciting contests featuring great skating and glittery skills. Players fly up and down the ice, pucks zip past both goals. It's high-energy, entertaining stuff, what pro hockey at its highest level is all about, the reason you want an NHL team. But how can they keep it up?

One thing that's true of the NHL these days is that every player is in superb condition, and every one of them can skate and skate fast. The pace is breathtaking, and when you look down the bench you see that this is literally true for the guys who just came off the ice—they're gasping. Shift after shift. And not in the way Bathgate and co. did in pre-season in the '60s: from being out of shape. Go back and look at the celebrated video of Bobby Orr skating through an entire team, circling the net, and backhanding in a goal—he's almost not moving, by today's standards. These guys are stretching themselves to the limit of human endurance.

In Washington the teams trade goals through the two opening periods and go into the third with the score 3-2 Caps. The Jets score with less than eight minutes to go—Brian Little again—and the game goes into overtime, where Washington score to win. But the Jets have come back to answer every Capitals goal, and as the teams file off the ice you have the feeling that if the game were to go on another five minutes, they'd tie it up again. Overtime loss, one point. A good result against a fine team.

The Hurricanes and Jets also play at a furious tempo. It's still amazing to me that the game can be played at such high speed, shift after shift, period on period. If you go back and look at footage from the '50s and '60s, even the game's stars seem to be skating in sand. Many defencemen at the top of their game—Leo Boivin, Bobby Baun—seem "fat" by today's standards. It's possible the same could be said of Byfuglien; but the difference is he can dash up the ice with the best of them. The game moves at something like twice the speed as in the '60s, and is much faster than even fifteen years ago. Every single player can fly down the ice. It's becoming clearer by the season that what's required for success in the NHL nowadays is speedy young players—skilled with the puck, yes, capable of quick decision making, too—but most importantly, fast: it's the ticket to success. And the Jets, among the youngest teams in the league, are punching that ticket. So are Edmonton, Dallas, and Florida, while older teams, Tampa Bay, Calgary, Anaheim— older on average by only a few years—flounder in the early going of the season.

At least in these early days, youth and speed are speaking loudly; will poise and experience have the last say by March and April?

In this game the lead changes hands, Carolina in front to begin with. but the second frame ending 2-1, Jets; and they pot one into the empty net. Final: 3-1.

For the first time in the season the Jets have a record of .500. Twenty-two points in twenty-two games. They've finally made up the three losses that opened the schedule.

It's been a long two-month grind to get to an even record. And it will not be easy to maintain in the Boston Garden.

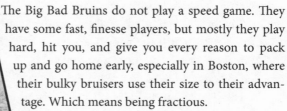

The Big Bad Bruins do not play a speed game. They have some fast, finesse players, but mostly they play hard, hit you, and give you every reason to pack up and go home early, especially in Boston, where their bulky bruisers use their size to their advantage. Which means being fractious.

The Jets are not intimidated. They score just at the midway mark of the first period, and then again only a minute later. The Bruins look a bit frazzled. But then Byfuglien is given a questionable penalty—he's becoming a target for NHL referees—and the Bruins score to bring the period to a close at 2-1.

The Jets do not look out of place. But the Bruins are a force. They're big and they're mean, and they don't like being behind on the scoreboard. They take over in the second period, scoring a short-handed goal before the ten-minute mark and again within a few minutes. Is there anything worse than a short-handed goal? You're up 2-1, you have a chance to score on the powerplay and extend the lead to two goals, and then *whammo*, the lead disappears altogether, you not only have not scored—you have been scored *against*. Nothing is more deflating. It's much worse than a goal given up on a penalty call, because there you can blame the refs and feel righteous indignation about being stiffed; with the short-handed goal, you've blown it all on your own, the blame falls squarely on you, and usually that's difficult to handle.

The Jets do not deal with it well. They take a number of brainless penalties toward the end of the period and stagger to the dressing room at the break, looking like a team that already knows its fate.

But the coaching staff does a good job in the intermission and they come out with renewed vigour for the third, first killing a four-minute penalty, then throwing everything they have at the Bruins, outshooting then 16-10, but giving up an empty net goal to finish the game 4-2.

Not a bad result for a three-game road trip: one win, one loss, one tie.

Now comes a five-game home-stand, playing on our turf.

SNAPSHOT: Local Rink

We're at the local rink, Andrew, Kristen, and I, just down the road from our house. March 1999. Andrew has just turned eight, a big-boned boy, a tall boy and strong who can skate with power. Three of his buddies are with us today, brothers Zachary and Joel, and Joey. We're playing a little game of shinny, Andrew and I against the others.

Joel has just scored on a set-up from Kristen. He's a good athlete, Joel, compactly built, speedy, and with an athlete's sense of timing. After scoring, he high-fives with Zachary and Joey and Kristen. I dig the puck out of the net and pass it to Andrew at the bottom of our faceoff circle.

"Let's get that one back," I say.

"Yeah," he says, "let's do that."

He skates doggedly up the ice, concentrating on the puck, aware that Joel and Zachary are going to check him. Kristen is watching me. This is not her sport, really, she was a collegiate athlete in field hockey. But she's game—and tenacious. The puck bobbles a bit on the blade of Andrew's stick. Just before the centre red line and just before the brothers close him down with their check, he flutters the puck over to me. I go wide, trying not to skate fast. I tower over these boys, I'm conscious my size is intimidating even to Kristen.

When I get to the top of the faceoff circle at the other end of the ice, I dodge past Kristen, then glance over to gauge where Andrew is. He likes playing on the local rink with his pals—and with me, too, though he's shown no interest in playing organized hockey. Neither has his classmate, Joel. Both belong to Jackrabbits, a cross-country skiing club, and they play on the local soccer squad in summer. Hockey teams, though, are not their thing.

That's all right with me. Coaching for fourteen years, I've witnessed enough of minor hockey to be pleased he's not involved in all that, overly ambitious coaches, noisy and belligerent parents. And getting up at 6:30 for practices at early hours in municipal arenas. Not for this chickadee. Kristen and I attend all his soccer games in summer, and she coached the team for a number of years. We're proud of our son in the way of parents and we enjoy watching him and his mates grow and grow up.

I glance quickly in his direction again. He's just at the top of the faceoff dot, stick on the ice. He knows what I'm going to do. Possibly the others do too—lay a pass across to him in front of the net. Instead I take two quick strides, cross behind the net and then lay a pass onto his stick. He shoots. He scores. Then he stumbles and crashes into the goalpost, tumbling over and taking Joey with him. They jump up, laughing. Kids don't get hurt when they go down. If that had been me, I'd be in pain for three days.

Joel digs the puck out of the net and says something to Zachary and Joey—team strategy, they'll be coming right back at us.

As we skate back into our end, I say to Andrew, "Nice shot, Andy."

"Nice pass, Dad," he says.

My heart expands in my chest. It doesn't get any better than that.

You know the old bromide: if you don't like the weather in Calgary, there's a simple solution—wait fifteen minutes.

If you don't like what you see from the Winnipeg Jets on a given night, there's a simple remedy: wait for the next game.

It's been a see-saw season. One night the team plays well; the next night they stink the joint out; on the third night they're mediocre. Will they be golden on the fourth? No one knows. They could win 7-5; they could lose 7-1. More likely, they'll fall behind 2-0 in the first period, then scratch back and go ahead 3-2 by the end of the second, only to let the game slip away 4-3 by the final whistle. They win three consecutive games against teams they should not beat, then they go into Columbus and lose, looking like bums.

Axiom: don't get too high when they win; when they lose, don't get too low. Talk about old saws.

After playing four high-quality games out of six against good opposition to claw their way back to .500, against Ottawa the Jets look flat from the opening whistle. The jump in their skating that is becoming their trademark is not there. So it's no surprise Ottawa score first. Sigh. Here we go again.

In the second period the Jets come out with a little more energy, scoring two quick goals, but before the period ends, Ottawa answer with two of their own, making the score 3-2 in their favour going into the third.

The Winnipeg coach has said he's disappointed in his team's inability to finish. They get ahead, but they can't close the opposition down. They fritter away leads; they take penalties that allow the other team back into the game. The third period against Ottawa is a textbook example: the Jets score two quick goals to go ahead 4-3, but then surrender two goals over the following ten minutes to lose the game.

They can't play defence; they don't know how to shut a game down.

Grumble, grumble from the fans.

The coach looks unhappy. But then he always looks unhappy. Or skeptical, or uninvolved, or cross. It's difficult to tell, he's not the expressive type, and in that he resembles a father who is alternately downcast or cool, but never pleased or kindly, a father his charges must look to for endorsement, only to discover a blank wall staring back at them. What must be going through the heads of the players?

Some coaches are Great Santini types, who drive their children to succeed, but who are unaware of the pain they're causing, the mayhem they provoke in someone else's psychic life. They push, then they push some more, these Iron Mikes. They're not easy to like, though sometimes we can admire them. Other coaches seem older and more manic brothers, with emotions like firecrackers, hearts on sleeves, clapping players on backs, chomping handfuls of crushed ice, racing up and down behind the bench, themselves as high-maintenance as their most needy players.

Do we like Firecracker Freddy more than Iron Mike? Do we prefer him to the Professor, the coach who strokes his chin as he contemplates the performance of the team, registering miscues, making mental notes for the next team meeting, but loath to show a sign of emotion? Depends on what kind of father we want—or need. We might prefer the kindly uncle, redolent of cigar smoke, likely to have movie tickets or the latest PlayStation hidden in the folds of his coat; we want Uncle but we almost never get him.

We get Iron Mike and play our guts out for him Monday—and on Tuesday hate him when he chews our heads off. We get Firecracker Freddy and try to be as good as he was in his day and are crushed by our inadequate performance. We get Professor Fish Face and have no idea where we stand, or if we measure up, or what the hell is going on.

We want Uncle, who values and indulges us—and we get Stepdad, who doesn't give a shit.

It's a messed-up relationship, doomed from the start.

But it's what we have. And then on one day...

Maybe it's inevitable that both players and fans look, in their coaches, for the father we all need, the father we never really have, the father who says *trust me, I know what I'm doing and in the end it will all come out right,* and who delivers on that promise, guiding the team to a ten-game win streak, devising the plan that wins the Cup and makes velvet our sorry selves, so we can rest content in the conviction that Dad will maneuver the boat through the storm in darkening skies and return us finally safe and happy to the harbour we thought we would never sail into.

SNAPSHOT: "Doc"

We're at Trinity College prep school in Port Hope, Ontario in 1990. I'm coaching a midget team, invited by the hosts to play in a mini-tournament for other such schools. We're in the final against the hosts, down 3-2. It's the intermission between the second and third periods and the boys have skated over to the bench.

I'm accompanied by Ian, assistant coach and father of one of the boys on the team. On this occasion I'm not very happy with the way the team is playing, sluggish, as if they're intimidated by the Trinity squad. We're not a great team, SJR has high academic standards, so the boys I get to choose to make up the lineup are already pre-selected in a way that does not place a high premium on athletic prowess. But the boys are good enough, if they play to their ability.

We've made the trip to Port Hope—airline flight, bus ride—accompanied by a handful of parents and the headmaster, a robust ex-pugilist and private education go-getter who finagled to hire me onto his staff because of my doctoral degree, and gets a kick out of the kids' nickname for me, "Doc." He knows I'm something of a loose cannon, both inside the classroom and out, behaviour he likes to think of as "creative chaos." He's standing behind our bench with the handful of parents and the head of Trinity School, slightly elevated in bleachers that look down on us.

When the boys are settled in front of me, I say to the captain in a loud voice, "What's going on out there, Mark?"

There's a pause. The boys are listening. It's not usual for a coach to begin this way, though they can tell from my tone of voice that I'm not happy with them.

Behind me, I hear the headmaster say quietly to the others, "Listen to this."

"Don't know," Mark answers, "we're—"

"I'll tell you what's wrong," I say in a hard voice. "You're playing like crap." I do not yell this, it's stated flat, a judgement, not an accusation.

"Like crap," I repeat.

"Yeah, Doc." Mark rotates his head the way some athletes do, a tic, a way of shaking off criticism, or letting you know he's ready to bang heads, a holdover from primordial history when this gesture was a life-and-death masculine call to arms.

"You can play better," I say, moderating my tone. I look up and down the bench—Ted, Rob, Chris. "I know it, and you know it and your parents know it."

"Right," Mark says. He looks at his vice-captains. "We know it."

"So get out there," I say, my voice rising, "get out there and play the way you can play."

"Yeah," Mark says, his voice rising too as he turns to his teammates, "let's play the way we can play." He bangs his stick on the boards and the other boys join in.

And less than five minutes later Mark himself scores from a scramble in front of the net, and shortly after Rob takes the puck down the left wing and hammers a slapshot from the top of the circle into the Trinity goal, and we hold on to win 4-3. Both of them look up to me after they've scored, smiles as big as sunsets on their faces. I tap them on the shoulder. Can there be anything better? At the final horn, the headmaster leans down from the first row of seats above us and punches me in the shoulder.

I know and he knows.

This is what we come for, this is what we live for.

This could be a memorable tilt. The Phoenix Coyotes, once the Winnipeg Jets, return to the city that the franchise was pulled out of in 1996.

Almost all the players from the 1996 team are gone; but a few remain, and among the others, spokesmen were caught on TV during the past season—a season when the team was financed by the other teams in the league—saying they did not want to move back to Winnipeg. Those remarks went down like castor oil in the prairie capital; they were perceived as yet another affront to a city smarting from the 1996 departure. There will be no love shown to Gary Bête Noire's Coyotes on this night.

From the outset the crowd is very involved: when a Phoenix player touches the puck, there's loud and protracted booing; when the Jets take control, the chant of Go Jets Go reverberates around the arena. The Coyotes are a good road team, but they look a little flustered. The Jets score before the ten-minute mark. The cheering is thunderous. The Coyotes touch the puck and the booing is even louder than before.

During a break in the action, Shane Doan's face is shown on the scoreboard in the MTS Centre. The one-time Jets stalwart is given a standing ovation. Two minutes later he's on the ice, and when he touches the puck, there's a resounding Boo! This is what it means to be a fan: consistently inconsistent. Or maybe it's as the novelist says: living in our era means holding two opposed views at the same time. To Shane Doan we say: we loved you when you were a Jet, but this whole Phoenix thing sucks.

Prior to the game, the Phoenix players said they expected a cool reception. A spokesman said, "Any energy in a building is good, we'll feed off that energy." He was trying to put the best face on things. No one likes to be booed. It hurts. Who doesn't want to be loved? And who isn't wounded by outright hatred? And despite the claim, it's nearly impossible to seize negative vibes and flip them—jiu-jitsu–like—back on themselves, transforming acid energy into sweet by an act of will. In short, that kind of talk is bull. But saying you will feed off negative energy is a good defence mechanism. Maybe the only one if you're in the position of the Coyotes.

Their coach has said he doesn't understand why Winnipeg fans would be angry at his players; with one exception, they are not the same guys as the ones who left in 1996. He's either thick, or he's trying to bamboozle Winnipeg fans. We do not hate the players. But in the way of pro sport, they are the sole target for our anger, they have to take it on the chin for the NHL and Gary Bête Noire. Because first, the NHL pulled the team out of the city—and we'll never forget that and never forgive it. And second, the Coyotes are in desperate financial straits in Phoenix, so much so that the league is effectively paying the team's bills, which means—wait for this irony—that Winnipeg fans are (oh, Gary, shame on you!) paying to keep the Coyotes in Phoenix, subsidizing Doan and the other players, who have said publicly they don't like Winnipeg. Did Bête Noire and his cohorts make such a deal possible in 1996 to the original Winnipeg Jets? No. Should we not feel anger that they didn't, and that now they're asking us to provide "professional sports welfare" to keep a team in Phoenix because it's "good for the league"?

No wonder Gary Bête Noire shows his face here only if he can cower between Mark Chipman and David Thomson, our heroes, our saviours. No wonder the Phoenix coach looks abashed when he claims not to comprehend our anger.

On the ice, his team puts in a good showing. They outshoot the Jets in the second period 16-9 and come close to tying the game, but the score at the start of the third remains 1-0. Deep intake of breath. It's the Jets. Bigger leads have been squandered. Following the loss to Ottawa, the Jets coach said bitterly that his team had "found every way possible to lose the game." Will that be the case in the third period of this game?

Get through the first ten minutes.

They do, bottling up the middle of the ice, keeping the Coyotes forwards to the outside on their attacks, limiting shots on goal. Are they learning to play defence? The GST line is back together, forechecking furiously, keeping the puck in the Phoenix end; Ladd & co. are picking up where they leave off, neutralizing attacks between the blue lines. Even Byfuglien is playing sensibly, minimizing the times he's trapped in the opposition end. When the final buzzer goes, the Jets have been outshot 33-31, but they've won 1-0.

The cheering of the fans lasts for minutes. The players salute the crowd at centre ice. It may be the best all-round game the team has played. These are the moments when your heart thumps in your chest, emotions running high, reminiscent of the opera.

SNAPSHOT: TOWERING PASSION

There's an element of the opera to a hockey season: emotional highs and lows, one close on the heels of the other; the sense that greater forces are influencing the action; the colossal passion of the scrap that becomes a brawl: enraged coaches, savage beatings, blood, mayhem. It's so deliciously, so exquisitely overblown.

Life itself has the architecture of the classical drama: the opening scenes that introduce the central characters (family, friends); the long middle section of action that complicates as it unfolds (careers, relationships); falling action, leading to the denouement (ultimately, death). Sport seasons imitate this arc. The early games of "feeling out" are followed by an increasingly intense section where the teams sort themselves into contenders, pretenders, and also-rans, a lengthy part that narrows to the telling push and the playoff that produces a grand finale. And they can be taken the same way, as tragedy or comedy. Do we view life as a dreadful unfolding and our passage as unfortunate and mournful? Or do we see in the eternal round of what the poet called "begotten, born, and dies" a comforting pattern, the old ceding the stage to the young in the way of nature, fall and winter giving way to spring and s u m m e r, our winter days enriching the promise of those who come after, our children and our children's children?

SEC: XX ROW: XX SEAT:XX

HOME GAME 26

JETS VS
DEVILS

DECEMBER 03, 2011

SEC: XX
ROW: XX
SEAT: XX

Do we see the end of a hockey season through the eyes of gloom, or do we perceive that one season inevitably leads to the next, a great design unfolding, and while it unfolds the opportunity for us to enjoy the ride: revel in the great goals, the wonderful wins, the nights of exhilarating entertainment?

Saturday night is called *Hockey Night in Canada* on the CBC, but because I'm in Tucson, Arizona, I'm watching plain *Hockey Night*. Should alarm bells be going off in certain quarters of the "true north strong and free?" Is Canada once again being subsumed by the Evil Empire? If the Company of Young Canadians was not defunct, those spiky-eyed patriots would be keeping an eye on this, Bête Noire.

I'm looking at the schedule for this Saturday night. There are twelve games on tap. How many, I wonder, will be won by one goal; how many go into overtime, how many be decided by shootouts? The league is very tight; parity is not just touted by the NHL offices; it's a fact. At the twenty-five-game mark, only seven points separate the East-leading Penguins from the Capitals, holding down the final playoff position. In both conferences, twenty-six teams of thirty are within three points of break-even records.

The New Jersey Devils have played 24 games and have 25 points; the Jets have played 25 games and have 24 points. It's that close across the board.

The Devils play the "neutral zone trap," a defensive strategy where two of the three attackers hang back near the blue line in the opposition end, so that when a turnover occurs, they can act as defenders. The four defenders then string out along the centre line and thwart the opponent's attack. The game bogs down. The team playing the trap has little interest in attack hockey; the team they're employing it against find it very difficult to mount attacks. Puck carriers are slowed down in the neutral zone, or even prevented from going through it; the play stalls. The result of the game hinges on: (a) a miscue turnover that leads to an odd-man attack and goal; (b) a fluky deflection off a stick or a skate; (c) a powerplay tally. Final scores in such games are often 1-0, 2-1, 3-2 in a shootout.

In the NHL the most avid practitioners of the trap have been the New Jersey Devils and Minnesota Wild, both coached by ex-Canadiens, who learned it from Scotty Bowman, its first NHL advocate, who employed it in Detroit in the '90s. But there was an earlier version utilized in the '60s and '70s in Montreal. Then called the "left wing lock," it was not employed with quite the ferocity it is today, when games can be brought almost to a standstill—have, in fact, literally, been brought to a standstill.

The opening faceoff has hardly occurred before the Jets score. The MTS Centre erupts. But only a few minutes later the Devils score. Then the game settles into a staid pattern: the puck goes up and down the ice but attacks are restrained, most of the action is in the corners and between the blue lines. The Devils are not playing a vicious form of the trap, but their forwards are playing "high in the zone," prepared at a moment's notice to drop back and be checkers. The pace of the game reflects it. At the end of the period the shots are six each, the score 1-1.

I say to Andrew, "If it wasn't that we're watching the Jets, I'd find this game utterly boring."

"Both teams seem to be skating in sand."

"It's like they're asleep."

"It's like they have no interest."

The second period follows the template: close checking, few chances, play at the pace of a plough horse. The Jets trying to force the issue, the Devils waiting for the fluky goal, the miscue, the powerplay. They get it with only a couple of minutes remaining in the period. They're gifted a 5-on-3 opportunity and score. But the Jets respond in the final minute of the period with a shorthanded goal, making it 2-2 at the end of two. But the Jets are still down one skater. So into the third period.

Kill the remaining minute of the penalty. Get through the first ten minutes.

They do. Then in the fourteenth minute the Jets score. Then pot one into the empty net, Evander Kane, his fourteenth of the season. The kid is impressive.

Final score 4-2; shots on goal: Devils 19, Jets 20.

A good result but an unsatisfying game.

Did I not say there was a Grumbler in all of us? Even when the Jets win, it's not always good enough. But a .500 record after 26 games, that's pleasing.

SNAPSHOT: On the Fly

Another day, another game. This book is proving a challenge to write. There's so little time between games for reflection and sober analysis. Like the players, I'm on the trajectory of a yo-yo—up and down—everything moving fast between the game just finished and the game on the immediate horizon. It would be nice to have time to cogitate on what's unfolding in the Jets' season, but that is a luxury the schedule does not afford. I'm writing on the fly.

What's coming out are impressions. The Jets win; the Jets lose. The coach looks poised; the coach makes mistakes. At the start of the season I see great promise in Byfuglien; he's a force like Bobby Hull, the one player on the squad capable of inspiring the crowd. Ten games in his plus/minus is a ghastly minus ten and he's a liability, pinching at the opposition blue line too often, giving the other team odd-man advantages; or taking penalties that cost the team powerplay goals. In the pre-season Ladd catches the eye. He works hard and plays with determination, a strong checker, an inspiration to teammates. But ten games in he's proving a liability, too, coughing up the puck in his own end, taking foolish penalties in the opposition zone, trying too hard, not contributing much on the offensive side.

One day the defence look solid, winning 1-0; the next they fall apart and lose a game they were leading 4-2. Which are the real Jets?

The coach has a strong line, Glass, Slater, and Thorburn, fierce forecheckers who neutralize the opposition's number one unit, retain the puck in the opponents' end, and contribute the occasional goal. He breaks them up. Wellwood, his most effective forward, he bounces from line to line. Little and Wheeler keep their spots on the number one line despite contributing nothing. He finds a line that plays well together—Burmistrov, Antropov, Kane—plays them as a unit for a couple games, then breaks them up.

Byfuglien's a bum, Ladd's a liability, the coach doesn't know what he's doing.

The team is like the girl with the curl right in the middle of her forehead: when she's good, she's very very good; but when she's bad, she is horrid. They look like they will be lucky to not finish last in the entire league.

But then.

Just shy of the twenty-game mark, Byfuglien begins to put his game together, takes fewer chances, makes effective rushes into the opposition end, scores goals, and adds assists. His plus / minus is still minus ten, but he's making a positive difference in games. Ladd continues to flounder, looking more like a sixth forward than a top-line guy, but Wheeler has begun to make an impression and Little is scoring.

The coach has put the GST line back together, and Kane, placed in Ladd's spot, is flying, alongside Little and Wheeler. The coach is getting results. The powerplay is beginning to click. The defence are playing a steady game.

The coach's quiet, patient strategy is paying off. The players seem calm and in possession of themselves. They're playing efficiently, his tactics are succeeding. He *does* seem to know what he's doing.

Now the team is eyeing the last playoff spot in the conference. I think they have a chance to have a .500 season, maybe make the spring playoffs. One thing for sure, the Jets are telling a great story this season—all the ups and downs of a classic potboiler, characters emerging and tailing off, the final outcome in doubt. Whew. I am impressed.

But who am I? One fan. One observer with a keyboard. One guy who has played the game all his life and been a spectator of the Jets for almost forty years.

I was off the mark earlier and may be just as wide of the mark again. There's little opportunity for sober reflection. I'm John Wayne, firing from the hip, the book is being put together on the fly. It's exciting, but it's not the most judicious way to create a balanced portrait. *Hold onto yer hat there, pardner, it's gonna be a bumpy ride!*

SNAPSHOT: LAUGHINGSTOCK

I'm scouring through NHL statistics, checking the number of games that on that given *Hockey Night* were decided by one goal—nine of the twelve, it turns out, none by shootout, an oddity. My eye falls on to the "standings" list. Poor Columbus; after 26 games played they have 17 points. What must it feel like to be *their* fans?

Well, we Jets fans know, don't we?

In 1980/81, their second season in the NHL, the team went through a horrendous streak. From October 17 to December 23 they did not win a single game. They opened at Washington, where they lost; and then they lost to Pittsburgh. Back at home, they beat Chicago, but then that was it. They tied Quebec, lost in Buffalo and Minnesota, tied Boston at home, lost to Chicago and Pittsburgh, tied Washington and Calgary, then lost to Edmonton, Toronto, Quebec. By now it was November, their record was 1-9-4, and going to the arena was both a joke and a sorrow. This once was a proud franchise, winners of three AVCO World trophies. To keep up our spirits, we laughed as we crossed the parking lot on our way to the arena doors, the north wind whipping our hair and the team's performance our hearts. They tied Boston, then lost to Montreal, Vancouver, Los Angeles, Buffalo, and Philadelphia. 1-14-5. Our stomachs roiled with acid. We had laughed once—"how are they going to lose tonight?"—but that was all behind us. It was sickening, depressing. We felt like we'd been in the ring with Sonny Liston for three rounds. Season ticket holders stopped going to games, the crowd in the end blues brought witty banners and wore brown bags over their heads. The Jets lost to the Islanders, lost to Hartford, tied St Louis: 1-15-7. Surely we'd reached the bottom, the nadir point. Into December we dragged our sorry asses to the arena; colleagues laughed at us, friends avoided the subject, loved ones patted our heads in sympathy. But it was not the bottom. Losses to Calgary, Rangers, Calgary, St. Louis, Hartford, Minnesota, Islanders, Islanders again. Now we really had a hate on for those rapacious NHL owners, we would have stoned them if they'd shown their faces in Winnipeg, this was really too much. But they didn't. And we lost to the Rangers and St. Louis before finally beating Colorado on December 23—Merry Christmas!

A league record: thirty games without a win. The losing was not over. Through the dark and cold winter followed loss upon loss. The team finished the season 9-57-14, not a league record; in NHL history two other teams managed to do even worse.

But Jesus H.

I was at too many of those games. We shook our heads, we laughed, we wept, we pulled our hair, we cursed, we laughed again. We felt like throwing ourselves in front of a bus.

But.

Never once did I or the people who went with me to games—friends, my wife—think of *not* going to a game, of selling our tickets. To stop being fans. We hung in there with the team, absurdly, comically, pitifully, knowing after a while that beating anyone was beyond the pale, accepting the lashes of defeat upon defeat—almost, at times, welcoming them.

We did, though, start to take a cruel satisfaction in imagining how many goals the team would concede on a given night: Edmonton?—at least four. We began to take comfort in a desperately fought-for tie, a goal by a rookie, a plucky performance against a powerful team, leads taken into the second period before being frittered away, a fetching babe singing the anthem, a particularly witty banner. In the media a certain notoriety developed that would not otherwise have been awarded to the city and the team. Toronto did not care about the mediocrity of the Oilers, Nordiques, or Whalers, all also admitted from the WHA to the NHL that year and doing poorly. But the losing streak in Winnipeg, now that was news!

And so we accepted our role as laughingstock. What else could we do? In April, we renewed our season tickets.

SEC: XX ROW: XX SEAT:XX

HOME GAME 27

JETS VS BRUINS

DECEMBER 06, 2011

SEC: XX
ROW: XX
SEAT: XX

How many penalty advantages will be gifted to the Bruins tonight? You know going in that the referees will make it easy for them to win. It's not clear that this is a conscious policy in the NHL, but it's clearly what does happen, whatever the stated policy of the league, the conscious intention. Last season the Bruins' giant defenceman, Chara, ran Montreal forward Max Pacioretty into the stanchion at one of the benches, giving him a serious head injury and knocking him out of action for weeks, but he did not receive a penalty or a suspension afterwards. Any other player in the league who committed this infraction would have been severely punished. Chris Neil, or Raffi Torres, for instance. This season the Bruins bruising forward Lucic outright "ran" Buffalo goaltender Ryan Miller, hitting him in the head, knocking him out of the game and giving him enough of a concussion to put him on the sidelines for more than half a dozen games. Penalty on the play? Suspension?

Neither. And this in a year when the new league mouthpiece, slick and slippery Brendan Shanahan, is tossing out two- and three-game suspensions like candy at Halloween.

Though they're bad-tempered and often resort to dirty tactics, the Bruins are the NHL's blue-eyed boys, their "protected" team.

So is it a surprise that after the Jets score first and take the lead, the Bruins are gifted three consecutive penalties? No surprise at all.

The Jets survive those first three penalties but by that time the momentum of the game has swung to the Bruins. Only the Jets fans' constant Go Jets Go! and the Jets' fierce penalty killing take them past the referees' obvious favouritism.

It's sickening, really, to witness such ineptitude.

Four nights ago, in a game between Anaheim's Ducks and Philadelphia Flyers, the referees unaccountably gave the Flyers a four-minute advantage in overtime, leading to a goal that cost the Ducks a precious point. In an interview after the game, Teemu Selanne, not a typical griper and complainer, was visibly upset, and he said, "Giving a team an advantage like that, it just doesn't make sense. It's just—"

He stopped himself. Whatever word he was thinking—"stupid," "ridiculous," "laughable"—he stifled. The league has a shut-your-face-if-you-know-what's-good-for-you policy about players criticizing officials or executives, so Selanne knew better than to jeopardize his own chances of playing in the next handful of games. Sleazy Shanny, who could not see a problem with Lucic's check on Miller, would have been all over Selanne for the dreadful infraction of speaking his mind.

Big Brother is watching. STFU.

He was right. He did not quote Lord Acton saying that "power corrupts," but he may as well have. NHL referees let their power to affect games get the better of them, are too often full of themselves, rather than full of interest in the game. They screw up; and at league level their screwups are neither questioned, nor redressed.

The league offices, of course, have a vested interest in seeing certain teams win: those in the big northeast cities, where the TV revenues are large, the sports shows originate, the wealthy owners live and pile up cash from sales of tickets and team merchandise. But what about the referees? They have careers to cultivate and protect, careers that can be helped along nicely by not offending owners and league bosses resident in New York, Toronto, Philadelphia, Boston, Chicago—whereas what is going to be lost by behaving badly to Edmonton, Colorado, Winnipeg, Phoenix? Maybe this sounds paranoic. But it's worthy of some mulling.

The NHL is not a bush league; but it has a long way to go to being a first-rate league. As one Anaheim fan said about Brian Pochmara, the referee that night, "If the NHL isn't going to severely discourage this, well, it just isn't professional grade." On this one they rate a solid B minus, where sound professional leagues, like the NFL, rate an A.

Wake up, Gary!

In the event, the game is a tough-fought battle, up and down the ice, and the Jets go into the third period ahead 1-0.

Get through the first ten minutes.

But they don't.

Before five minutes elapse, the Bruins score. It's no shock when a few minutes later Boston's Krejci plasters Jets defenceman Stuart into the boards without being given a penalty. Can you be this blatant about favouring one team over another?

Apparently you can—if you're Gary Bettman from New York and the team is a northeast team whose winning is "good for the league." Boston, Philadelphia, their players get away with things players from Colorado and Calgary do not. Ovechkin spears Ottawa's Chris Neal in the gut and it's Neal who gets a penalty for "delay of game."

The Jets score to go ahead 2-1, Brian Little, his third in three games. Is he turning things around? Less than three minutes remain in the third period. Can the Jets hang on?

The Bruins press; pucks zing around the Jets' goal, they ice the puck; the Bruins crash the net, Pavelec hangs on to the puck. The linesmen refuse to give the Jets a break when they shoot the puck out of their zone and the Bruins defencemen lollygag down the ice, letting the puck trickle over their goal line, so icing is called against the Jets. The Bruins pull their goaltender and put six skaters on the ice; the Jets win draw after draw, scramble the puck into the corners. Here's where Little and Slater shine.

It's nail-biting time.

Somehow the Jets hang in. The shots at the end of the period are 40-35, in favour of the Bruins, but the important stat is the final score: 2-1. The

Bruisers from Boston have lost in regulation time for the first time since October. To our Jets.

Hallelujah!

When the Jets lost to the worst team in the league, I said, "If you lose to the worst team in the league, are you the worst team?" Is it then fair to ask: "If you beat the best team in the league, are you the best team in the league?" The answer then boiled up from a fan's bile; now it seems obvious that neither is true.

Emotions are so easily engaged. It's all happening on the fly.

SNAPSHOT: Fickle Fan

I'm watching *Center Ice* in Tucson when the news comes over the TV: the NHL is going into the upcoming season under realignment. The Jets, this year in the Eastern Conference, will next year be switched to something temporarily being called "Conference B," a collection of eight teams, including Dallas, Chicago, Detroit, and others, mostly occupying a narrow band that runs north to south down the middle of the continent, mostly in the Central time zone. It's a big change; it will mean a lot less travel for the Jets next season, though it might mean more for Detroit.

Team managers interviewed on the TV sport shows concur that realignment is best for the league. They support the plan. The Jets' Mark Chipman says, "I judge it to be a positive development for our franchise." He points out that a lot of games now will occur in the local time zone, much easier on the players and a plus for Jets fans watching on TV. And he seems very pleased that two of the eight teams in the Jets' new conference come from the NHL's Original Six: "Those are high watermark organizations that you aspire to play and be like."

He's right on all accounts. Less travel is good; more Central Time Zone games on TV is also good; and having Detroit and Chicago visit Winnipeg frequently will be pleasurable, though not more than a lot of other teams—Vancouver, Montreal, others.

I study the Jets' conference again. Columbus is there too, St. Louis, Minnesota, Nashville. From these eight, four will make the playoffs. A competitive pool; though by no means an "easy" one; but not a "group of death" either.

In looking at the teams to be bundled with the Jets, it occurs to me that during this season I've been a lot more interested in teams that I would not otherwise have given much more than a passing thought in other years: Islanders, Carolina, Florida, Tampa Bay. Each night I've checked the overall league scoreboard. Did Tampa Bay win? What happened between Buffalo and Carolina? How did New Jersey fare? I don't have an intrinsic interest in these teams. The Devils play boring hockey, and I've never felt any excitement about the two Florida teams, even though Tampa Bay once won the Cup, and they have several first-rate players. No, it's not intrinsic interest I have in the fortunes of these teams. It's embarrassing to admit, but my interest is purely in how they're doing relative to the Jets, because each of them is competing with the Jets for playoff spots. So if Florida loses a game against, say, Phoenix, a non-conference rival, that's "good," but if Carolina beats Minnesota, that's "bad," even though I dislike Minnesota's style of play and feel a long-standing loyalty to plucky Carolina, because they're the one-time WHA Hartford Whalers.

To be a fan of a big-league team puts you in quite bizarre positions, cheering for teams you dislike—New Jersey—against others you would in altered circumstances admire: Ottawa. And these positions change on a nightly basis. If Toronto is playing Calgary, I'm cheering for Calgary to win: fewer points for Toronto. But if the next night Toronto is playing Washington, I'm pulling for Toronto, because Washington is a team the Jets are competing with for the final playoff spot. So go Leafs! (Tonight— but maybe not tomorrow.)

My loyalties shift on a nightly basis. And for the meanest of reasons: not the inherent integrity of other teams—their style of play, the attractiveness of their stars—but for how their fortunes affect my team. It's quite bent, really, like so many things connected to being a supporter of a given team rather than a fan of the game per se.

Fan of the game? That naive fair-mindedness ended when the Atlanta franchise was transferred to Winnipeg and we threw our lot in with, threw our very hearts in with—again, after sixteen years—the Jets.

"Our Jets forever."

Another game against the struggling Hurricanes, who've had to deal with a coaching change and rumours that their star player, Eric Staal, is on the trading block.

Going in, Kristen says, "I have the feeling the Jets are going to blow this one. They've been playing well, they've had a couple of days off, they're going to be sleepy."

"It's tomorrow night against Detroit that they should relax."

"Yeah, in Detroit, a strong team, that's the one to lose. Whereas tonight."

"But that's not how things work out, is it?"

"No. Show up tonight not ready to play and lose 5-2."

"Then turn around and lose again in Detroit tomorrow. Probably a squeaker."

"Exactly. I have the feeling the old Jets are going to show up tonight."

Sigh. This is what it's like to be a fan: glass half-empty. Battening down the psychic hatches in anticipation of a loss.

In the stands someone holds up a placard: KANE THE CANES. There's a joker born every minute.

The TV commentator says, "Carolina are going to come out on fire." But the puck has barely been dropped when the Jets score, Byfuglien banking it in off the goaltender from behind the net. What's he doing behind the other team's goal?

It's the Jets who are doing the storming: shot after shot. Only four minutes later, they tally gain. Carolina's coach calls a time out; the crowd is already going after the opposition goaltender: *War-rd, War-rd.*

Then the game settles into a composed contest, defences playing well in their own ends, attackers pursuing pucks in the opposition zone, goaltenders making stops and forcing faceoffs that slow the pace of the game. At the end of the period the shots stand 19-7 Jets, a fair reflection of the play.

Much the same happens in the second period. The Jets continue to carry the play, outshooting the Hurricanes 12-8 and scoring on two powerplays. Professional play from both sides, but not an inspired performance. But then that suits the Jets just fine. They're ahead by a good margin: 4-0. They don't need to dazzle the fans with entertaining hockey.

They do, though, need to hang on in the third period. Four goals should prove a comfortable lead, but just the previous night Montreal blew a three-goal lead and ended up losing to Vancouver 4-3. There's a cautionary tale.

So it's take a deep breath time when Carolina score before the ten-minute mark. Oh, oh. This is the Jets, right? No lead, however large, is ever comfortable. Less than four minutes later, Carolina tally again and it's game on. Damn good thing that was a four-goal lead and not three. The Hurricanes press. Most of the play is in the Jets end; the shots are piling up in Carolina's favour. Pavelec once again is "standing on his head," save after save, some of the heart-stopping variety. And the Jets are hanging on. At the final horn it's 4-2, a good professional victory that takes the Jets' winning streak to four and puts them two games over the .500 mark, something that seemed impossible to wish for only a month ago.

The team seems to have gelled into a steady professional outfit. The coach's low-key tactics seem to be working on a nightly basis. At about the one-third mark of the season, the playoffs no longer seem a remote possibility. Can the glass really be half-full? Go Jets!

The vaunted Red Wings, winners of four Stanley Cups in the past fifteen years, and a powerhouse boasting names like Lidstrom, Zetterberg, Datsyuk, Franzen. Interesting how those names fifty years ago, when Detroit was also a force to be reckoned with, were Howe, Lindsay, Abel. The NHL is truly international now. Those WASP names of fifty years ago have been replaced by Russian, Slavic, Nordic names. Among the Jets' most reliable players are Burmistrov, Antropov, Pavelec.

And it's arguable it was the Winnipeg Jets that began the trend to full "Europeanization."

That trend began in the 1970s when Swedish players first appeared in the NHL, Borje Salming and Inge Hammarstrom, playing for Toronto in 1973. But the trend in the NHL was sporadic. There was generally the xenophobic feeling that European players were not gritty enough to play here—skillful, yes, but without the tenacity to compete in the long NHL schedule against hard-nosed Canadian players, weaned in our robust junior leagues. They were, it was often said, too much like soccer players, soft, more accustomed to fancy play than grinding it out in the corners.

When the WHA began, it corralled a few big-name NHLers, notably Bobby Hull and Derek Sanderson. But a lot of the players in the fledgling league were from the minor pro leagues, guys who had been paying their dues in the AHL. And juniors, who the WHA took on even before they had played a single game in the AHL or other minor pro leagues: Wayne Gretzky was among these, brought into the WHA as a member of the Indianapolis Racers at age seventeen. Rick Vaive, of the Birmingham Bulls, Dennis Sobchuk, of the Cincinnati Stingers and fresh from the Regina Pats, who had won the Memorial Cup, emblematic of junior hockey supremacy in Canada. For their rosters of players, the Winnipeg Jets cast their eyes to Europe, making in just a few short years Bergman, Nilsson, Hedberg, Sjoberg, Labraaten household names. And many more would come: Ketola, Riihiranta, Lindstrom, Steen.

While many teams now boast rosters comprised half of Europeans, it was the WHA Jets who first saw the possibility of that talent pool.

In recent decades, the Red Wings have made the most of it.

When the commentator on the TV broadcast tells us the Jets did not arrive at the hotel in Detroit until 4:30 AM following Friday's game and flight from Winnipeg, Kristen says, "Oh, oh."

"There's gonna be some tired legs out there tonight."

"You think they'll get pasted?"

"I don't know what to think any more. They could lose 7-1 or squeak out a 3-2 victory. Most likely they'll lose 5-2."

Before the first minute elapses, the Jets score. Good grief, they're a young team, but they can't be that resilient, can they?

They aren't. Detroit score twice within fifteen minutes and the period ends 2-1. But the score does not really tell the tale. The Jets look tired. Almost all the play has been in their end. The shots on goal stand 12-9 for the Wings.

In the second period the trend continues: Detroit net two goals before the five-minute mark. Then another two in the following ten minutes. The game is just past the halfway mark and it's 6-1. And these are not cheap goals. Detroit is playing with verve and beauty, criss-crossing in the Jets end, working triangular passing plays that free a man in front of goal. They're smooth skaters and slick stickhandlers. And they play a fluid game. In one way, it's a pleasure to watch, dazzling hockey from a skilled and disciplined team. But 5-2 now looks like a score Jets fans would gladly take. At the end of the second, the shots are 25-18. The Jets are not playing badly, but the Wings are putting on an eye-catching display. They cut their engines in the third period and coast to a 7-1 victory.

Kristen mutters, "That winning streak came to a crashing end."

"Jets crash," Andrew says, laughing. "Good one."

"Maybe it was good for them," I say.

Andrew agrees. "Reality check."

This happens sometimes; a team gets spanked and bounces back, where had they merely lost a close one, they might drift into a half-dozen mediocre losses. But there are other possibilities.

Kristen asks, "What's to say they won't unravel now and go into a funk?"

"That's up to the coaching staff."

SNAPSHOT: DRUBBING

A December evening in 1990, the Dutton Arena, home ice of the prep school where I teach—and coach. I'm coaching the team that won the tournament in Port Hope, a group of fifteen-year-olds—grade tens—and we've just lost a game by 9-1, a sound drubbing.

Usually I go directly into the dressing room following games, but tonight I hold back a few minutes, fussing with water bottles, the team's puck bag, the medical kit, anything to calm my hands and still my flailing heart. I'm chattering with my assistant coach, Ian, a fine fellow with a good tactical sense of the game and a sympathetic disposition, important to both the boys on the team and me.

The team is registered in the Double A league, above themselves in one sense. We've placed them in AA, the school's head hockey coach and I, so they can develop both the skills and the grit to play in the city high school hockey league when they're in grades eleven and twelve. But it's been tough sledding. Double A is the division in Winnipeg's minor hockey system that draws teams from population bases of around 60,000, fairly substantial cities on their own. Boys try out for AA teams, and the tryouts are highly selective: only eighteen boys from an area of the city that large, in each age group, makes for stiff competition. Players are big, fast, skillful.

At the prep school I get to make up a roster of eighteen from a total of the forty boys registered in one grade, so the pickings are occasionally sparse. We end up taking "marginals." Still, this is a pretty good team, and at the start of the season we had high hopes for them. But things have not worked out well. After fourteen games, we've won three, lost nine, and tied two. Though I cautioned the boys at the start of the season that playing in AA would be difficult, and they agreed in a team meeting they were willing to take it on, they're kids, really, and these things can be dispiriting. Some of the boys are taking it hard. Some of their parents, too. And I'm beginning to wonder if I've made a mistake.

I say to Ian, "We took it on the chin tonight."

"Some lucky goals against. I thought the boys played well."

I have a habit, when anxious, of jingling my car keys in my pockets. "They did, they did." Jingle, jingle.

"It was only 4-1 at the end of the second."

Ian's an optimist, it's one of the reasons I took him on to work with me, an optimist and a balanced man, more balanced than I am. If either of us is going to lose it, it's liable to be me. And he's good with the kids. I'm tough Dad to his easy-going Uncle.

I sigh. "Is that three losses in a row?"

"Four. But then there was winning at Trinity College. That was big for the boys."

"It was. We need another shot in the arm like that."

"A tournament? Maybe in the country? Brandon?"

"No, they load up their teams in the country. We end up playing all-stars and getting thumped. And rural kids, they're tough as nails."

Ian laughs. He comes from farm-folk himself.

"I've been thinking of maybe setting up a game against a Triple-A team, but a year younger." AAA is the division above AA, the best players in the city system.

"Huh. South End?"

"The Transcona kids are middle of the pack."

"Yeah. South End's fighting with St. Boniface at the top."

"Right. Think I'll call the Transcona coach."

We're halfway back to the dressing rooms, nodding at parents. "Tough loss," one of the fathers says, more to Ian than to me. Ian is more approachable than I am, he tends to do the liaising between us and the parents. I walk on, jingle, jingle.

When we've passed out of earshot of the parents, we pause at the dressing room door. We're both still thinking of a game against a Triple-A team.

"We can beat them," I say, "it will be good for morale."

"It will."

"But it would be bad to lose."

"Well…"

"You got that right. It would be bad to lose. But we should win on size alone—though they'll be faster and more skilled."

Ian nods. He knows more than he's saying, he knows it's not only the boys who need the shot in the arm.

"And it wouldn't be a disaster if we did lose. They're Triple A, the boys can look at it that way."

"We can sell it that way."

"Win-win," I say and laugh. I move my car keys to a different pocket.

"Yeah," Ian says, pushing open the dressing room door, "we could use a little of that around here."

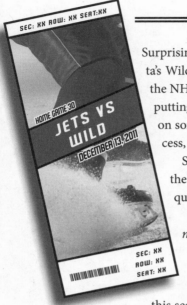

SEC: XX ROW: XX SEAT:XX

HOME GAME 30

JETS VS WILD

DECEMBER 13, 2011

SEC: XX
ROW: XX
SEAT: XX

Surprisingly, the Jets' neighbours to the south, Minnesota's Wild are atop the Western Conference standings in the NHL. They have always been a hard-working outfit, putting grit before grace in their style of play, relying on some form of the neutral zone trap to achieve success, but not offering much in the way of pizzazz.

So expect a close game, and fear a dull one. After the blowout in Detroit, be prepared for the Jets to be quite focused and determined.

And—of course—*get through the opening ten minutes.*

The game starts at a good pace, rushes up and down the ice, fierce checking in both ends. Maybe Minnesota has opened up their game this season. They've got some players with flair: Koivu, Heatley.

The crowd is animated. Go Jets Go! This is the thirtieth game of the season, just past the one-third mark of the schedule, and very little of the glitter has worn off the return to the NHL. If anything, there's a feeling of confidence building: the team is playing better than .500 hockey, beating the stronger teams in the league as well as the others, holding their own up and down the Eastern Conference, playing mostly sound hockey. No one is prepared to make ambitious claims for the Jets' prospects, but a quiet confidence is developing: the playoffs are a possibility. If the forwards carrying the attack—Kane, Wellwood, Little—stay healthy, if Pavelec can continue his good run in goal… In the meantime, the team is playing entertaining hockey.

It's becoming clearer that the team's style is a mirror of the historic Jets: flair and verve, emphasizing skating and skill. The team stands in the middle of the pack when it comes to goals scored (84), though they've allowed nine more goals than they've tallied, indicating they're offensive minded rather than defensive. (The teams at the top of the table boast differentials of plus ten and more.) Among them are the Wild, who have scored one less time than the Jets, but have allowed a dozen goals fewer.

They're a tight-checking outfit and it's obvious in this game. The first period ends with no scoring. And then Minnesota pounce on a power-play advantage to take a 1-0 lead, typical of a "trapping" team. The second period ends 1-1, the Jets having replied with less than five minutes remaining. Neither team is giving much away, the attacking forwards being held to the outside where shots can be more easily parried. There are flurries around both nets, but both goaltenders are making timely saves—and the Jets have had a goal called back.

Can they hang on? It's a fifty-fifty proposition. Either team could score—or, the way they're playing, neither. A tie might best reflect the play on the night.

As it is, the Jets break through just past the fifteen-minute mark of the final frame, putting the puck in the Wild goal just as an extra man advantage in their favour expires.

In the final minute the Jets take a penalty and have to hang on desperately, down four men to six as the game comes to its finish: 2-1 against the Wild, leaders of the Western Conference. Not a bad result, following the drubbing in Detroit; though not an exhilarating game from the entertainment perspective. But what do we want—results in the standings, or pleasing hockey? Answer: we're fans; we pay good money to see our team in action; we want both.

13 December 2011

Team	GP	PTS
Philadelphia	29	41
Boston	29	39
New York R	28	38
Pittsburgh	31	38
Florida	31	38
Toronto	30	35
Buffalo	30	33
New Jersey	30	33
Montreal	31	33
Winnipeg	30	32
Ottawa	31	32
Washington	29	31
Tampa Bay	30	26
New York J	28	24
Carolina	32	23

Though they changed their coach after a stumbling start to the season, the Capitals have continued to play mediocre hockey and they come into this game with fewer points than the Jets. How can this be? They're a team loaded with talent, including the once-incomparable Ovechkin, the unpredictable but sometimes dazzling Semin, reliable and highly skilled Backstrom. The Jets don't have one player of this ilk, though Kane is moving into their echelon.

So what explains Washington's poor performance?

Can this be the Don Cherry Effect?

Cherry, a long-time xenophobe who has nevertheless been allowed by CBC to air his extremist views on national TV for decades, is fond of claiming that European players, especially a certain type of Russian—swift skater, fancy stickhandler, poor checker—do not have the grit to play through a complete season in the NHL. They're good—better than good—in the regular season but wilt under the pressure of playoffs and often "disappear." Their coaches and fans, accustomed to seeing them dominate games, scoring buckets of goals, dazzling crowds and TV watchers alike, witness them being manhandled in the post-season, where a greater premium is placed on checking than scoring. Cherry might cite Pavel Bure as a past example of this phenomenon. In the current period, Ovechkin seems to be heading down the same road. Though the Capitals have been the cream of the league in many seasons, winning the President's Trophy in 2010 for most points in the season, they have never won the Stanley Cup.

And now they appear to be floundering during the season. Ovechkin has only 21 points, 18 fewer than the league leader, 8 down from his contemporary Russian, Malkin, 9 less than the Ducks' aging Selanne; the Jets' Kane has 3 more points, as do other youngsters such as Eberle and Seguin. Semin, once thought to be the match to Ovechkin's brilliance,

SEC: XX ROW: XX SEAT:XX

HOME GAME 31

JETS VS CAPITALS

DECEMBER 15, 2011

SEC: XX
ROW: XX
SEAT: XX

and certain to lead the Capitals to several Cups, is struggling to get into the teens, with a Spartan 11, trailing numerous defencemen.

The shine has gone off the two Russian stars.

But they're still both potent offensive forces, and it's early in the season, and a streak is possible at any time, and ... the Jets had better be wary tonight.

Get through the first ten minutes.

Both teams do, the Jets playing an inspired game, the Capitals looking more organized and more dangerous than the last time the teams played. And the play is entertaining: at one point the action goes for more than three minutes without a stoppage. Both sets of forwards are carrying the puck to the backboards; both goalies making routine saves; the defence clearing the front of the nets effectively. This is wonderful hockey, high entertainment, great drama.

There are few penalties—and lots of exhilarating rushes. Maybe too many going in the direction of the Jets goal. The defence are pinching and occasionally getting caught. Against a team with the explosiveness of the Capitals, they're playing with fire. The second period ends scoreless with the shots about even: 22-19 for the Jets.

"Well?" I say in the intermission.

"Looks like whoever scores, wins," Kristen says.

"Yeah. Should favour the home team."

"But you never know."

"No, you never know."

At the intermission a girl is waving a sign: MARRY ME ONDREJ. What do players think of these things? What does Ondrej Pavelec's girlfriend think?

The Caps come out strong in the third. It looks as if the ice is tilted toward the Jets end. Ovechkin is playing with passion, a winner-take-all brand of hockey that is going to land him with a serious injury one of these days. Every time he touches the puck, the crowd lets out a long *boo*. It's nail-biting stuff, highly entertaining, but you can feel the apprehension building in the crowd: how long can the teams play like this without one of them giving up a goal? Without the Jets giving up a goal?

I look at the time clock. Less than five minutes remaining, both teams with 25 shots on goal. I say to Kristen, "I guess we settle for a point tonight."

But then the old Jets bugbear strikes again: Ladd coughs up the puck between the blue lines, Ovechkin sweeps in and scores. Hardly a minute remains in the game.

Precious points thrown away.

We go home deflated. So close to victory. But then so far.

"That close," I offer as we go through the door.

"They're Charlie Brown," Andrew says, helping us to hang coats in the foyer. "So much hope—but then..."

"A good game," Kristen says, "both teams playing at the highest level, looking like they know what they're doing, looking professional."

SNAPSHOT: Professional

A Saturday afternoon in early summer, warm enough for outdoor barbecuing but still springtime cool enough that we take our steaks indoors to eat with salad, potato, and beer. Indoors is the hall of a Catholic church in St. Boniface. It's the "windup" party for the Hooks, an old-timers team I play for in the '90s, a nice group of mostly working-class guys who don't take themselves seriously and have a lot of fun playing the game, sharing a few beers in the dressing room, shooting the breeze before and after ice-times.

Balancing paper plate and cold bottle of beer, I take a seat beside my nephew, Shane, who also plays for the Hooks, and across from Darryl, one of the better players on the team and a guy who always has something interesting to say.

We chat for a while: the weather, the recent heart attack of a guy who used to play with the Hooks, the prospects of the Jets remaining in the city. It should be a hot summer; Buddy is resting and recovering and wishes he could join us; it looks like the Jets will be moved to another city—Phoenix?

After a while Shane gets up and fetches us another beer. When he's sitting again, Georges, who acts as manager of the team and has arranged this gathering, stands up and clears his throat. "On behalf of Hook," he begins. Everyone chuckles.

Hook is an older man, maybe in his seventies, the original manager of the team who drops by the dressing room once or twice a year and hangs out with his "boys," most of whom, now, he does not know. At the windup he usually gives a little speech but he's ill this year, so the honour has fallen on Georges. He has a cardboard box in front of him on a folding table and he rummages in it as he talks. Out come trophies, the kind kids get at the end of a hockey season. Georges is smiling and laughing.

Hook has decided, he informs us, to give each of the *boys* an engraved trophy, and keeping with a tradition long-established in minor-league hockey, he has assigned a designation to each recipient. Guffaws go up from the team. Titters of disbelief. A few cheers. Georges puts up one hand for silence as he holds up the first trophy.

Scoring Leader: Jamie. A matter of statistics. As well as being skillful, Jamie never misses a game. When Jamie stands to fetch his trophy, a hooting cheer goes up.

Most Gentlemanly: Bob, a soft-spoken cop and the undoubted choice. "Way to go, Bob," someone calls out as he makes his way forward.

Inspiration to the Team: the absent Buddy, recovering from heart attack. Palms bang on tabletops. A murmur of *where is Buddy?* floats around a nearby table.

Best Defenceman: Darryl. No argument there. But it would have been nice to be named. Darryl gives a dramatic bow as he receives his trophy.

Best Forward: Shane. No argument there either, though others in the room would like to have been chosen. Shane holds the tiny trophy over his head as if he were displaying the Stanley Cup at centre ice, a ridiculous parody. As many boos as cheers.

Most Reliable Player: Scotty. Someone shouts out: "Got that right. He can be relied on to drink the most beer." Scotty gives him the universal finger.

Best Checker: Paul.

Most Skilled: Matthew.

This has the earmarks of junior high. Guys are squirming in their seats. This is beginning to feel like those times when sides are chosen up and you fear your name will be called last and only grudgingly. ("All right, then, we'll take Ralphie.")

Georges breaks the ice with Most Valuable Player: Georges. Clearly not true, the only category so far of which that is so, but good for the laughs.

How many more designations can be left?

Shane has his trophy on the table between us. A little man on a pedestal with a hockey stick in hand. It's engraved with his name and "Hooks, Best Forward."

Defensive Forward: Al.

Fastest: Other Al. Hoots and cheers. This Al is a powerful skater and he likes to carry the puck from one end of the ice to the other. He has one move, and once you know it, he's easy to check. But he is fast—and he keeps trying.

Most Professional: Wayne. I stand, unsure it's my name that has been called and even more unsure what is meant by "professional"? That I show up on time; that I pass the puck when someone else would shoot; that I tap my teammates on the shin pads if they make a mistake? I think of myself as steady and reliable, prone to the occasional mistake, and capable of modest achievement. Is that *professional*? Maybe it's a joke. Maybe Hook ran out of designations. I decide on: *go about my business without fuss*. There's clapping as I step forward, but no hooting or jeering. Maybe this is part of designating someone *professional*. I shrug when Georges passes me the trophy with a smile. He's fumbling in the box with the remaining trophies.

Professional?

Teemu Redux.

The sports page blazes the headline: Go FLASH GO. Teemu-mania has struck the city. When the Anaheim Ducks' flight arrived at the airport at 2:30 AM Saturday from Minneapolis, where the Ducks had been playing the Wild, fans were waiting to cheer their hero and get Selanne's autograph. The word on the street is that a nine-dollar ticket (who knew there were tickets at that price?) is going for $400. Next to the opening game against Montreal, tickets to this game were the most difficult to procure. Inside the arena, banners dot the stands: TEEMU WEE LOVE YOU, GO FLASH, TEEMU TIME.

It's not so much a hockey game as a love-in. Before the game starts, there's a spontaneous standing ovation for Selanne, chants of his name. Nine guys sitting in a row have painted on their naked chests each letter of Selanne's name and the jersey number he wore as a Jet: 13. What does Selanne, who has not played in Winnipeg since 1996, who left in disappointment bordering on despair when he was suddenly (and callously) traded that year, think of this outpouring of affection, fifteen years later? What do his teammates think? What do the Jets think? Their fans are cheering for the opposition—at least one member of the opposition.

The relation between fans and players is a complicated one. When Shane Doan returned to the city some weeks ago, he was given a standing ovation when his photo was flashed on the centre-ice scoreboard. But each time he touched the puck, he was booed. Message: we liked you when you were a Jet, but now that you're a Coyote…

There seems to be no such ambivalence regarding Selanne. Yet he only played here for six seasons, a small portion of his twenty-year career. Somehow he reached the hearts of Winnipeg fans in the way some athletes do. He's one of ours, seems to be the feeling, though he was born and lived in Finland for twenty-some years before coming here, though he has lived in California for the past fifteen years.

Each time he touches the puck, a loud cheer goes up.

We love this guy, though it may not be clear to Anaheim fans why. He began his career here; he set a rookie scoring record in this city, making him part of hockey history, as well as our history; he was part of "The Young Guns," with three other rookies: Tkachuk, Zamnov, Davydov; he always made himself available for charity events and autograph signings; he was soft-spoken, and despite his brilliance on the ice, a modest man, seemingly a regular guy; he was a Finn with a Finnish wife and Nordic attitudes to big cities, the welfare state, cold weather. He was the son you wanted your son to hang out with, the boy next door you wanted your daughter to marry. He was everything you ever wanted to be yourself and the polar opposite of all those loudmouth, big-ego athletes who are subjects of countless "sport-shouting" TV programs, heartless million-aires whose multiple failures as teammates and human beings are always someone else's fault.

Each time Selanne crosses into the Jets end a roar of approval goes up.

But an even louder cheer greets a Jets goal early on. That loss to Wash-ington in the final minute two nights ago stung. Fans need to have their faith in the team restored. So when a second goal is scored less than two minutes later, there's an almost palpable relief in the arena. Game in hand. The Ducks are not a strong team, the Ducks struggle on the road, the Ducks are tired after the game in Minneapolis and the subse-quent late-night flight. They don't look very organized, their goaltender has let in at least one soft goal. The goombah contingent is jeering out his name—*Ell-iss, Ell-iss*.

But the Jets are not playing great either. Where the last two contests were speedy affairs with heart-in-mouth dashes both ways on the ice, this is a slow game, a game that features lots of turnovers in the neutral zone, errant passes, flubbed shots. Neither team is showing much energy. And the Jets seem off-balance at their blue line. So it's no surprise when Anaheim score a fluky goal on a rainbow pass into the Jets end, and that they then follow it up with a long strike up the middle, resulting in a breakaway and a second goal. The period ends 2-2.

Other than the cheers of *Teemu*, the game has been anything but entertaining, outright dull, actually, and poorly played. And now the result hangs in the balance.

That's redressed in the opening minute of the second when Burmis-trov scores on a laser shot from the top of the circle. Thank god. The Ducks have a terrible road record, but all season they've been a come-back team—as those two goals in the first period showed. Fortunately for the Jets, the Ducks are leg-weary on this night, and though they have a couple of chances in the remaining minutes of the second, it's the Jets who put the puck in the net and restore their two-goal lead: 4-2.

But it hasn't been much of a game: slow, fumbly, chaotic. Both teams look more like minor leaguers than top-rank pros. And the defensive messiness in both ends resembles junior hockey. Some games are just bad games. You shake your head, you take a deep breath and think, *at least the Jets are ahead;* you quaff another ale.

The Jets score a fifth early on in the third period and the air goes out of the Ducks. Still the fans keep waving their banners: TEEMU, WEE LOVE TEEMU. Now would be a good time for him to score: everyone would feel great, and the goal would not threaten the outcome. He has a golden chance from the top of the slot, but the puck goes flying past the post. A groan goes up from the crowd. But he does assist on a powerplay tally at the midway point of the period, and for a brief time the Ducks pour on the pressure, trying to get within one.

The game ends 5-3. Just one of those games. Satisfying for the fans to see two points go on the board for the home side but otherwise not much to be excited about. In an 82-game season it's going to happen every now and then. Maybe it's surprising that it doesn't happen more often.

SEC: XX ROW: XX SEAT:XX

HOME GAME 33
**JETS VS
ISLANDERS**
DECEMBER 20, 2011

SEC: XX
ROW: XX
SEAT: XX

There's clatter and banging in the arena before the start of the game, loud rock music over the PA system, 15,000 faithful fans blatting horns, starting up cheers, waving signs, strobe lights playing over centre ice and the Jets logos at the faceoff dots in both ends.

The Islanders are one of the weaker sisters in the league and a team below the Jets in the standings, so on form the Jets should beat them; but the games are played on the ice, not on form, and the Islanders have a fast, young squad that plays quality hockey on some nights. If the Jets aren't careful, they could blow this one.

They start fast, buzzing the Islanders goal, but that burst of energy flames out after three or four minutes and the Islanders begin to take the play away from the home team. They have one and then two odd-man rushes into the Jets end, and if it weren't for good saves by Pavelec, could have two or three goals early on. Where would the Jets be without this guy? The Isles put one in before the ten-minute mark.

The Jets do not look good. Breakouts die at the blue line, passes through the neutral zone are flubbed, attacks fizzle out in the Islanders zone. And the Isles keep getting gifted odd-man rushes at the Jets goal. It's not pretty. Against the Ducks three nights ago the Jets looked disorganized and tired, and this game resembles that one. We puff out our cheeks. The guy next to us quips, "I didn't know the Jets had so many one-legged skaters." As the period winds toward a close, I think they'll be lucky to get to the intermission behind by only one goal. And then against the run of play, they score at the eighteen-minute mark. "A miracle," the guy beside us says.

"That was pretty ugly," I say to Kristen.

"They started strong but when they didn't score seemed to lose interest."

As the play starts again, I say to Kristen, "When they play poorly in the first period they sometimes storm back in the second."

But they don't. The slow and bumbling play continues and it's no surprise when the Islanders score again before the five-minute mark. Hoo boy.

One of the things that dogs teams struggling to be genuine contenders is their failure to play at high intensity for the entire sixty minutes that constitute a game. Young teams are especially prone to this inconsistency. It's not easy to reach that level of efficiency. In fact, it's difficult to forecheck doggedly, to mount attacks that threaten the opposition goal without trapping players deep in the opposition zone, to keep the shots of opponents' forwards to the outside in your own end, to protect your goal and minimize scrambly play in front of it, to break out of your zone speedily and effectively, to not take penalties. Each of those things is difficult to master, and to put them all together for an entire game is a daunting task. Throughout this season, the Jets have done it from time to time. But more often they play in patches, a good five minutes followed by a scrambly three; a strong three minutes followed by five of erratic play. Coaches witness this on-and-off performance and are driven crazy by it; they know the team can play well in patches, but they don't know the magic formula that will raise the level of play to that height for an entire game. Fans are not so forgiving. They're grumblers, and it doesn't take long for rumbles of discontent to shudder through the arena. "Kane, you bum," "Do something, Byfuglien."

Ladd dispels the worst of the grumbling with a laser shot under the bar of the Islanders net before the midway point of the game and the period ends 2-2. Ladd again; he has a habit of scoring key goals, and this one, his eleventh of the campaign, might help the Jets salvage something on this night.

Still, you can't help feeling the Jets are lucky to be in it. You fear they're going to blow this one—and for no good reason. The Islanders are not brilliant; but the Jets are floundering.

Maybe it's the time of year. Around Christmas a lot of teams that start the season on the jump run out of gas. The demands of the professional schedule get to them: the travel, the nagging injuries, the pace of the games they're required to play night after night, the ups and downs of their individual play—am I forechecking well enough, should I be shooting more? These things add up. Older players know how to pace themselves through the 82-game schedule, but younger players expend a lot of energy on side issues, flailing emotionally as well as thrashing physically. They poop out. It's mid-season doldrums, which are equivalent to the falling off of energetic play that can occur within a single game. The same stumbling to execute well night after night. Consistency may be the hobgoblin of little minds, as the writer says, but it's also what makes winning sports teams.

So the third period begins with a familiar plea: *Just get through the next ten minutes.*

Both teams do, though to their credit, the Jets begin with a flurry that nearly produces the go-ahead marker. They outshoot the Islanders 6-0 at the opening of the period. But then both teams settle into a tighter game. There are rushes and good chances around both nets. The Islanders hit the post. The Jets respond with a three-on-one attack that ends with a good shot and a better save. With five minutes left on the clock, overtime looms, and one point seems acceptable.

A woman behind us screams: "Put New York away!" It's a cry of desperation.

A guy behind us yells: "I got thirteen hundred bucks riding on this!"

The game ends 2-2; the overtime does not produce a goal; the Islanders record two goals in the shootout to take the extra point. Another game the Jets may regret not winning come spring. But that's the way it goes.

"Not a bad game," Kristen says as we're leaving.

"But not a good one either."

SNAPSHOT: SPORTS FEVER 5

We go back. At the start of the season, we have few expectations. Maybe the team will play well, maybe they will be entertaining. Whatever the case, the city is in a Jets frenzy and we want to be part of it: the talk around the water cooler, the buzz on the Blackberry, the yakking in the dressing room before our own games.

Our modest expectations are realized. The Jets drop the opening three games, one at home, two on the road, at least one of which they could have won, another that was gifted to their opposition by inept officials. We drop our heads. Same old Jets, same old NHL. It's fun to attend the games, exhilarating in the stands, the city is wild for its team, yet it's just as painful to lose as in the past. But still, it's a buzz to be back in the bigs: Go Jets Go!

The team rallies and through October plays impeccable .500 hockey—losing one night, winning the next, occasionally posting a tie. We're up and down like yo-yos. One game the team flounders in their own end and it seems they can do nothing right anywhere on the ice. Crikey, we think, they stink, they're no better than the Moose. Two days later they play a near-flawless game at both ends and win by one goal and post a shutout. All right, we think, this is better, the team is on their way to doing good things, respectability. Somewhere down the road they could make the playoffs. They take the lead in the very next outing but collapse and lose 5-2.

Our hopes are dashed but we come back. We're not going through the horrific winless streak of 1981. But we're riding an emotional roller coaster. It feels like a grade-nine crush: one day the elusive love of your dreams smiles your way in the hallway, but on the night of the Halloween party dances with someone else.

Is that what draws us back—the elusive but inevitably defeated promise? We dare to hope?

The long road trip goes reasonably well but the match on returning home is a stinker and then the team goes on the road and loses to the weakest lineup in the league. Now we're really down. And *up* looks a long way off. But we go back. Is it the fascination of the once-brilliant gazelle floundering in the jaws of the lion that lures us? Possibly. Every time the team stinks the joint out, the fans come to the next game and cheer louder: Go Jets!

It's as if our belief grows stronger the worse the team performs.

In psychology there's a name for this phenomenon. Believers in quacks who predict the end of the world on a given day do not turn their backs on the quack when the fateful day comes and goes with no catastrophe. Against all logic, they believe more fervently when a new doomsday is announced by the same quack. What the?

We return. The team goes on a mini winning streak, three victories in a row, then four in five games with a tie thrown in as well. Is that the .500 mark they're flirting with? They lose two, then win four more in succession. This is heady stuff, the Jets record is above the .500 mark and the team is playing professional-looking hockey, as well as entertaining us every outing. Is this the same squad that looked so awful in Columbus only weeks ago?

Once again, we dare to hope.

We go back. We cheer lustily. Go Jets! The team stands in ninth place in the conference, only one point from the last playoff position. Who would have imagined back in October when they dropped their first three games and had a record after ten of 3-6-1? The playoffs? Are we talking about the Jets?

Is this why we go back? Because the team is winning? But we go back when they're losing too. We feed on losses almost as greedily as wins. No, it's not winning game upon game that brings us back, but something more complicated and aberrant in our psyches, our souls—somewhere like that—what brings us back is the elusive possibility of winning, embedded in the knowledge that the team is as likely to lose as win, as likely to play crappy hockey as brilliant, as likely to disappoint us as to please us; for some mystifying reason we like dancing on the knife edge between ecstasy and heartbreak. Wasn't there a philosopher who pointed this out—that we enjoy swinging between the extremes of joy and depression? Really?

You tell me.

_____

What sweaters are fans wearing tonight?

In the old days of the NHL Jets, a number of fans showed up at the games against Toronto and Montreal sporting the jerseys of the Leafs and the Canadiens, cute in one way, but irritating too. They tended to cheer brashly for their teams, they were loudmouths in the concourses, there was a common feeling that they should be punched in the mouth. Imagine the fans of Arsenal swaggering around in Old Trafford as if they owned the place. They'd have been thrashed in the stands and beaten to death in the streets. But it was Winnipeg, mild-mannered Winnipeg, and we let them get away with their audacious strutting on our turf.

Our turf. This is how being a fan affects the psyche. Our team, our turf. It's not the game as a game that interests us, or sharing the arena with fans of other teams; it's us against them, it's winning at all cost and the hell with sportsmanship and the beauty of the game.

This one starts off at fast pace, the stumbling Canadiens eager to make up for a bad loss to Chicago only twenty-four hours ago. There's a flurry in the Habs end that just falls short of producing a goal; then one in the Jets end that produces gasps and sighs from the crowd. The play goes end to end. The Habs take a penalty and the Jets score. Montreal look rattled. The game has hardly begun and they're behind. They're showing signs of fatigue from the Chicago game and late-night travel, and their ranks are depleted from injuries, especially on defence, where they've struggled all year to maintain a healthy corps.

The Jets score again and the heart goes out of the Montreal attack. By

SEC: XX ROW: XX SEAT:XX

HOME GAME 34

JETS VS CANADIENS

DECEMBER 22, 2011

SEC: XX
ROW: XX
SEAT: XX

the end of the period they're behind 2-0 and the shots are 13-6, Jets. The game seems to be in hand.

Seems.

The Jets score again in the opening minute of the second. Behind us a guy calls out: "News flash, news flash: Habs stink!" But at the halfway point of the second, the Jets take a four-minute penalty and the Canadiens have their chance to get back into the game. Their powerplay cannot get going. Kaberle at the point muffs a shot and then throws a blind pass across ice that nearly results in a breakaway for the Jets. Grumbler behind mutters, "That's what you get for three million bucks a year."

The Habs look out of it. But they're gifted another penalty and they fire shots on goal without result. All those fans wearing their *bleu, blanc, et rouge* have nothing to cheer. They're not cheering, but then again neither are the Jets fans. The arena is eerily quiet, partly because the Jets have had to kill five consecutive penalties and the only thing to cheer is their efforts to ice the puck.

In the third, things are much the same. The Jets are playing a checking game and the Habs look like they'd rather be somewhere else. Near the midway point of the period I say to Kristen, "I'd forgotten how humdrum games can be when you're three goals up—or three down." A little later she says, "Less than six minutes remaining and they've still got the shutout."

"Kristen," I say, wagging my finger, "How could you?"

I'm talking about the hex, of course, speaking the word *shutout* before it has occurred, putting a jinx on the goaltender. I glance at the clock to see how long it will take for those fateful words to perform their black magic. The Habs do come close twice before the game ends but the shutout remains intact and the final score is 4-0.

It hasn't been much of a contest. The travel and their injuries showed on the once-proud Canadiens, who now find themselves behind the Jets in the standings. Winners of twenty-four Stanley Cups, it's been years since they've been a force in the league. What are their fans feeling?

SNAPSHOT: MIKE THE HABS FAN

I'm watching a televised game on *NHL Center Ice*—I'm not sure which—on an ordinary weekday evening when I see words tracking across a hard roll on the bottom of the screen, *Cammalleri traded to Calgary in mid-period,* and before I've had time to think *wow, traded in mid-period, what can possibly be going on there?*—before any other flash of neurons has occurred in my brain, I think *Mike.*

Mike is a guy I taught with at the prep school twenty years ago, a big friendly historian from an Irish background who played goal on our old-farts team and then moved to Edmonton to continue his doctoral studies. Bearded, with a hearty laugh, a good teacher, a fine friend, an able sportsman, accomplished cook, Mike was above all a Habs fan.

He came from Winnipeg and he attended occasional Jets games; he followed their fortunes with enough interest to engage in conversations in the Common Room with his usual intelligence and wit, but he was not a supporter of the home team. His loyalty stretched back before there were Winnipeg Jets, to his youth, when only six teams existed in the NHL, when everyone had to choose between the Leafs, Rangers, Bruins, and so on, and his favourite was the Montreal Canadiens. The Habs.

Like Roch Carrier, he had a Habs sweater as a boy, not one of these nylon or polyester concoctions that are sold today, but one of those *sweater jerseys,* made primarily of woolen fabrics. He adorned his back with it, as he adorned his head with a Habs toque, long before it became fashionable to wear your team's ball cap. Most important, Mike adorned his heart with the *bleu, blanc, et rouge* of the Canadiens.

When the Habs were faring well, as through the golden years of 1975-79, Mike was aglow. He loved to talk about the great dynasty of the '60s and could wax poetic on the subjects of Beliveau, Lafleur, and Dryden. When the Habs stumbled, as they did through most of the '80s, he took it hard. Their surprise victory in the Cup final in 1993 was a cause of unexpected joy. When Montreal won the Cup, he treated us to rounds of Boilermakers at a local bar. To the Habs!

He knew everything about their storied past: how many Cups, which coach did what, greatest rookie. He was a historian, after all, but more important, he was a fan. He lived and died with his team, breathing their wins and losses; his loyalty was unshakable. Over the years I knew him, the association between the two, *Canadiens–Mike*, became so strong that I can no longer think of the one without immediately thinking of the other. A Pavlovian response: Habs = Mike. I know this may be difficult for non-fans to understand. Surely there are connections more important in the life of a grown man than those to a sports team? Mike has a wife, Deb, a son, Chris, and a fine career as a historian. But if I hear over the TV that the Canadiens have been sold by the Molson family, that the coach has been fired, or any other matter to do with the team, my mind is instantly triggered with one thought: *Mike*. He has become for me one with them. I suspect I am not the only one among his acquaintances of whom this is true.

Maybe he would be happy to know that, to think that all over the country there are people—women he once dated, guys he played on teams with, former colleagues, people he may never see or speak to again—who hear the word *Habs* and think at the same moment: *Mike*.

Isn't that an ego stroke, something very few of us get?

Game 35 of the 82 on the schedule, nearing the halfway mark. Officially, the Jets stand ninth on the table, much better than most fans would have aspired to at the outset of the season; and they're only five points back of the Penguins, one of the league powerhouses. Can they close that gap on this midwinter night? Can they vault into the final playoff spot, however briefly, as they close in on the holiday pause in the schedule? What a Christmas present that would be! Their coach would be most pleased: *Joie pour* Claude Noel! *Joyeux Noël!*

The game starts fast, both teams focusing on attack, the play continuous. And the crowd is very lively: Go Jets Go! Near the end of a Pittsburgh powerplay, Slater gets a breakaway from centre ice and hits the crossbar. The crowd groans. I say to Kristen, "We may regret that miss later."

The puck goes up and down; the goaltenders make saves; shots on goal; the teams exchange powerplays. There's a scrap after the Jets lay a bodycheck on the Penguins' Malkin. The clock ticks past the midway point of the opening period. Sighs of relief. The scoring chances in the early going favour the Jets but the shots at their end are piling up. Then the Penguins score. The crowd is deflated.

If only that breakaway shot had gone in.

At the end of the period the shots are 14-5 favouring the Penguins. Score: 1-0.

The guy behind us says, "I don't get that shots on goal count." He's right, the play has been even, and the Jets have had the better scoring chances.

The second period begins with the Jets pressing. But following an initial flurry the game settles and the Penguins are bottling up the neutral zone, forcing the Jets forwards to dump-and-chase. The Penguins get more shots but right at the midway point of the period, the Jets score: 1-1. Still the period ends with the shots 26-12 in favour of the Penguins, an ominous sign.

In the concourse Kristen asks, "Well?"

"The next goal wins."

"You think?"

"The Jets are fading. Did you see the shots on goal? If they don't score first, it's going to be uphill sledding."

Before half the crowd is seated, the Penguins score. Twenty-two seconds.

It's odd how games go. A hit crossbar here, a garbage goal there, and a game that looks like it could go one way, goes the other. Sometimes the result is just a matter of breaks. Coaches say there's no such thing as luck, you make your own breaks, but those are the adages of men whose job it is to convince teams that they can rise above deflected pucks, crazy bounces, dodgy officiating, a skater who loses an edge and falls at an inopportune moment. Everyone else knows better; everyone else knows Fortune smiles on you sometimes, and sometimes it does not.

Sports is filled with these adages. *Never give up; a good team is a team that makes itself good; you win if you give 110 per cent.* Over time these old saws become mantras that coaches, players, and fans alike come to believe in. We talk ourselves into believing them, and—miraculously— sometimes that's how things work out. And then we really do believe them. It gets you thinking that the mind is a powerful entity that makes it possible for us to transcend the limits of our mere physical beings, we come to think life can work out to *mind over matter,* that if we want something badly enough, we can make it happen—a morsel of metaphysics that defies logic but which nevertheless seems to be part of our mental makeup and destiny.

Before the five-minute mark, the Penguins score again: 3-1.

Maybe it was possible to come back from a one-goal deficit, but not two. The Jets must be thinking the same thing. Forty seconds later the Penguins score again. It looks to be all over. But there are fifteen minutes remaining and anything is possible. Can they come back? We've seen them show resilience before, but this does not look like one of those nights.

We settle in, chins resting on fists, gloomy silence in the arena, fans getting up from their seats to buy drinks, a general ennui brooding over the crowd.

The Penguins play shut-down hockey; the Jets seem unable to break through. The remaining minutes tick down. There are banners every- where in the arena: ALL I WANT FOR CHRISTMAS IS TO BE ON TV, RETURN OF JETS BEST PRESENT EVER.

The guy behind says, "The Jets are making it easy to lose this one."

At the end of the game the shots favour the Penguins 39-19, a 3-1 loss.

All the Jets needed to do was play hard for twenty minutes, but, as on several nights in the past month, they fall short whenever that elusive playoff spot looms too near. They lack finish, they lack the killer instinct.

As we leave the arena, a guy in front of us sums the evening up: "On another night some of those early chances would have gone in."

SNAPSHOT: MAGIC

Christmas Day, 1988. I have the key to the arena situated on the grounds of the prep school where I teach and after Christmas dinner I walk over to the arena with my wife at the time and my in-laws: Doug and DJ, and my wife's brother, Don. We're carrying skates in our hands, extras of mine as well as others that I've scrounged up for the occasion. We've got hockey sticks, too, and a handful of pucks. It's a lovely December evening on the prairies, crisp and clear: "Good King Wenceslas" stuff, stars above twinkling, seeming within arm's reach, ghosts of breath rising in the frosty air.

Inside the arena we put on our skates and go onto the ice. My wife teeters a bit, as do her mother and father. "It's been forty years since I've been on skates," DJ says, laughing, balancing with the aid of her hockey stick. But she's a prairie girl, both game and familiar with the single blade of steel under her feet. "Whoa," Doug calls out as he rounds behind one goal, heading toward a collision with the boards before righting himself. She and Doug are in their sixties, hale and fit, so in a few minutes they're making their way around the ice easily, if not at great speed. Don has played hockey since he was a boy growing up in this very neighbourhood, though he now lives in Toronto, and in a few minutes he's zipping up and down the Olympic-size surface and zinging pucks at the goals.

I stay near my wife for a while, skating alongside until she's confident of her balance, and then get a puck and start passing it back and forth with her. At first she tends to whack the puck rather than slide it towards me, and I remember this is how children make passes, striking the puck as if shooting it, instead of using the wrists to slide the puck along. Sometimes when she makes contact with the puck, she half loses balance for the second or two after the puck leaves her stick.

In a few minutes we're joined by Doug, who, like most Canadian boys, grew up playing the game—in Fort Frances, where his family ran the local hardware store, the place where you bought skates in the days before sports equipment emporia dotted the commercial landscape. Doug takes one of the pucks, skates toward the net and fires the puck in, bulging the back netting. I yell out, "He shoots, he scores!" And my father-in-law, an internationally respected architect, turns and looks at us with a smile bigger than the Jeux de Pommes on his face. "Ha!" he calls out, "the rocket of

Fort High strikes again." He retrieves the puck and makes a loop around the faceoff dot and fires it into the net again.

As a boy growing up in Northwestern Ontario I did this for hours— aiming to put the puck just under the crossbar, or top left corner, top right corner, off one post, then the other. Standing still at the top of the faceoff dot, gliding in from the slot, making backhand shots, skating backwards to the faceoff dot then wheeling and firing in the same motion, whistling slapshots from the blue line. Hours of potting goals.

"Take a shot on goal," I say to my wife, sliding the puck to her stick. She slides it into the net along the ice. "All right!" DJ joins us and puts a few in herself.

"All right," Don says, coming up to us, "Time for a game."

He and I reposition the nets against the sideboards, so we're playing across the width of the rink, not its length. "You take Doug and DJ," I say to Don, "and the two of us will play together."

He's a fast skater, Don, and a nifty puck handler, so he maneuvers around the ice skillfully, laying passes to his parents, who shoot at the goal and go crashing into the boards with their daughter when they miss, scrabbling for loose pucks. I try not to use my weight to advantage, or my strong stride. But I swoop wide of the net and slide passes onto my wife's stick so she can score. Sometimes Don intervenes, but just as often he lets her shoot; and she scores a couple of goals. So do Doug and DJ. Don and I try to neutralize each other, occasionally scrapping for the puck with intent.

In fifteen minutes we're all sweating and I'm glad I brought a water bottle, so we pause, resting our butts and elbows on the boards at the players' benches. When he's had a drink, Don goes back to skating and shooting, firing wrist shots into the top of the goals, trying snapshots and slapshots.

"I've had it," DJ says.

"I could use a Scotch," Doug adds.

We watch Don for a few more minutes. He skates well, knees bent, torso over his stick, fast hands when he stickhandles and shoots. "All right," DJ calls out after a few minutes, "final whistle." I turn off the arena lights but a bright winter moon is shining in at the windows. We take off our skates. Don is still breathing heavily and the rest of us have sweat on our brows. I lock the doors behind us. On the walk home, our shoes crunch on the snow. The stars overhead are brilliant. It will be cold toward dawn. We approach the house. "Man," Doug sighs aloud, clapping me on the shoulder, "what a night, Wayne. Magic."

Four days following the uninspired loss to Pittsburgh, two days after weighty festive Christmas dinners and carousing with families, the Jets are on a one-game road trip to Colorado where the team is hot and the air thin. With all of that clouding their skies, there's little chance the Jets will play well and less that they will win.

When we settle in front of the TV, I say to Kristen, "What do you think?"

She shrugs. Like most Jets fans at this point, she's baffled. On a given day they can be world-beaters; but it's just as likely they'll stink the joint out. "Let's hope for a good game."

I'm less optimistic. "Anything could happen. But I'm guessing a 4-1 loss."

"Jets win," Andrew says confidently.

I raise my eyebrows. "Put a fiver on it?"

"Maybe not." He laughs. "I'm closer to my money than that."

We both laugh.

The Avalanche have been playing well overall and particularly at home. They start fast. They're a young team and they play with speed, moving the puck quickly out of their own end and through the neutral zone. And they're skilled: their lines do weave patterns as they attack, going wide left into the Jets zone but leaving a trailer high to the right in the open ice between the blue line and the top of the faceoff dot. When the puck is zipped across the ice, that attacker has a clear line to the goal. One shot follows another. The Jets hold their shape, but most of the play is in their end.

Get through the first ten minutes.

The Jets do not get a shot until the halfway mark of the first period, when the shots on goal stand 7-1. At a break in the action, Claude Noel is

SEC: XX ROW: XX SEAT:XX

AWAY GAME 36

JETS VS AVALANCHE

DECEMBER 27, 2011

SEC: XX
ROW: XX
SEAT: XX

pictured chewing his lower lip. But he isn't saying anything, and he certainly is not yelling at his players. After the loss to Pittsburgh, he said, "I'm not going to criticize the players; they've played well through December." It's not the first time he's publicly expressed such sentiments. He must be the most composed coach in the history of the NHL.

Against the run of play, the Jets score with less than five minutes remaining in the period, a now-familiar zinger of a wrist shot from Kane into the top corner. "This guy can shoot," Kristen says gleefully. Yes, I think, such crystallized moments of action stop time, and that's what makes sport glorious.

I'm also thinking, Still could end up 4-1.

I ask, "What do you think of the way the Jets are playing?"

"They're playing well. They look organized and they're covering off their men in all three zones of the ice. The defence really seem to know what they're doing. On that long road trip early in the season, whew, they looked bad. But now they look well coached." She makes a point of emphasizing the final words. We both laugh. She's read what I've written about Claude Noel and his assistants, and I know she has.

"That was then," I say. "I agree with you. Now they're playing well. And they do look well coached."

Maybe the extended road trip in October was a learning experience, a bonding experience. Stuff happens in dressing rooms that's hard to explain if you haven't played the game. Maybe the coaches have learned, as well as the players. Whatever, this is a different team from the one that began the season looking to be over their heads in the NHL, a bit lost. This is a team going about its business with purpose and determination.

Just into the second period, the Jets score again, not a pretty goal but ...

"Aha," Andrew says. "Did we shake on that fiver?"

The Avalanche look a bit deflated and the game settles into a less frantic pace, both sides forechecking hard and looking organized in the neutral zone. Not much is being given away; most of the shots are coming from the outside, the goaltenders are blockering pucks into the corners and pouncing on loose rebounds. Then with less than five minutes remaining in the second period, the Jets score again: 3-0.

"Well," I say to Kristen in the intermission, "They're not going to lose 4-1."

"They're gonna win," Andrew says.

They score early in the third. The Avalanche played on the previous night and it's beginning to show. They started the game at a torrid pace but they're leg-weary, and now that they're behind 4-0, there's not much to play for. Though they don't give in or give up, the final score is 4-1, the shots 33-26 in favour of Colorado, Pavelec's shutout lost in the final few minutes, a shame since he's saved the Jets' butts on numerous occasions already in the season. Still, a good game for the Jets, but the Colorado fans must be unhappy that their team had to play on consecutive nights and looked ordinary after the opening period. Once again, the schedule has had more of an influence on the game than it should have. Not only did the play deteriorate in the final stages, the result was unduly affected. It's a shame. The games mean a lot, even at this earlyish point in the schedule, and the fans have paid a lot to witness a sub-standard performance.

But this is what it means to be in the "bigs." Not everything is velvet.

SNAPSHOT: College Days

It's spring of 1977 and I'm on the bench at Bison Gardens, the arena at the University of Manitoba where the college team practises and plays and where various squads compete in intramural leagues. I'm part of the team registered as St. John's College, and I'm breathing heavily at the end of a shift.

In the fall I was teaching a class in freshman English at St. John's and at a break one of the male students came up to me and said, smiling, "You look like a guy who's played hockey."

"I do?"

"You've got that nick on your chin. Stitches."

"Stitches, yes. Guilty as charged."

"We can use someone with size on the St. John's team."

I laughed but the next week found myself pulling on a black and yellow jersey with SJC stitched across the chest. One game followed another.

It's three years since I last suited up with the Carling Buffalos in Regina and the Indian Head Chiefs in that rural town. I've put on a little weight. But it's coming off; and the legs grow stronger each time out. I jump over the boards, changing on the fly, and pick up a pass as I maneuver into the opposition end. We're playing one of the fraternity teams, whom my teammates hate: smartass bully-boys, they think of them, guys in college to party, sporting mustaches and driving swishy cars. In my day I might have got into a scrap with one of them. I'm an oddity, a "professor" among a squad of students ten years my junior, a grad student writing a doctoral thesis on the poet Robert Frost, the blue-collar towns of my childhood and youth far behind me. As I drift into the opposition end I elbow one of the frat boys aside and head towards the corner, glancing across at the net. I score as well and as often as anyone on the team, but I'm a passer first and a shooter second. A burly defenceman moves toward me and as he does I saucer a pass a few feet in front of the net; a teammate scoops it in. Take that, frat boys.

As I pass behind the net, I register a thought: it's still as big a thrill as ever.

The little boy who grew up in the mining town banging pucks against the boards and playing on the town's Pee Wee all-star team now attends gallery openings, drinks fine French wine, is invited to conferences to give papers on American literature. But poke him the right way, flutter a team jersey in his face, and he's lacing on skates in a drafty arena. Where is he headed? To the University of British Columbia, he thinks, he's said that in a newspaper interview when he received an award and a fellow-ship a year or two earlier, though the job market in colleges has tightened up severely in the past few years. There may be no room for him, for a whole generation of young academics. His classmates at the University of Toronto who used to quip *publish or prairies* would now be grateful to find positions in Regina or Calgary. He may take a job teaching at a prep school in the city, a step some would consider a step backward but he's never been that fixed on *career*. His ambitions don't run that way, as they did not run towards a career in pro hockey.

I come back to the bench after the goal. Though we're a goal behind, the guys on the team are smiling. We didn't expect to win. We're putting in a good show. The frat boys are good players, you have to grant them that. Nothing's at stake except our egos—and that doesn't matter much. We're on the way to careers, to white-collar occupations. I look down the bench: doctor, dentist, lawyer, accountant. None of us need to make it in hockey. We read books, we debate issues over paper cups of coffee and we're happy just to be out here, exercising, putting ourselves to the test.

The frat boys score again. Make a big deal of slapping each other's shin pads. It would be nice to beat them. It would be nice to knock a couple of them into the boards and give them a little comeuppance. But no more of that. Tomorrow there's a lecture to give on poets of the nineteenth century: Walt Whitman, Emily Dickinson. A paper to work on, a book about Frost to read. In the evening a meal at La Lanterne Rouge, they do a flavourful *coq au vin* and a somewhat salty *boeuf bourgignon.*

Hockey is fun; hockey is what we do as leisure.

Still, those frat boys do get under your skin.

Coming into the game the Jets occupy eighth spot in the Eastern Conference standings, the final playoff position, ahead of Washington, ahead of Montreal, ahead of Tampa Bay, only a point behind the Toronto Maple Leafs. Egad, who would have thunk it?

It's been a great run through December, the team rising steadily, week after week in the standings, but now begin the heebie-jeebies: can the Jets maintain the high-tempo game they've been playing for the remaining forty-three games? Can they stay with the experienced teams in the league, who have been playing a bit of wait-and-see thus far but will turn up the gas in the second half of the season? Most important, can they maintain their focus now that they're in a playoff position—their composure—that elusive quality of playing consistently for sixty minutes every night, night after night? Hold down the penalties, play smart hockey.

On this night they're up against the Los Angeles Kings, a team that just came off a 2-0 victory in Chicago, but also a team that struggles in the first period, having scored only 15 goals in their previous 37 games, whereas their opponents have scored 26. The Jets' record in the opening frame is 40 goals. Then too, in 28 of their 37 games, the Kings have scored two or fewer goals. And it's well-known that most games are won by the team that tallies first. Conclusion? The Jets need to play their fast-skating, high-tempo game and get the first goal, they need to take advantage of such statistics, but then, as the philosopher once said, we use numbers to create the illusion that we're in control of our destinies.

Statistics are just that. On any night, anything can happen, whatever may have occurred in the past. The Kings could score three goals in the opening frame; the Jets could be shut out. Both teams could play slow, dull hockey.

This game starts fast, both teams moving the puck quickly out of their zones. And they're hitting too. Los Angeles is a big team, featuring bruisers like Penner, who at 6'4" throws crushing checks. But the Jets are up to it, focusing their bodychecks on the Kings defenceman Doughty, who takes two solid hits in the opening ten minutes.

The crowd feeds off the energy of the players: Go Jets Go! On this night they have chosen Doughty as their whipping boy: every time he touches the puck, there's a loud chorus of boos. Appreciative cheering when the Jets goaltender makes stops during a Los Angeles powerplay that brings the first period to a close: 0-0.

The second period is contested in much the same way, both sides going at each other physically, banging and crashing along the boards and in the corners. There are high-quality attacks coming through the neutral zone and constant traffic in front of the nets, scrambles that threaten to produce goals, hard shots from the points and good saves from the goaltenders. The shots on goal in the first period were close to even and that trend continues in the second. Toward the end of the period, the Jets are tagged with two penalties at the same time, giving the Kings a five-on-three advantage, the fifteenth time the Jets have been so penalized.

"Well, that's it," I say. Whoever scores first this late in a tight game is bound to win.

But the Jets hang on, holding their shape in front of the net, blocking shots, Ron Hainsey and Mark Stuart throwing their bodies about heedlessly, forwards winning just enough faceoffs to catch their breath and icing the puck for line changes. In a frenzy in the Jets zone the Kings clank the post; a few minutes later the Jets hit the Kings' crossbar. The second period comes to a close at 0-0. A scoreless game but an exciting one.

Now comes the big test for the Jets. Though they have improved in the past month, they do not finish well. Their third periods are a weak spot. They've been outscored 37-25 overall, and in five overtime games they have won only once.

Score before the ten-minute mark.

Both teams come out intent on that. The forwards barge through the neutral zone, carry the puck towards the net. But the defences are doing their best to ensure that shooters are kept close to the boards, shutting off attacks in front of goal. There aren't as many shots as in the two previous periods, and most of them from wide of the faceoff circles, and though the Jets are given a five-on-three powerplay advantage, the best they can do is hit the post. Regulation time ends with the score 0-0.

Not great for the Jets. They've won only one in five overtimes; and by contrast Los Angeles has won five times in five such situations. But statistics are only statistics, and the Jets score just past the first minute of overtime.

Jubilation for the players, ecstasy for the fans. The Jets have 41 points in 37 games and are now positioned above Toronto in the standings, officially holding down seventh spot.

And the Maple Leafs are the Jets' next opponent, two nights down the road. Is the script for the season being written in Hollywood? It's turning into such a gripping story: what can possibly happen next?

SNAPSHOT: "EVERY GUY"

Is it time for the question: *who am I?*

There's a certain amount of hubris involved in writing any book, committing to paper the thoughts of one individual among many who have had similar thoughts, the same feelings, and who might even have greater facility with the language, a broader or more far-reaching intelligence, a greater breadth of experience. Surely there are many who have played as many games of hockey, coached for years, watched the Jets in both the WHA and the NHL, gone on road trips with old-fart teams. What makes my limited pool of knowledge and experience of special interest—who am I to think I have a unique take?

I suppose that's the point, isn't it? I don't. I'm Everyman, one guy who has sat in countless dressing rooms listening to banter about the game; coaching kids in damp and drafty arenas and overhearing their screaming parents; attending pro contests on nights of bitter cold when the team was playing poorly and the franchise drowning in red ink. I may not be unique, but I am representative: one of the many, the voice of the common man who has taken a puck in the teeth in a game of "shinny," and laid his money down to buy tickets in good times and bad, and seen the flash of delight on a child's face when a goal went into the net, and stood in the stands at a Jets game and screamed deliriously, or roared *boo* at thuggish enforcers and inept referees.

Yes, I'm one among the many, a voice and a scribe.

And so many can say: *been there, done that.*

In an odd way, we make up a team ourselves, having shared the joy of putting the puck into the back of the net; of standing elbow to elbow, cheering and clapping when the Jets won the AVCO Cup; of sitting in a dressing room and chuckling when some wag pinions Bettman or Pronger with a witty riposte; of going on road trips to play games and finding out on the way that you're part of a benevolent "gang" that will always have a moment of personal history in common; of helping a generation of youngsters appreciate the game we love and become better adults along the way for it (hold on now!).

We share an obsession and we recognize it immediately in others, the way eyes light up when we talk about the night Selanne scored that remarkable goal—the third of a hat-trick, actually; we acknowledge a fellow out there on the ice when he pots a goal and his buddy gives him a high-five; we look into the mirror of another retired coach's face and recognize our own secret wishes come to life when he talks about a youngster he coached who has gone on to have a career and family and who took the time one day in a coffee shop to come over and say "hello."

These are celebrations of a collective dream that those of us who

cherish the game are all a part of. Not me uniquely, but me representa-
tively: one among the many, a voice that feels the need to utter *this matters,* and a scribe who affects to speak for us all.

Don't some things just need to be said?

A man behind the Toronto goal in the MTS Centre is
holding up a sign that reads: I'D RATHER GO 15 YEARS
WITHOUT A TEAM THAN BE A LEAFS FAN. It's a very
Winnipeg sentiment. When it was first announced
that the Atlanta franchise was being moved north,
there was a one-liner going around the city: "Now
that Winnipeg has an NHL team, Toronto wants one
too."

In any case, here they are again, coteries of supporters in their Leafs jerseys at the MTS Centre.
This turncoat phenomenon is galling. There are,
of course, fans of other teams in every city. But
this feels different to me. I suppose it's because
we see ourselves as perennial underdogs in
Winnipeg, the last team mentioned on TSN's nightly
roundup of scores, the city that was dispossessed of its team. Those of us
here chafe at these things, at the way Toronto rubs our noses in our provincial status, and at fans in our own home town sporting the jerseys of
the despised—but wealthy and powerful—Leafs of Toronto. So however
varied our backgrounds—and some of us are light years apart in class,
political attachment—we are a community that sees our fates entwined—
at least when it comes to playing the lackeys of the Great Grey City.

Toronto is the city we love to hate.

Toronto teams are the ones we love to beat.

So it's no surprise that the fans are crowded into their seats well before
the start of the game, cheering. *Go Jets Go!* is popular, but nowhere near
as popular as the prolonged jeer directed at the Leafs goaltender: *Rei-mer,
Rei-mer.* Several nights earlier when the Los Angeles Kings were at the
MTS Centre it was *Bern-nier, Bern-nier,* and constant booing aimed at

SEC: XX ROW: XX SEAT:XX

HOME GAME 38

JETS VS
LEAFS

DECEMBER 31, 2011

SEC: XX
ROW: XX
SEAT: XX

the Kings' defenceman Doughty. We were told at the first intermission that he didn't understand why the crowd was picking on him. He was told that Winnipeg fans singled out the best player from the opposition team and "honoured" him this way.

Maybe he was all right with being singled out for this treatment: it was oblique flattery, backhanded acknowledgement of his star status. Maybe he understood, too, that what he was witnessing was a tribal chant, not so much meanness directed at him personally as a way that Jets fans came together at the start of every game to say we are one, we are the Jets gang, a brigade of the like-minded building through cheers and jeers a united voice that shouts during the national anthem "True North," a community that behaves like a community of believers but who more importantly throw their passion behind their team in a united kinship in order to carry the team through adversity and boost them on to victory. The proverbial "extra man."

In a society that has grown out of religion and is increasingly skeptical of politics, sport offers the opportunity to enslave the heart in a relatively harmless spectacle. We dip into politics at election time, choosing sides, posting signs on our lawns that declare our emotional attachments. It's like wearing team colours to the home games. But the engagement is short-lived and lacks the intensity of fandom. There are too many scandals, too much crassness in the realm of speeches and votes. We maintain our attachments with resignation bordering on ennui.

But after religion and politics comes sport: Go Jets Go! All I want for Christmas is the Jets to beat the Leafs.

The teams are up for it. They start fast, playing the speed game, with quick passes through the neutral zone and resolute forechecking. The energy level is high, every player skating at top pace. At times it's breathtaking, the play is so intense it's reckless and you can't help but wonder if the players are putting themselves at peril of injury with their heedless dashes toward the opposition net, risking a fateful fall, rashly hammering the opposition in the corners, crashing into the goal posts, tumbling into the boards behind the nets.

The Leafs score toward the end of the period on a powerplay but that does not slow the play—or the crowd: Go Jets Go! What are fans in Toronto thinking as they watch the game on TV? "Toronto the Good" the city was once called, because of its staid WASP behaviour and austere common laws: "Toronto the Quiet."

The Winnipeg crowd is as loud and boisterous at the start of the second period as they have ever been. In one sense, I can't help but observe, fans come to the MTS Centre to hear themselves cheer—almost as much as to watch the game: like players on a stage, we're revelling in roles. Whatever, the joint is rocking. And the Jets feed off it, scoring an early powerplay goal and adding another shortly after: 2-1. The shots on goal at the end of the first period were 15-8 in favour of the Jets, and by the mid-point of the second they're 22-10.

Against the run of play, the Leafs score to tie the game. But shortly afterward the Jets score again to lead 3-2. The game has hardly hit the halfway mark.

The result could go either way. The Leafs are playing good hockey and seem poised in all three zones. Their coach, former Jet Ron Wilson, once a crowd favourite in Winnipeg, has them playing a smart, organized game. And the Jets are matching them stride for stride, attack for attack. It's an exciting contest, high entertainment value, if a bit heart-in-mouth. Is it even worth asking if we'd prefer an engaging game or a two-point result for the home team?

Matters remain much the same in the third period, both teams playing attack hockey and defending well in their own end. At the second intermission the shots stood 28-12 for the Jets but the play was more even than that, the scoring chances about equal. And the Leafs come on in the third, pressing for the equalizing goal, and almost getting it on two or three occasions. But the final is 3-2.

The Jets are jubilant, Winnipeg fans euphoric. Winning is good, but beating Toronto is better. And the team is in seventh place in the standings. What a way to go into the new year.

SNAPSHOT: FRESH START

It's a new year, 2012, the first calendar year that the "new" Jets will spend entirely in Winnipeg. Have the players made New Year's resolutions? The coaches? From the time of the team's arrival in the city the coaches have been tight-lipped about their expectations for the season, about the like-lihood of the team making the playoffs, wishes and dreams, all of that. Publicly, it's been "wait and see."

You can't help thinking, though, that Claude Noel and Kevin Chevel-dayoff and Mark Chipman have to have been secretly wishing and hoping through the past four or five months. They would be unusual team execu-tives if they had not.

But the onset of the new year triggers certain questions. New years, like new seasons, are a time of new beginnings, when everything is fresh, the baggage of the previous rounds has been put behind and laid to rest—when the eyes can turn forward to the future. At the start of a new year, the start of a new season, everyone is not only ready to turn a new page, but exonerated from the blotches on the old. Maybe this will be the breakout season for the high-round draft pick, maybe this will be the year the team makes the playoffs, the coach gets the long-term contract, maybe the Cup is within reach. Over every new year hangs the scent of renewal, the alluring fragrance of promise.

This is one of the things that draws us to sport. The possibility that resides in fresh beginnings. For our lives are filled with fresh beginnings, too, the beginning of a new relationship, the start of a new job, the birth of a child, moving to a different city, tackling a new project. Sometimes the arc of a sport season runs parallel to one of our own seasons: it must for college students who are going through orientation at the same time as training camp, September, and digging into classes about the same time as hockey's regular season opens, October. Teachers, professors start up again every year in the same way. And businesses—lawyers, accoun-tants—have their year-end at 31 December, so they start a new fiscal year with the New Year.

There probably are—no, clearly must be—people for whom this new Jets season not only parallels their own life, but provides inspiration for it: people who *because* of the Jets' arrival in the city have decided to chuck their tiresome job / give up on their frustrating relationship, whatever, and begin again with the "new" Jets, hoping for the kind of renewal the team has brought to the city as a whole and its supporters as individuals.

Fresh starts are a part of life we may take for granted when our lives are trundling along year after year, same-old, same-old. But pro athletes live in an entirely different world, where training camp may see the fulfillment of a lifelong dream, making the big team; or, just as often, the realization that the dream will never be realized, the pros will forever be out of reach. For the aging athlete, the start of the season may be the start of the last season; for the injured, it may mean physical torture followed by the mental agony of not being up to one more season of brutal contact, coaches' harassment, and constant travel. Rookies find themselves at the very dawn of something indescribably thrilling; veterans are hanging on for one last hurrah.

Beginnings are often endings. And endings are sometimes new beginnings.

Like pro athletes, we dip into these realizations when we change jobs or see a relationship come to a close, or lose a parent, or welcome a child. New eras are all around us, occasionally drawing attention to themselves, but most times slipping past unnoticed as we go about our workaday lives of obligations and responsibilities, going to the ATM, driving the kids to soccer. But sport, with its training camps, its halfway points in the season, its run for the playoffs, its cup final reminds us of how important fresh starts can be, how our lives turn on them, and how much more energetic, fuller, and richer life can be than we had only heartbeats ago thought possible.

Last year the Atlanta Thrashers began the season well, occupying a playoff position at the Christmas break. But then they fell apart, winning only five of the next twenty-four games and finishing a dismal thirteen points out of the play-offs. Management and the players alike have been eager to discount this poor performance, mouthing phrases such as "different team, different city," to dissociate the Jets from that collapse, but breakdowns of this type follow organizations around, and the Jets team will have to demonstrate to the city of Winnipeg that things really have changed, that they're not going to fold in the second half of the season and "thrash" their way to the finale.

It's going to be a tough call, because teams tend to tighten up in the final forty games—and the Jets are going to play a lot on the road, where they have proven not be a strong outfit. They have proven, though, to be a resilient one, and young and talented, so everything is in the hopper, all is to be proved.

A four-game road trip to open the new year should test the team's mettle. At this juncture they have 42 points and stand in tenth place, three out of the playoffs.

In the games against the Canadiens and the Leafs, the Jets look lost, playing at a slower pace than is typical and struggling to generate the energy that usually typifies their efforts. Both the Canadiens and Leafs grab early leads and then settle into tight-checking mode, content to be ahead and make the Jets come to them. And the Jets are unable to penetrate their defence and mount much offence.

It's frustrating for Jets fans: they're used to seeing high-tempo skating and exciting games, but these are road games where they're outclassed by opponents who are more deliberate in their style and more patient.

In Montreal, the Jets lose 7-3.

In Toronto, they play a team like themselves, just above the .500 mark, contending for the final playoff positions. Halfway through the season, now, it's obvious there are teams that are out of it, and equally a handful that stand above the rest. Barring injuries, the teams at the top will make it. But of the half-dozen in contention for the final three spots, two or three will swoon while two or three claw their way into the first round. Will the Jets be there? The Leafs?

After the 7-3 beating in Montreal, the coach noted bitterly that the team was complacent going into the road trip, happy with its December performance: "As soon as you get comfortable, that's what happens."

It may be so. Certainly in these two new-year games they've looked a lot less energetic than through December when they won ten times and looked good doing it. But it's not feeling comfortable, I think, that's the issue. Overall, they look sluggish. For five- and ten-minute stretches they can—and do—play at high tempo, threatening to take over games. But then they sag; they look tired. And their opponents pounce. Through December they played their hearts out—and their asses off. And they may have burnt themselves out. Feeding off the energy of the crowd at home, they rose to the occasion, giving everything they had, game after game, pleasing their rabid fans and achieving quite remarkable results: improving their record to four games over .500 and advancing in the standings from thirteenth to sixth at one point. But that may have come at the cost of flaring out once those results were achieved. There may be a ten-game interregnum when they stumble and fall back in the standings before re-igniting their jet engines and playing at the highest level again.

In the event, they go down to the Leafs 4-0.

Coach Noel may not want to admit it, but his young charges may not be as sound a team as they appeared to be in December. Coaches are not paid to think that way—or to say such things. But this is a young and inexperienced squad and they may have made the error of "going too soon," only to find themselves lapped before the finish line. But who's to know really? They're now four points out of the final playoff spot at exactly the midpoint of the season, forty-one games to go.

Will the game at Buffalo in two nights reveal how things stand?

5 January 2012

Team	SP	PTS
New York R	38	54
Boston	37	53
Philadelphia	38	50
Florida	40	48
Ottawa	41	47
Pittsburgh	38	46
Toronto	40	45
Washington	38	44
New Jersey	39	44
Winnipeg	40	42
Buffalo	39	40
Tampa Bay	39	37
Montreal	40	37
New York J	37	34
Carolina	41	33

The game against Buffalo starts at a good tempo, first the Jets putting on the pressure and then the Sabres. Both teams have speedy skaters, and a bit of a track meet develops, shots coming in and the goaltenders sharp. When the Jets take a penalty, they do a fine job of killing it off, aggressively forcing the Sabres in both ends and creating several chances for themselves. Then the game settles into a well-played pro contest, close checking in the neutral zone, tight stickwork in the corners, safe passes along the boards, north-to-south methodical action, with few chances taken. For the Jets, Byfuglien has been out of the lineup for the third straight game and it's obvious they miss his power rushes and energetic checking. Erratic, yes, but creative, too.

By the midway point of the period, both teams are playing a sound road game, frustrating for the Buffalo fans, but sensible of the Jets, who need a game where they don't give up a handful of goals or look disorganized in their own end. For Jets fans it's not very exciting, but it's heartening to see the team not giving up wild scrambles in front of their net. And needless penalties. The period ends with no score and the shots even and low.

"Well," I say, "at least they're not behind." After the drubbing in Montreal and the weak game in Toronto, getting out of a period without being scored on seems an accomplishment.

The second unfolds in much the same way, scoring chances at a minimum, both goaltenders playing well. For neutrals this game could seem lacklustre, but a lot is at stake and neither team wants to commit the error that leads to a goal.

It comes on a powerplay just past the midway mark of the period, the Sabres cashing in on the man-advantage opportunity. Here we go again. It's difficult not to see this as the beginning of the end for the Jets, who have not scored a goal in almost two hours of hockey. Grit your teeth, hang in there, they're playing sound, sensible hockey and are only one goal behind.

Right at the end of the second period the Jets are given a five-on-three advantage, and following furious action around the Buffalo goal, score: Blake Wheeler from his knees in front of the Sabres goal with only five seconds remaining. God, this guy has turned things around—and the Jets need it. Going into the third: 1-1.

With so much at stake, neither team gives up much in the third. Minutes tick by, and though there are chances at each end, there are no odd-man attacks, and pucks are cleared away from both goals with professional prudence. With less than five minutes to go I say, "Looks like we're settling for a point."

Andrew grunts.

"You don't think so?"

"I think it's better than nothing. It hasn't been very inspired play."

Better than nothing, maybe, but when you're tied toward the end of a game on the road, you should win, especially when you've lost two straight on a road trip. But neither team tallies and it's into the overtime, where, surprisingly, Oduya, one of the Jets defencemen, scores. You can almost feel pulsations of relief vibrating through Winnipeg. Maybe, maybe.

One more game before the road trip comes to a close.

SEC: XX ROW: XX SEAT:XX

HOME GAME 42
JETS VS
BRUINS
JANUARY 10, 2012

SEC: XX
ROW: XX
SEAT: XX

It's in Boston on a Tuesday, where the Bruins are in an ugly mood after losing to Vancouver on the weekend. They start fast, attacking the Jets goal in the opening minutes, pushing for the early lead, but when they don't get it, the game settles into high-tempo play with even scoring chances and a lot of bodychecks, and it's the Jets who score first toward the end of the period. The Bruins counter in the dying seconds and the teams go into the second tied 1-1.

The second period follows a similar pattern, the Jets scoring very early and the Bruins tying the score before the Jets take the lead 3-2 just at the midway part of the contest. It's high-energy stuff, the Jets trying to force the attack, the Bruins checking with ferocity.

It's the sort of game that makes clear why it's so important for teams to have full squads of players in the American league to provide backups for the NHL roster. At any point a skater could go down with an injury from a vicious check meted out by the opposition. There was a time in pro hockey when the premium was on the swift skater and slick stickhandler, guys in the style of the Richards, Syl Apps, Stan Mikita. There were big strong defencemen in the mould of Dick Harvey, Tim Horton, yes, but rosters overall were filled by smaller men who carried the puck from one end to the other on the strength of adroit skating and controlled it in front of goal with deft hands and agility. Back then the difference between contenders and pretenders was these guys who played with elegance, weaving around their opponents, laying out smooth passes, working inspired give-and-go routines, dipsy-doodling. Even the fans of opposition teams were awestruck by the grace of a Lafleur rush or the skill with which Bobby Orr maneuvered in his own end and then captained an attack down ice. *Wow, did you see that!* There were big brutes who acted as enforcers—Ferguson, Cashman—but they were there to protect the skilled guys, who carried the play and were at the centre of the game. Now they have been replaced by seriously large specimens—guys standing 6'4" and carrying 230 pounds, brutes. Chara and Lucic. They barge down the ice on power rather than finesse, knocking over opponents and intimidating them with size alone. Where once the rare big forward—Jean Beliveau—oozed style, there is now only physical force. It's almost a cliché today that there's no room in the NHL for a small man, and guys like Daniel Briere and Martin St. Louis have had to prove themselves over and over against an increasing number of thugs who have little respect for the game and none for their opponents. They're vicious and amoral, ready to smash the other guy, knock him out of the game, send him to hospital, end his career. There's a generalized ferocity to the game now, where in earlier eras that level of violence was confined to one or two plays a game. It's the money at the root of it. We pay players millions and expect them to go out there and win—at all costs. And it means that many games are now little more than gladiatorial battles. We seem to want this; we seem happy to live in the drama of high stakes—who will go down next, our guy or theirs? We're unaccountably willing to let stars be injured and driven from the game, the fate of Eric Lindros ten years ago and today perhaps Sidney Crosby.

In this game, crunching bodycheck follows crunching check. Tendons are being stretched out there, bones fractured, joints dislocated. Skaters are hobbling to the benches; trainers and physios are a-bustle; ice and tape—and possibly drugs— pervade the dressing rooms.

In a way it's surprising the Jets are ahead after two periods. The Bruins have been dominating other teams all season. In the past 28 games they've won 23 and they've outscored their opponents in every period over the 38 games they've played thus far, amassing a total differential of +68.

So when they score in the opening minute of the third period it's expected, but it's deflating for Jets fans. Here we go again. Before five more minutes elapse the Bruins have taken the lead and by the midway point of the period they tally again to make the score 5-3. In the meantime two Jets have gone down with injuries and not returned, tough checking forward, Glass, and steady defenceman, Bogosian. That thuggish play the Bruins have made their trademark has paid off again. And the Jets limp home with only two points out of eight on the road trip and down two key players with injuries, Bogosian "lower body," and Glass a smashed up face.

SNAPSHOT: CHICLETS

I'm prone in a dentist's chair at 8:10 on a Friday morning in late winter, 1994, pale light coming through a narrow window on my right, the bright beam of an overhead dental lamp forcing my eyes to blink. I close my eyelids against it and the pain in my jaw. Ugh. The usual equipment is in my mouth: clamps holding my jaws apart, hoses hooked over the lower lip to evacuate saliva and water. My dentist bustles into the room, followed by his assistant. They've made a place in their morning routine to take me before the first scheduled patient at 8:30.

"So," Ron says, "You don't have to tell me, I know how this happened."

"Uumph."

"Stick in the mouth, huh?"

"'Uck."

"Ah, puck. Stick, puck, not much diff." Ron *tsk-tsk*s. "You'll never learn," he adds. "How old are you now?"

"Uumph."

"Well," he says, peering into my mouth, "somebody did a good job of sewing this all up, anyway. You should see some of the messes that come in here some days. I'll tell you."

"Uh-huh."

To his assistant, Ron says, "Freezing is in."

"Okay," Lori says. "Good." She smiles at me and shakes her head, a mother concerned about a wayward child.

Ron positions the light over my head and begins to poke about in my upper jaw with one of the steel probes that resemble the tool used at Christmas to dig nuts out of shells. When he probes deep, my hands clench into fists. Blood must be running.

I've known Ron and Lori for almost fifty years. Every filling, every extraction in my mouth has been done by Ron. Every cleaning has been done by Lori. I know their story, they know mine.

"Just a little wider," Ron says, as he repositions his probe and prods the gum.

I comply and close my eyes. Eight hours ago I came home from the Emergency ward at the local hospital, holding a plastic bag of ice against my jaw and lip. I had been there for more than two hours. The young doctor who smelled of Lifebuoy soap had sewn twelve stitches into my lip, eight on the inside, four on the outside. He'd played hockey when he was in high school, he'd told me, but he had given it up for tennis. "You don't lose teeth in tennis," he'd said breezily. "Usually."

The anesthetic he'd given me was local to the jaw. I'd driven home on my own. When I came into the house, dark except for the light in the foyer, silent, the furnace humming, the refrigerator ticking, I'd gone into the bedroom and sat on the edge on my wife's side, waking her. She'd asked, "What is it?"

"I don't want you to be alarmed," I said, taking her hand and moving it toward my head. "Just feel this." I brought her fingers carefully to my jaw.

"Oh," she said, "that stupid game." It was not anger in her voice but sadness, resignation. Gingerly she ran her fingertips around my mouth. "You all right?"

"I'm all right." Pain throbbed through my jaw with every heartbeat, a jolting electric current that ended in the temples with an exclamation point.

"You've lost some teeth."

"Yeah."

"Poor baby. Will you be able to sleep?"

"After a while."

"You'll need a bridge."

"I guess."

We sat for a while in the darkness. I thought about the eighteen stitches I'd taken in the skull in high school, the six under my jaw a decade later.

"You've lost two teeth," Ron says decisively. Almost to himself he adds, "Let's just hope ..."

"Uumph." There's muzak quietly thrumming in the background, a Carole King tune.

"Were you wearing a mouth guard?"

"Uh-huh."

"Yeah, but not a mouth protector. Why don't any of you guys wear mouth protectors? You wear helmets but you should wear mouth protectors."

"Uumph."

"But you won't, will you, it's not manly. Ridiculous game. Now golf ..."

"Uumph."

"Yeah, what's the point of my saying that. I'll fix you up and you'll be back out there next week. Am I right?"

"Uumph."

"Yeah, I know, but—" Ron interrupts himself while he prods in my bleeding gum. "Huh, just as I feared. This tooth here is broken off above the gum line."

"Baahdh?" My hands clench into fists at my sides and I take deep breaths.

"Not too bad. But I'm going to have to dig for it."

"Huh," Lori sighs. She pats my shoulder.

"Yeah, gonna to have dig for it before I can get hold of it and pull it outta there." Ron says this cheerily but he's shaking his head. He's a small, tight, precise man who is expert at what he does in every way. And he's seen everything there is.

I study the ceiling, then close my eyes. Unclench my fists.

"I gotta get something," Ron says. He puts the steel tool down and goes out of the room, followed by Lori. Below the thrumming of the muzak, I can hear them conferring in another room. The words are not audible to me, but I know what they mean: pain, more expense, extra time in the chair, more pain. Electric currents run through my jaw. My hands feel hot, hotter than they've ever felt before. I close my eyes and breathe deeply.

But he's right. He'll fix me up and I'll be back on the ice by the weekend.

When he comes back in, he says brightly, "Good thing you were wearing that mouth-guard, my friend, or there'd have been Chiclets all over the ice."

Has the skid out of the playoff spots begun?

The Sharks are one of the league's solid franchises, playing better than .500 and standing third in the Western Conference. They're big, they're experienced, and above all they're disciplined. From the opening faceoff, they carry the play to the Jets. Their coach has said that in Winnipeg they're looking at playing two games: the first ten minutes and the following fifty. He knows that the Winnipeg crowd is loud and boisterous and the Jets feed off its energy. And in the NHL, where the first goal is the crucial goal, it's important to score first—or at least not get scored against.

His team plays hard, bottling up the middle of the rink, forcing the Jets to dump the puck at centre ice and chase into the corners to retrieve it. The game is not exciting. The Sharks don't want it to be. They want to take the crowd out of it—and they do, bottling up the Jets in their own end, stymying attacks before they get going. At the halfway mark of the opening period they have allowed the Jets only two shots on goal. The score is 0-0. In the concourse at the intermission, a friend we stop to talk to says, "This is the quietest the crowd has been all year."

The Sharks are having their way. The Jets look ordinary, the crowd has fallen silent, hoping for the breakthrough, anticipating the worst. A doufus in the crowd nearby yells, "Do something, eighty." It doesn't take long for some pissants to start picking on one of the Jets, this time Nik Antropov (#80). Byfuglien is still out injured, along with Bogosian. When the Jets get a powerplay, they look lost without one of them on the blue line.

In the second period the Sharks continue their disciplined play. For a few moments the Jets have them on the run in their own end, but they produce few shots, for all their effort, and most of those are blocked before they get to the net. Halfway through the game the shots on goal are Sharks 18, Jets 12. "It looks like there's less ice out there tonight," Kristen says.

"It's *national anthem hockey,* I say, "all the play in the neutral zone, the two teams lined up on the blue lines."

"Do something," a guy behind us moans.

In the crowd there's a placard being waved: HARPOON THE SHARKS.

Occasionally the cry of Go Jets Go! starts up, but the team cannot do much and their frustration is transmitted into the crowd as apprehension. The longer this goes on, the more likely the Sharks are to score first. They do, in the fourteenth minute of the second period. It seemed inevitable.

The crowd is restless, perturbed. Their high-energy team has been thwarted.

"C'mon Jets," a woman behind us calls into the silence.

"Get off the toilet, eighty." Now that Blake Wheeler is on track, it looks like the malcontent contingent has decided to make Nik Antropov the new whipping boy.

"Hit somebody at least," another voice chimes in.

But it's mostly the Sharks doing the hitting, the Jets rallying for a rush or two and a brief flurry in the San Jose zone. But they mount no real threat. Then in the third minute the Sharks score again. It's all over. Fans begin to do the Mexican wave, a sure sign that the game on the ice has lost interest. Final score: 2-0. Shots: 37-22.

Some nights you're just beat by a better team. What the fans will say is: *get off your butts, boys*. What the coaches will say is: *we never got our game going*. The fact is the Jets were beat by a better team on this night: stronger, more determined, better organized, more able to execute their game plan. Four losses out of five games played does not signal the end of the Jets' world, the fans' dreams, but we've passed the midway mark of the season; the playoffs are coming; with thirty-nine games remaining, the Jets are in tenth place, two points out of the playoffs. This is where the better teams begin to gear up and show their class; this is where weaker sisters tremble and fall off, puff balls in a prairie wind.

SNAPSHOT: RINGER

An evening on the prairies in 1971, the sun is setting and the sky is a painter's palette of purples blending into oranges near the horizon. I'm at the wheel of my '68 Mustang, driving out of Regina to a hockey game in the town of Fort Qu'Appelle. It's a lovely evening, the breeze coming in at the window carrying the odours of the land mixed with pungency of bales of hay stacked in fields. Bucolic, idyllic.

Just past the town of Balgonie, I turn off the Trans-Canada Highway onto a side highway that goes north and east, into the Qu'Appelle Valley. My hockey bag is in the trunk. I'm driving to Fort Qu'Appelle to play a game with the Indian Head Chiefs. In Regina I play in a beer league but the Chiefs are in a superior league and, as usual, I'm excited by the prospect of playing for them. I'm called into these games only rarely. Usually the Chiefs, who are allowed to dress two players not from their immediate area, go with a speedy forward and a puck-moving defenceman. I'm neither of those; I'm steady on the blue line, but on some nights that's what a team needs.

The land rolls in the Qu'Appelle Valley, little undulations where the car slows for the ascent and speeds up for the descent. Behind is the town of Balgonie, ahead Edgeley. I glance at my watch. The game starts at 7:30. I have lots of time.

On the radio Jackson Browne is singing about lost love, a melancholy dirge that I hum along to. I'd prefer a hard rock number on a game night, but I'm confident one will come on soon. The Stones, maybe, Peter Frampton, something to get the heart hammering.

Out the window the land stretches for miles in every direction, broken only by one-mile roads that crisscross the prairie, at this time of year denuded of the crops that are the lifeblood of this place. The roads that cross the highway are gravel. Cars and pickup trucks stir up dust as they approach the highway. When they pass, going in the opposite direction, drivers raise one finger off the steering wheel, a rural form of greeting.

The Mustang comes up behind a pickup at one of these intersections and I lift my foot off the accelerator. The driver has pulled over, the red tail lights flicker in the gloom. I approach cautiously. Maybe engine trouble? Inside, there's a man in his early twenties and as I drift up beside the pickup he glances across and touches his forefinger to the bill of his baseball cap, another form of rural greeting. I raise one hand in greeting and drive on.

My throat is dry. I've brought a can of Coke with me and I open it, *ppff*, and take a slug. The glow of a yard light far in the distance catches my eye, a halo of pale light. Otherwise the land is still and empty, only the thrum of the Mustang's engine, its headlights cutting through the darkness.

I slow for Edgeley, a once-prosperous prairie centre, now not much more than a ghost town. Boarded-up buildings, a gas station where the highway crosses the main street, a dog sniffing the base of a tree, in a yard of a ramshackle house a beige tarp pulled over what appears to be a snowmobile. I clear my throat.

When I drive through these prairie towns in falling gloom I feel a kind of sadness for these dying towns—and the life that went with them, a simpler life than I lead, than most people I know lead, a life of hard work and unpretentious pleasures: gatherings at community centres for weddings, barn dances, town fairs, church on Sundays, shooting the breeze in the coffee shop. There's a stillness over the land at sunrise and a quiet in the woods dotted among these fields—"bluffs" they're called on the prairies—and beauty in the sunsets when the meadowlarks and robins whistle their songs along with the twitter of blackbirds. But perhaps I romanticize.

I should be thinking of the game, of bodychecks and one-timers and slapshots rather than drifting into a Zen-like reverie. There are realities to this place and time that are not idylls: I'm a hockey player, a hired gun of a kind. Snug and cozy as these little towns might appear, the inhabitants who gather at their arenas call us ringers and hurl abuse at us. So there's a contradiction at work—for me, anyway.

In Regina I'm a professor of English at the university. I spend my days marking the themes and essays of college students, and in classrooms talking to the offspring of farmers and bourgeois families about novels and poems. We moved here a year or so ago from Toronto when I completed my master's degree and where I've begun my doctoral work. The boy who banged pucks against boards and grew up alongside miners' sons owns original paintings and fancies himself an intellectual. He's more likely these days to be reading *The New York Review of Books* than *Hockey Weekly*.

But that's how life unfolds: working-class kid turns budding professor; small prairie towns are lovely and cruel. All lives are filled with contradictions; these are just several of mine.

More than a month has elapsed since these two teams last tangled, the Jets on that occasion winning 4-2 at the MTS Centre. Since then New Jersey has risen steadily in the standings, improving their defensive play and getting better performances from star forward Ilya Kovalchuk, once a member of the Thrashers who defected from the team after becoming disenchanted with Atlanta. There are probably players on the Jets' team who took that as a slap in the face; there are no doubt fans who hold a grudge. So there will be no love shown to the rangy Russian during this contest.

The crowd begins the game in a surly mood: unhappy with the Jets and intent on taking their frustration out on Kovalchuk. Right from the opening

faceoff the *boos* directed at him are loud but not overly mean. No one calls out: *go back to Siberia* or the slanders typical at European football stadiums. The worst comes from a voice nearby: "Kovalchuk, you suck."

Like the Bruins and Sharks on the two previous nights, the Devils have come to play shut-down hockey. They too are a big team and begin the game forechecking in the Jets end and bottling up the middle of the ice, the third forward hanging back to form with the two defencemen a group of three along the New Jersey blue line. There are almost no shots on goal. Despite the Jets' determination to carry the play to the Devils, they can mount only two shots by the ten-minute mark. Another of those nights.

Despite the Devils' tactics, the Jets score late in the period, and though they only have six shots on goal, the first period ends 1-0. The Devils are probably fairly content; they'll play for a powerplay opportunity, a fluky goal, a turnover by the Jets that becomes an odd-man attack. They're not just big, they're patient.

They continue to play heavy hockey in the second period, forcing the Jets to work along the boards where the Devils can use their size to hold up Jets attacks and slow the pace of the game. The Jets have nifty and speedy skaters but too many are simply outmuscled in the corners and around the goals: Stapleton, Burmistrov, and Enstrom cannot make any headway. And with both Bogosian and Byfuglien out, the Jets cannot counter the tactic in their own end, and the Devils control the play. The second period ends with no further scoring, but the Devils are wearing the Jets down. Still the score remains 1-0 Jets, the shots 16-12 Devils.

Will the Jets hang on? Their third periods are dreadful. Before this game, they had been outscored 47-27. They'll have to compartmentalize, win each five-minute segment and try to come out with a 1-0 victory. Is that likely?

The first five minutes go by. The Jets are playing hard and smart, boxing the Devils out in their own end, dumping the puck into the corners of the Devils end, forechecking with intent. This is as well as they've played defensively all year; they give up little; it's not very exciting, but Jets fans are happy to be ahead. But they need that second goal, they need the cushion. Just at the midway point, the Devils score. Sigh. We've seen this movie before. The crowd goes silent. Now the Jets are playing for the single point that comes with a tie, maybe a lucky goal in overtime or a shootout victory. Within three minutes, the Devils light the red lamp again. The Jets have gone soft in the third period one more time.

They start to play hard. The crowd responds. Go Jets Go! But New Jersey are experts at holding a one-goal lead. "They're not coming back against these guys," I say. Kristen says, "C'mon, you have to believe." I suppose I do. Like many Winnipeg fans, I give up too easily, I pack it in emotionally. The vocal part of the crowd does not: Go Jets Go! They try, dumping and chasing, and the shots on the Devils goal mount up. But with no result.

"New Jersey, you suck," the guy nearby calls out. He's become louder over the course of the game—and more belligerent. A security guard comes up the stairs into the section. Time is running down. The Jets coaches are sending signals toward their goaltender, Pavelec. He'll be coming out soon for an extra attacker.

"C'mon, Jets," a guy nearby calls out in a break in the action, "score, it's my birthday, for heaven's sake."

They mount a furious attack in the Devils end, the puck flies past both posts, the crowd *oohs* and *ahhs*, but the final buzzer goes by without a goal being scored.

Three losses in a row. The Jets played a good game, they did not fumble it away but they lost anyhow. How long will the losing go on? Are they into a serious slump? What can be done to break the black aura hanging over the team?

SNAPSHOT: Parrot Towel

It starts innocuously enough. I score two goals at Sunday morning shinny and when I'm drying off in the locker room after showering I notice Kristen has thrown the bright blue towel with the silly parrot icon on it into my bag. The vivid colours of the parrot towel arrest my attention; the two goals give me pause: can this be my lucky towel? The next Sunday I score the winning goal and now it's almost impossible *not* to carry the parrot towel to every game. But should it be washed? Should it always be folded and laid on the top of the bag before zipping up, as it was on that first occasion, the moment of magic? These become important issues.

The scoring stops but the parrot towel remains a fixture in my bag. I like its gaudy yellows and reds and oranges, its azure background, and the parrot's goofy, oversized beak. But more important: it brought me those goals. It's magic.

Three years later I'm still rubbing its image over my skin following games. I can hardly remember why I'm carrying it.

It's ridiculous, the conviction that something you do, some phrase you repeat can determine how you play, the outcome of Sunday morning shinny. But …

As the Jets come on the ice for every game, the first man to emerge from the corridor is goaltender Ondrej Pavelec. And just before every game is about to begin, Andrew Ladd swings through the top of the Jets zone just above the blue line, then sprints to the bench, or takes his position for the opening faceoff. Moments of magic.

A guy I played with years ago in a beer league scored a hat trick one night, a rare occurrence for anyone, unheard of in his case. He did not change the undershirt he wore beneath his shoulder pads for the remainder of the season. He did not wash that undershirt. He became a butt of jokes. Toward the end of the season he dressed in his private ghetto in the far corner of the locker room, the stench of ripe cheese radiating from his body. And he never did score another hat trick.

The Jets are in a funk, a two-game winless skid. When I come into the arena I'm thirsty and stop at the bar for a drink. No more ten-buck beers, thank you. A cup of soda water—four bucks! At the seats I nod to Grumbler and look around for Smitty: not at the game tonight. Just after the second sip, the Jets score. I notice because Kristen bumps my elbow, jumping up to cheer, and a little soda dribbles down my chin. The Jets go on to win, the home winless streak ends. At the next home game I pause at the bar before going up to the seats. I'm not thirsty; soda water does not interest me; it costs four bucks. But the Jets won. I buy a cup of soda water.

How can this be? I'm a rationalist, trained in the best traditions of Western thought, I think of myself as an intellectual. I think of religion as a system of magic and hope laid onto a foundation of fear and bigotry that has had its day, has, in fact, become dangerous in our post-Cold War world. And yet I fall back on the supernatural tics of our primitive ancestors to get the home team to win a hockey game.

I notice that when the Jets come on the ice for a game, the last man to hit the ice is backup goaltender Chris Mason. He and his goaltending teammate form bookends of magic.

When I tune in a road game and find the Jets are ahead, I think, *turn off the TV*. If they got ahead and I wasn't watching, I'll jinx them by leaving it on. My hand lingers on the remote, the play goes down into the Jets zone, the puck whizzes past the net, almost a goal. My fingers tremble on the buttons. How can my *not* watching TV affect the result of a game taking place thousands of kilometres away? Should I cross my fingers too, should I buy a lucky rabbit's foot, should I never shave again?

But I'm doing these things already.

Get through the first ten minutes.

Holy Mary, mother of God, pray for us now …

Mantras, incantations, magic spells.

When I was a boy Johnny Z and I used a pocketknife to slice into the knuckles of our index fingers and pressed them together until the blood that dribbled out mixed together. A secret pact, magic that would bind us together as brothers for life. The New Zealand national rugby team, the "All-Blacks," a frightening outfit by any standard, enact a ritual war dance in front of opponents before every match, the *haka*, powerful magic that has taken them to three world championships of the seven that have been contested, or so it is claimed.

Who am I to argue with that?

Who is any fan to argue with that? We bring to the games our banners and towels and wave them, putting in the charm for goals. After the Jets score a goal, the incantation goes up in the crowd, *Bir-on, Bir-on*, the hex is put on the Rangers goaltender. Ward off the bad, bring on the good.

When the old Jets went through their terrible slump, I tried wearing a lucky shirt, I tried walking into the arena by a different door, I tried parking in another spot in the parking lot. Light beer, lucky socks. Soda water, lucky shorts. I blush to admit. But what else can we do? We invest hours and days and months in the fate of a sports team, Berkshire-Hathaways of emotion in an world that is out of our control, believing that magical incantations, that rites will give us power over our world, just as our prehistoric ancestors fell back on barbaric ritual to deal with the shadowy mysteries locked deeper down in the cave that troubled their ingenuous lives.

Coming into these two games, the Jets are missing their highest point-getter, Wheeler, and their two strongest defencemen. And though reeling from losses to two teams that proved bigger, stronger, and more organized, the Jets come out against Ottawa playing high-energy, resolute hockey, bottling up the neutral zone, content to play chip and chase, single-minded in front of their goal. There isn't a lot of bodychecking in this game, and that seems to suit the Jets. They have room to skate, they are not being pressured on the boards and in the corners. They go ahead early in the contest and take a lead of 2-0 to the second intermission.

Jets fans heave a sigh of relief. But we're aware that Ottawa have come back from being down on six occasions in third periods this season, so they will not lack confidence about that. And the Jets have gone soft on any number of occasions. In the third, the Senators storm Winnipeg's end of the ice. On one shift they hit the crossbar twice, but luck is on the Jets' side and they survive, despite being outplayed in the third. 2-0 is more than could have been hoped for. And the Jets have played one of the most disciplined games of the season. This unexpected victory after the three losses gives reason for optimism coming up against the Devils, a team that beat them soundly only a few games ago.

For the second of the two road games back-to-back they're still without three key players, Byfuglien, Bogosian, and Wheeler, and it's beginning to show. Every team has injuries—it's a gruelling eighty-two-game schedule with many back-to-back set-ups, so guys get injured. But some teams can struggle through these setbacks easier than others. Some teams have more depth. The Jets have a lot of young and promising players, but the core of the team, the group of five or six that make winning possible, is small. When they're without three of those guys, they're not a very strong team, the bench is thin. They can win on a given night—they proved it in Ottawa, where they used speed, grit, discipline—but stringing a number of such games together is difficult for this team, as it is for most in the NHL. With thirty teams in the league, the talent pool overall is thin. And most organizations find themselves with a handful of quality players and ten or twelve other guys who can fill out a lineup but not carry a team to win after win. This is true of the Jets, whose top five forwards—Ladd, Kane, Wheeler, Wellwood, Little are competent pros (though none a genuine star)—are good enough to win their share of games and squeak into the playoffs in the spring. They also have good pros like Slater, Thorburn, Glass, Antropov, Fehr, and a promising youngster, Burmistrov. But that latter group is not up to carrying a team; they're forwards seven through twelve. When the top six guys are not getting the job done, the team stumbles. And much the same can be said for the defence: Bogosian and Byfuglien are key members of the squad; on any given night, the rest can do a good job—even show the qualities of long-term pros—but if they are left to carry the team, then every single one of them has to perform flawlessly on a given night for victory to be possible. Any falling off from that standard spells doom.

And so it is on this night in New Jersey when both teams come out playing a hard brand of hockey and trying not to give anything up. Check, check, check. The Devils score on their final shot of the period at 18:59, a disheartening goal for the Jets. They give another one up early in the second, and before the ten-minute mark surrender three more goals and the contest is over. New Jersey go into a shell, and though they give up a goal in the third period, they keep the Jets to a total of twenty shots for the game and win 5-1.

"This being a Jets fan," I say to Andrew, "is hard on the gut."

He grunts. "Stapleton punches above his weight."

"There's that."

"And Kane, I like the big guy."

"Kane is impressive."

What else is there to say? (1. Anger at the home team gives you a gut ache and gets you nowhere. (2. Sometimes you just lose and you have to put it behind you because in two nights there's another game. (3. This is just a .500 team and to expect more is delusional. (4. When they get their injured players back, the Jets may put together a streak of wins, so… (5. Don't get too down, it's a long season, things may yet work out. (6. In two nights Buffalo is in town. Win that game.

SEC: XX ROW: XX SEAT:XX

HOME GAME 47
JETS VS SABRES
JANUARY 19, 2012

SEC: XX
ROW: XX
SEAT: XX

It's frigid on the prairies, minus 30 Celsius on the walk to the MTS Centre, and a cold wind is blowing through the Jets season. Once four games above .500, they're now only one game above, and a loss on this frosty night might spell the beginning of the end of the Jets' playoff hopes. We've been told that the three injured players are all game-time decisions. The coach says injuries are no excuse, other teams have injuries too. And he's right: the Sabres have a handful of key players out; and they lost a one-sided contest in Chicago last night, so they might be leg-weary. Best for the Jets to start fast and give the Sabres no reason for hope.

They do, skating hard from the opening faceoff, dumping the puck into the Sabres end, forechecking fiercely, shooting and crashing the goal. The fans are into it, too, chanting Go Jets Go! and working their hex on the Buffalo goaltender: *Mil-ler, Mil-ler.* The Sabres counterattack; they're a fast and disciplined squad, but the play is mostly in their end of the rink. By the midway point of the period, the shots are heavily in the Jets' favour: 10-3. And they score shortly after. Huge sigh. Opening goal statistics are eye-opening. When the Jets score first their record is 15-7-2; when they don't it's 6-12-3. They continue to apply the pressure; the shots mounting up, reaching 19-9 before period end, but the score remains 1-0.

This is a team that has trouble scoring, lacks finish. Their strength is skating; they carry the puck well to the opposition end; they forecheck effectively; they crash the other net. But they don't score often. They're a lunch-pail outfit, admirable in the eyes of blue-collar Winnipeg, but not polished in the shooting and finesse areas of the game, like the Red Wings or the Canucks. Each goal the Jets score comes at the price of tremendous effort. And so they count one goal after nineteen shots.

As if to underline the point, Buffalo tally to tie the score on their first shot of the second period, their tenth overall. There's a sickly silence in the MTS Centre. But it does not last long. Go Jets Go! The crowd is as lively as I've seen it. Beside me Andrew says, "This is something." Behind us a guy calls out, "C'mon, Antropov." He's the new whipping boy. These days Wheeler is afire, creating chances from eighty-foot rushes where he beats a defenceman at the faceoff dot before sweeping in on the goaltender: magical, memorable stuff. From the opening faceoff he's been using his big body effectively along the boards, and he's made several exciting rushes up the ice. Missing two games did not hurt him. In fact, his five-day layoff demonstrates how much these guys put out on a daily basis, how the travel and the checking take their toll. Despite his injury, Wheeler looks fresh compared to his teammates, he's energizing the Jets and carrying the play.

They score on a powerplay that he assists on just past the midway point of the period: 2-1 Jets; shots on goal: 23-13. Behind us the guy says, "Wheeler is flying out there." It's great to see. Ineffective at the beginning of the season, he played through the dark days and has emerged as one of the Jets' bright lights. The coach stuck with him. It's heartening. It's what we find uplifting about sport, our spirits buoyed by hard work, by self-belief, by stick-to-itiveness. Maybe Antropov will prove the grumblers wrong too.

The Jets go into the third period up 2-1. Will it be enough? They've been outscored 51-27 in third periods, so it's hold-your-breath time. And the Sabres come out skating hard. They know the Jets' poor record in the final frame; and they're desperate themselves. But they take a penalty and the Jets score; they're jubilant, their fans relieved. Now the chant of *Mil-ler, Mil-ler* is raucous, the chanting of Go Jets Go! strident. The team senses victory; the crowd senses blood. And even though the Sabres put on a push that sees them outshoot the Jets by a large margin, it's the Jets who score late in the game to finish 4-1.

What a mystery this team is. How odd that these talented boys, who showed so poorly only days ago against the Devils and the Sharks, seem tonight to have the skills of Cup winners and the nerves of steel to match.

The crowd is on its feet. The players go to centre ice to salute their fans. Joy in Joyville. It takes so little. When they lose in New Jersey, we're in the dumps; but when they win at home against Buffalo we're elated. This is what it means to be fans. Tonight we love these boys.

SNAPSHOT: The Boys

You see them on the street sometimes, or in the lobby of a hotel, or waiting to catch a flight at the airport. Two dozen fit, muscled, and coiffed young men in smart suits and gleaming shoes. It's Blake Wheeler with his tie askew, smaller than he looks on ice, but still busting out of his jacket; it's Evander Kane wearing a silver suit so glossy it might be made from tin foil. They look so young! And yet so old.

Their talent is evident when they are ten and they are put on the all-star squad or the travelling team. Their coaches say, *You've got it.* Scouts travel to arenas to watch them. Make notes in tiny books. Their moms and dads scream in drafty stands, phone aunts and uncles for advice. They know they're special, they see other boys cut from the teams, heads hanging, dreams defeated. Sensing their future, they go to bed early, focus their teen energy on the training regime the coach provides in the weighty black binder. They don't smoke, they don't drink. When they fall and bang an arm, off to the doctor; if they have the sniffles or the cough, ditto. More boys drop off the all-star teams—not strong enough, not fast enough, not resolute enough. The group grows smaller but the will to make it grows larger. Training camps with former pros, video instruction, sessions with sport psychologists. Skating: winter, spring, summer, fall. Out on the local rink firing pucks at the boards, hundreds, thousands—or at the wall in the corner of the basement. If there are girlfriends, they're discouraged, if there are camping trips, canoeing, kiting, carousing, the coaches purse their lips and arrange bowling for the all-star team, a movie at the cinema with popcorn and sodas.

By sixteen they're on a junior team, playing twice a week and practising five, travelling on a bus, away from home, separated from friends; they wear the team blazer on the buses and in the motels; in their free time they sit in their rooms with video games and text their increasingly dwindling circle of friends from school and neighbourhood. Their family is the team. Their meals are arranged for them, their motel rooms. They are told what to wear, when to go to bed, when to get up, how to talk to the press. They are not asked to read, to study, to think about anything other than hockey.

When they make the national team that represents the country at the World Junior Championship, they weep into the phone telling Mom. Increasingly focused on hockey, they have no social life, no friends outside of hockey. Yearning to make the starting lineup, they do everything the coach asks: the diet, the training regime. Picked, they exult; left out, they despair. They study video of their performance and make notes on how to improve.

Isolated from everyone but other players and coaches, they worry about injury and become hypersensitive to criticism. When their knee hurts, it's off to the world-renowned specialist; if things don't go well, they're steered clear of the journalists. They call Mom and Dad to share their dreams. But not their fears.

They're drafted and step onto the podium with league and team VIPs, they pull the team jersey over their heads, snug the team cap over their locks. They're eighteen or twenty and they know only people in hockey and a handful of school friends who say they adore them but may only be after something—game tickets, money, drugs? Desperate to be loved, they suspect anyone who tries to get close. They hang out with other players and watch porn videos in hotel rooms or bring in trashy girls for orgies that end up in the early hours with punch-ups and hangovers. They marry the girl next door or a "model" working as a waitress at one of young eligible singles' restaurants (YES) they frequent. But they spend almost no time at home. They travel, they play, they train, they watch video. The only time they feel good about themselves is when they trot down the corridor leading to the ice on game nights. The crowd roars, horns blat, canned rock music blares from the speakers. Their hearts swell with pride; they salute the fans. If they play well, the crowd cheers and the papers print glowing words about them; if they play poorly, the fans scream abuse. The papers will say: could have done better; the papers will warn: down to the minors. The only people they can trust are teammates. They will stand by them. Otherwise, nothing. The coach can turn on them; the fans; the press. When they score, they hug their team-mates, they're in ecstasy, they cry out. Only on the ice can they release all their pent-up emotion—the yearning to belong, the need to be loved, the fear that they are not good enough. They are at once infantile and mature beyond their years. Desperate and haughty. Boys and men. And they swing between these poles daily, today up, tomorrow down, an endless roller coaster of joy and anguish that cannot even be satisfied by winning the Cup. What about next year? Will they be traded because they performed so well? Will management break up the team, knowing they will not be able to afford the payroll, now that their players have become stars? Everyone wants something from them, but in the motel room, they're alone. And they have such a short shelf-life. Where will they end up—behind the bench as a coach, doing colour commentary on TV? Their heads reel, they can't sleep at night, they sweat on the team bus, they've got headaches. The stable ones learn to go into themselves and to get by; the less stable ones get less stable. After they push the buttons on their mobile phones, the first word they utter is: "Mom?"

It's crowded and noisy in the concourses on another cold night in Winnipeg. But the fans are hot with energy. A knot of guys drinking beer from plastic cups is chanting Go Jets Go and laughing at themselves ironically. They're all wearing Jets jerseys with names on their backs: Kane, Burmistrov, Ladd. How many of these jerseys have been sold? It seems as if every second fan has a jersey; in the old days it was about one in ten. It's a testament to the passion for the team in the city, the near-frenzy for everything Jets.

SEC: XX ROW: XX SEAT:XX

HOME GAME 48
JETS VS
PANTHERS
JANUARY 21, 2012

SEC: XX
ROW: XX
SEAT: XX

These jerseys are a phenomenon of the theatre, I'm guessing. We put them on the way some folks dress up at Halloween, an opportunity to shed our everyday selves and put ourselves on stage: once en-jerseyed, no longer inhibited, part of a crowd that has been granted the liberty of screaming heartily (and sometimes vulgarly)—though at the same time in the strain of self-parody that actors on stage must feel on some occasions at least—here I am doing Hamlet, myself playing at Hamlet; it's serious in one way but also something of an affectation, too, a pose where I do not have to be myself while being myself also.

We take our seats, Kristen and I. "Listen to this crowd," I say.

She asks, "You interested in theories?"

"Always."

"Try this: the crowd is going to stay with the Jets, the fans will not turn on the team for three seasons, as long as they win at home."

"It's a good theory."

"As long as they win at home."

"And stay close to a playoff position," I add. "Win at home and stay close to a playoff spot."

"For three years."

So win at home, it is. The Jets seem to know this. They come out playing as if their hair is on fire, shooting puck after puck at the Florida goal, but without getting a result. Florida do, though, on their third shot. But the Jets keep going hard into the Panthers end; by mid-period they've tested the Panthers keeper ten times but still have not broken through on the scoreboard. This team has difficulty scoring. In their last ten games they've taken 295 shots but scored only 18 times, an average of about 6%. Low by the NHL standard, which is about 8.5%. So it's no surprise when the Panthers tally again before period end on their tenth shot to make the score 2-0.

In the intermission I ask Kristen, "You think they'll score?"

"I hope they score," she says.

"I hope they score before the Panthers do."

They come out playing hard again, responding with energy to the chants of the crowd: Go Jets Go! Skating with passion, chipping and chasing, shooting whenever possible, crashing the net. They mustered fifteen shots in the opening frame and keep up that pace early in the second. But with no result. Until they go on the powerplay and post another marker on their twenty-third attempt on goal. The crowd is electric with cheering. And the Jets continue their presence down low, press below the Panthers goal line, in the corners, looking for the turnover that will produce a second goal. The period ends 2-1, shots on goal 30-17. Florida is lucky to be ahead. But the Jets are once again going into a third period behind and their record in such circumstances is doleful.

The Panthers come out playing lockdown hockey, bottling up the neutral zone and forechecking vigorously. The Jets have difficulty taking the puck to their goal. In each of the first two periods they marshalled fifteen shots on goal but it looks as if they'll have trouble managing ten in the third. The fans keep cheering, the Jets continue to skate hard. And they're rewarded: 2-2 just past the five-minute mark, big Antropov getting his second of the night. A heartening comeback; when was the last time the Jets were behind two goals and tied the score? The fans are delirious, winning seems within grasp. And not only winning, winning on the strength of a comeback, the single most satisfying way to come out victorious.

But they blow it. Give the puck away in their own end. The coach calls these giveaways "pizzas," easy pickings for the opposition, and on this night all three goals scored by the Panthers have been *pizzas*. For a moment the crowd is deflated. Just when victory seemed within grasp, the Jets have given the game away. But they don't give up; they're aware they've goofed up, and they press on, despite Florida's efforts to check the game to a standstill. Florida played—and lost—in Chicago only twenty-some hours ago and came into Winnipeg on a delayed flight, so they should be tiring, but they don't seem to be. Still the Jets big players are demonstrating presence in the Panthers end, and Burmistrov scores with just over five minutes remaining. You have to hand it to the kid: he, too, punches above his weight. The Panthers go into a defensive shell. Regulation time ends with the score 3-3. The crowd is delirious. Once again the Jets have come back; one more goal and it will be a perfect game.

Though both teams have chances in the overtime—the Jets just missing the winning goal on three occasions—the result goes to Florida in the shootout. Not quite the perfect game.

SNAPSHOT: PERFECT GAME, OR, THE TREMBLER

For players, the perfect game begins with an early two-goal lead, builds into a more expansive advantage, and culminates in a 7-0 rout. All of their skills can be put on display—defensive and offensive—and the goaltender chalks up a shutout.

For fans, it's different. The perfect game is the Trembler—which occurs only rarely but with unmistakable features.

To start with, the Jets are at home and the crowd engaged from the outset. Blaring horns, loud cheering, colourful banners all contribute to the game's sense of urgency and the crowd's expectation that something important is occurring, that being at this game matters. *Bring it on!*

That enthusiasm may flag if the home team falls behind on the scoreboard, but paradoxically that's an essential ingredient in the perfect-game heady brew. One goal will do as the early deficit, but two is better, because it's fairly easy to come back from being one-goal down early with a fluky shot or a powerplay goal. But two down requires concerted effort over a lengthy period of time to rise above initial deflation. So first one goal has to be counted, the goal that raises hope and gets the fans off their hands and into the game vocally. It sets the stage for a second goal, the one that ties the contest and opens the possibility of the victory. If the first and second goals are separated by more than ten minutes, the appetite for the comeback is whetted. Too brief a separation does not allow enough momentum to be built up in the crowd, and the Trembler requires a crescendo to a climax. But a lengthy delay between the goals is not the best either. Energy in both the team and crowd must develop at just the right pace and just the right pitch. The absolute best "arc" in this respect for the game to form is for the Jets to fall behind 2-0 towards the end of the first period, then tally a first goal just past the midway point of the game, and score the tying marker early in the third and the winner with about five minutes remaining to the final buzzer. All the elements for an exhilarating win are in place; and the build-up from despondency to hope to exultation is heart-thumpingly gratifying. *Y-yes!*

Another layer of emotion develops from bad refereeing. Nothing gets the blood on the boil like the sense of being done over by the officials. In one way, we thirst for injustice; it provides us the excuse to be savages.

A fine edge of anger develops nicely over several bad calls, the kind of anger that is honed if the opposition score a powerplay goal that is felt to be undeserved. *Boo refs, boo!* Sustained booing cements the crowd as one and augments the teeth-gritting, ear-splitting rage that is perfect for transforming fury and indignation into self-righteous triumph. Without this sense of triumphing over the referees—*we had to beat them too*—the comeback lacks both the initial bitterness and eventual bliss of perfect final resolutions.

That's heightened by a good dust-up somewhere along the away. For those of us in the paying seats, the best comebacks hit an emotional peak when two players drop the gloves and go at it. All of that suppressed dissatisfaction at the score, the refs, even the home team, suddenly finds an outlet and pent-up frustration explodes. Up off the seats and onto the feet to scream insults at the opponents' fighter and lustily cheer the hometown champion. *Kill Boileau!* Of course, enjoying a scrap is not in the best sporting tradition, but for me—for most fans—sprightly tussles are an essential ingredient in the emotional mix of the perfect game. If nothing else can get you involved in a hockey game, a spirited scrap should.

Games that feature any two of these elements are the stuff of water-cooler talk: how about that game! Those combining three or more are "perfect" games, they send us home trembling at the knees, and transform mere spectators into rabid fans.

January marks the beginning of hockey's "dog days," the cold of winter when teams begin to knuckle down to the task of securing playoff spots, the experienced squads showing their moxie, the weaker teams dropping out of the race, the ones between scrapping furiously among themselves for the one or two positions up for grabs. The Jets find themselves in the latter group, though spinning downward.

And the Jets are on the road and their road record is poor: 7-12-3. They need to improve that.

The new mantra is: *score in the opening ten minutes*. They try, in Carolina falling behind 2-0 at the midway point of the first period and then firing shots and forechecking, but all to no avail. It's the same old story: a lot of "thrashing" around with no result.

They've been without Kane for three games now; he's a presence, he takes a lot of shots; he's their highest goal scorer. There's no point moaning over that, though. Or the continuing absence of their most productive defenceman, Byfuglien. They have to muster what they can from the team going out on the ice. But they don't muster much.

Given the gruelling schedule, the travel, the injuries, every team looks bad on certain nights. Even the Canucks, even the Wings. And the Jets do not actually look bad on these nights. In Carolina they carry the play for stretches, storm the Canes goal, but they go down 2-1. In New York they play a solid professional game: tight checking, good positional play, focus in all three zones of the ice, but the Rangers are a strong, disciplined team and the Jets do not have the power to make them screw up or the finish to make any impression on the scoreboard. This is a team the Jets could learn a lot from: how to play positional hockey, to capitalize on chances, to build and then maintain a lead. They're admirable pros; whereas the Jets flail around much of the time to little effect. The game ends 3-0, the Jets managing only sixteen shots in total, completely over-mastered by their opponents.

That's the frustrating part for Jets fans. Their team's best game falls short. Their inadequacies are more and more apparent: they're not big enough, they're not strong enough, they lack finish. They can skate with the best in the league, it's entertaining hockey they play; but it is not hockey that's taking them anywhere. Of their "secondary" forwards, skaters numbers seven through twelve, at least three or four are not NHL calibre; they will have to be replaced by players who are better pros: bigger and stronger, even if less skilled than the guys currently on the roster. The same is true of the defencemen after the best four. Unless Jets management makes these moves, Jets fans will have to settle for a team of also-rans, entertaining enough, but doomed to lose more than they win, and inevitably frustrating.

At the All-Star break they have fifty points, five out of a playoff spot. Not terrible, but not very encouraging either. They've lost three consecutive games, have won only seven in the past twenty. In the past ten games they have scored only seventeen times, while giving up twenty-five, for a differential of eight. The skid has turned to a plummet.

Is it all bad news?

Depends whether you're a glass-half-full person, or glass-half-empty.

At the outset of the season, it looked as if the Jets would do well to play .500 hockey and to perhaps contend for a playoff spot. They began poorly, losing three consecutive games, but they rallied and did fairly well through to Christmas, rising at one point as high as sixth in the Eastern Conference. They gave their fans a reason to hope. A playoff spot was not out of the question. They were at home a lot, and were playing entertaining hockey—and getting results. Yay, Jets! They were exceeding expectations, and fans were glowing. But then they went into a tailspin, a tailspin that has brought them back to .500 with the momentum of the season turned against them. Once again, it seems they will be lucky to finish the season at .500, unlikely to secure the final playoff position. All things considered, that's not bad. They're in the hunt. They commit a lot of gaffes and give games away. But at home they play an exciting brand of hockey and the MTS Centre rocks with cheering and excitement. The question for Jets fans to ponder is this: is that enough to justify a pair of season tickets at $8,000-$12,000?

SNAPSHOT: All-Star Break

As the teams, the managements, the fans enjoy a week off from the grind that is the NHL schedule—well, some fans go into a funk when there's no hockey to watch for six days running—it may be time to ruminate about those teams and what makes winners, contenders, also-rans, bottom-feeders.

What do those top two groups have that the others do not?

First, it's important to say the obvious: better players. Teams that boast a star or three on their rosters have genuine advantages. The Canucks have the Sedins and Kesler, Bieksa, Luongo, all top-quality players, and the management's job of building a strong team around them is a matter of intelligent choices, tinkering as the season progresses, and good luck in the injury department. The same can be said for the Red Wings, Bruins, Blackhawks, and a few others. It cannot be said of the Jets, who do not have one legitimate star player, so it's a team of hard-working mid-level talent; the Jets' better forwards on top-level teams would be numbers four through six.

Second: experienced professionals. Guys that have been through the grind a few times know what it means to play disciplined hockey, tactics that do not have players chasing the puck in their own end in little groups, like Atoms and Pee Wees, for instance. Instead experienced players let a defenceman chase a single attacker below the goal line and cover the other attackers, guys in front of the net especially. Not having opponents floating around free near your goal means tighter checking and fewer quality scoring chances, fewer goals against, more victories.

Third: good coaching. Coaches can teach discipline, both building a system in the defensive zone and helping players *unlearn* bad habits. Harry Neale once quipped, for instance, that there are two places where you never make a backpass—at home and away! Coaches teach wayward young talents to maintain their positions, to not try to do it all themselves, to be patient, to play within a system, even if it's not energizing the fans or producing instant results. Tactics, an overall strategy, a game plan, a professional attitude. Patience is the key, particularly on the road.

Fourth: a top-quality goaltender—or one on a hot streak. Thomas of the Bruins, Luongo of the Canucks, Lundquist of the Rangers regularly steal three to six games a season for their teams, and those points are crucial in the rundown to the playoffs. And a stopper having a hot season—Niemi of the Blackhawks the season they won the Cup when he was "unconscious," can make a good team a great team. The Jets' Pavelec is a fine goaltender, he's maybe singlehandedly stolen a couple games this year; and if he were playing for a team that didn't leave him on his own so often, he might be among the elite of the league.

Fifth: leadership in the dressing room. Solidarity in the locker room is a good thing, everyone happy, the whole squad pulling in one direction, being friends off the ice, sharing an ethos on the ice. It's not vitally important; teams have won the Cup with a toxic dressing room, as they have finished last with a positive one. A strong leader in the room can be useful too. Mark Messier was the prototype when the Oilers were experiencing their Cup years. But you don't have to be a bully to lead a team to victory. The Red Wings' Yzerman was a quiet leader, as was Beliveau in his day and Orr in his. They did their talking on the ice. And they respected their teammates in the locker room, and were in turn admired for it.

Sixth: energized support in the stands. Known as the "extra man," boisterous crowds lift teams and energize them. At home they can inspire intense commitment from the squad and even, it is argued, goals and victories. The jury is out on those latter two. Last season, playing before lethargic audiences, fans with little knowledge or sophistication about the game, the Thrashers at this point in the season boasted a home record of 11-11-3, for twenty-five points. The Jets, playing in a hockey-mad arena, are 15-8-2, for thirty-two points. Better. And it's fun to be part of a boisterous crowd; but it would be heartening to see the measurable impact of loud chanting before the teams hit the ice and booing the opposition's goaltender transform into results on the road, too, where the team's record is an appalling 7-14-4, wouldn't it?

Any team that has three or more of these factors going for it is likely to enjoy quite a bit of success. There will be bad losses, true, there may even be losing streaks when the team stumbles for half a dozen games. But quality players, sound coaching, and disciplined play will, in the end, win out. With a record of .500, the Jets are not out of the playoff race. They can re-energize during the All-Star break, get away from pro hockey— its daily pressures, its brutal travel schedule, its injuries; they can pull together and put on a push in the final thirty-two games of the season, scramble into the last playoff spot, maybe go on a lengthy run during the playoffs, as both Calgary and Edmonton did in the past decade and go right to the Cup final. As the famous novelist so tellingly put it: wouldn't it be pretty to think so?

30 January 2012

Team	SP	PTS
New York R	47	66
Boston	47	64
Philadelphia	48	63
Pittsburgh	49	60
Ottawa	52	60
Washington	48	55
New Jersey	48	55
Florida	48	55
Toronto	49	55
Winnipeg	50	50
Tampa Bay	48	46
Montreal	48	46
New York I	48	45
Buffalo	49	45
Carolina	51	45

You want to hope but you're filled with fear. With the Jets' post-break play beginning in Philadelphia on a road trip, the run to the playoffs does not look to start well. But then the Jets have played well against the Flyers, winning twice this season and five consecutive times stretching back to last season. Room for hope. But then, the Jets have lost three games in a row, have won only seven of twenty-five on the road. Which way to jump, then? Hope or fear?

The game starts vigorously, Philadelphia playing hard along the boards and crashing the Jets net, as is their style—crash the net first, intimidate second, fight third. It's been the Flyers' *modus operandi* since their Cup days in the 1970s and not much has changed in forty years. This is a team that looks like thugs and plays like thugs: obstreperous. And wins. Welcome to the NHL, new millennium.

The Jets are up to the challenge. Sometimes a team plays best against fierce opposition. Going into Philly the Jets know that they will have to give their all if they expect a result. So they scuffle around their own net when the Flyers crash it. Tit for tat. Crosscheck to the back, glove in the face; slash to the arm, jab in the calf. The opening ten minutes are contested like rollerball, both sides laying on the body, neither team registering a shot on goal until well past mid-period. It's not a match for the purists but it is being played at a spirited level.

Just past the fifteen-minute mark the Flyers score at the end of a powerplay, a typical Flyer goal, jam the crease, jab at the puck and the goaltender's pads until the puck goes over the line. Ugly as Scott Hartnell. The period ends with the shots 7-6.

In the second, the teams continue the hard play: blocking up the neutral zone, grinding the puck along the boards, scuffling and scrapping below the goal lines. The Jets score on a nice pass and shot, Antropov to hard-luck Chris Thorburn, who notches his first of the campaign. In a game of hack-and-harry, it's nice to see some skill on display. Near the midway point of the period both teams suddenly run out of gas. It looks as if they've got no strength, no energy. The Jets in particular sag, reduced to tactics like flipping pucks over their blue line and limping to the bench, hacking and hoping to clear their end, shovelling the puck toward their goaltender in the hope he can stifle the flow of play. This is the residue of the All-Star break, when players took the week off and sat on the beach or visited with families. Legs suddenly have no jump, bodies are drained. No gas in the tank.

In the intermission, I ask Andrew, "Think they can hang on?"

"Not a chance."

"It's only a matter of time."

"Yup. That it be."

Some players seem more out of it than others: Fehr, who has done nothing for the team, Brian Little, once again logging lots of ice time but not producing, Antti Miettinen, brought to the squad for "secondary scoring" but without a goal so far. "Trade all three," I mutter in disgust, "for one guy who can score."

"They're having trouble hitting the net."

"Throw in the proverbial bag of cement," I add, laughing, a bitter sound.

The Flyers don't look as exhausted as the Jets. They're carrying the play in the third period, outshooting the Jets widely. But then near mid-period the Jets catch a second wind and the game evens out somewhat; the Jets may be able to hang on. Still, it's the Flyers who are getting the good scoring chances. They outshoot the Jets in the third period 13-4, but regulation time ends 1-1, the Jets' Pavelec having made at least four game-saving stops.

"Man," I say, referring to the one point secured. "How did they do that?"

"*They* didn't," Kristen says with authority. "Pavelec did."

"Got that right," Andrew says. "Pavelec's saving their butts."

And he does in the overtime, too, and the shootout, where he stops all three attempts against—and Little, ironically, wins it for the Jets.

Some nights you just steal one.

Leaving Philly the coach said he was pleased with the team: they'd played hard, they'd shown discipline, they'd come out with two points. He was looking for the same in Tampa Bay.

It's a totally different kind of game. Where Philly was bone-crushing checks and crashing the net, this is two teams skating and playing at tempo. There's room on the ice to skate, that extra half-second to maneuver, make a play with the puck. This contest brings home how much hockey is a game of time and space, big, bruising teams trying to cut down the space in which niftier players can operate, slicker teams working for that extra second—or half second—of time in which to make glossy plays. The minutes fly past; very few stoppages, none of the Philadelphia-Boston style of scuffle and scrap at each whistle. This is what we come to see, what we pay good money to cheer: hockey at its finest, two teams going at it but without the Broadway Bully Bullshit. Passages of two to five minutes zip past without a whistle. But the fans are cheering, almost as many chants of Go Jets Go as Go Bolts. The first period ends 0-0. In the dressing rooms, players must be gasping.

Byfuglien, out with a knee injury since December, has returned to the squad. He was missed. He carries the puck with force, he knocks forwards down in the Jets end, it's hard to separate him from the puck when he's in possession. He's presence.

The frantic pace continues into the second period. "This is a good game," Kristen says, "a great game." Past the midway mark of the period, Tampa Bay begins to take over: rush after rush, the Jets seem to be standing still, are hemmed into their own end. The shots on goal go from an even 12-12 to Tampa 20-Jets 12. The Jets are under siege. It doesn't look like they'll make it to the intermission. Then totally against the run of play, Wheeler pots a goal with only 15 seconds remaining. Jets 1-0.

The late marker does not deflate the Lightning. They come out blazing in period three, their snipers, Stamkos, Lecavalier, St. Louis carrying the play, the Jets on the back heel in the early going. Tampa score just past the mid-mark of the period. Is it another of those nights when the Jets get ahead and then fold? Another third-period collapse? They don't. The game evens out, goes into overtime.

"Well, one point," Kristen says.

"Two in Philly, one here, not bad."

"Maybe two here."

"Maybe."

The four-on-four overtime produces swift rushes. The Jets are happy to control the puck when they get it, circle back to their own end, don't foolishly toss it away and give up possession. They're learning things, they're playing with poise. And for it they're rewarded: a goal by Wellwood with less than two minutes remaining, a goal set up by Byfuglien. Despite his erratic play, they've missed this guy, he's a central cog in their machine.

More and more I'm discovering just what it means to be chronicling the ups and downs of a team in a book that is a journal. Things that seemed important early may not be in the end; and conversely, things that seemed unimportant at the start of the season may become vital towards its conclusion. There's no knowing because it's all happening on the fly. I'm beginning to sympathize with the coaches.

Still, the road trip goes not badly. Two points in Philly in the shootout, two in Tampa in overtime. And both low-scoring games where the team played disciplined hockey and looked good. Byfuglien has returned and his contribution has been huge. They must be happy with themselves; they must be pumped in that dressing room.

SNAPSHOT: Yada Yada in the Dressing Room

I'm coming back into the dressing room from the showers after a game of shinny in 2010, towel wrapped around waist, when I hear a loud guffaw. It's Hal, who gives me a wink as I ease down onto the bench.

"It's expensive," Willy is saying, "that's the point. It costs too much."

"You pay for good ingredients," Taz replies, voice at the end of the rope. He runs a pizza shop and from time to time brings in freebies after games.

"Yeah," Willy insists, "but what I'm saying is, it's expensive." He sticks out his jaw, takes a sip of beer.

"Jesus," Taz says. "Do you not understand? You get what you pay for. And—"

"Dominos I understand, Gondola I understand. It's just—" Willy looks across at me, twinkle in his eye, the beginning of a smile crinkling his lips.

"It's good pizza," Hal tosses in, "what's the problem?" He chucks an empty beer can into the trash. *Clank.*

"What's the problem?" Willy's voice shoots up.

Taz is on the other side of the room, fulminating. "You pay for what you get. That's what I'm saying. Good ingredients cost."

"It's good pizza," Willy continues. "It's not that." He gives me a wink.

This could go on for fifteen minutes, round and round, it has in the past gone on for fifteen minutes, but Dave wants to make a point with Jonny. In the gap in the conversation he says, "You looked good out there, man, you pumped in a couple goals today." A guffaw goes up.

"Pumping, yes." This is Hal again. His blue eyes twinkle.

Dave laughs. "You been eating your Wheaties, man?"

Jonny has been out with a shoulder injury. This is the way it gets talked about, this is how his pain, his recovery is deflected and dealt with, what everyone in the room fears: months of anguish, surgery, recovery exercise, then finally the go-ahead to go back on the ice. At least not sidelined forever, not out of the game.

"Wheaties?" someone adds. "He's been eating something."

Another guffaw.

"Eating out. That's what he's been doing."

"Maybe pizza." Someone can't let a sleeping dog lie.

"Been scoring," Hal says. "You know, pumping."

Mike across says, "He's got the pump." He makes a gesture, a hand pushing down the handle of a water pump.

The meaning of all this is obvious, juvenile, yet it goes on, as if the word pump and its variants, used for sexual innuendo, had just been discovered.

"Oh, he's got the pump. So I hear."

Jonny says, "Not from me."

"Not from his wife."

A burst of laughter.

"Not what I hear," Willy says, but weakly.

"Maybe *your* wife."

"Maybe yours."

"Maybe from that waitress at Bar Italia."

"Or that babe at the Palomino?"

Jonny narrows his eyes. "I was not at the Palomino."

"Of course. Neither was I. Neither was he."

Hal asks, "What's the Palomino?"

"*Pal-i-mony*," Willy corrects. "Palimony Club."

"Babes in there just dying for it." Taz has roused himself.

"Old broads, you mean. Cougars."

"Better a hot cougar than a cold wife."

"Says you."

"Says you."

"Babes in there rub up against you in the hallway on the way to the can. Stick their tits right in your face. You can taste it. They can't wait for a bit of pumping."

"From you?"

"Who, then? You?"

This can go on for quite a while, sex talk that is not really sex talk at all but a way of talking about something important to the group—how injuries put you on the sideline, how good it feels to be part of the group, how everyone revels in the energy of the room; it's not about sex, as it is not about pizza, it's about the gang, about being part of the *boys*, about being—ever and always—rink rats.

Only three points separate the Jets and Panthers as the Jets come to the end of a five-game road trip. They've been playing pretty well, winning close ones, garnering important points in the race for the playoff position, but it's also true that all games in the division are beginning to look like four-pointers. So much to play for, so little room for error.

Florida is a good team: big, strong, fast, not reluctant to grind along the boards; they play a north-to-south game that is impressive. A real lunch-bucket outfit, with a star scorer or two. If they were the Jets, Winnipeg would be proud of them. They go ahead in the opening frame, but the Jets stiffen up in the second to tie the contest 1-1, but only a few minutes later Florida scores again. It results from the smallest of gaffes when Byfuglien loses his man in front of the net.

The game is made of such gaffes.

Hockey occurs in such a limited space and at such a fast pace that gaffes are inevitable. Consider how much more quickly pro players move on skates than running in football, where speed is limited to the tempo of running—and the fields, whether in the NFL or the European FAs are much wider and longer. Everything that happens in hockey happens fast. So decisions made on the ice must be made in split-seconds, quite literally: the defenceman skating backwards between two attacking forwards has a half-second to decide whether to force the puck carrier, in the hope of breaking up the play (but risking a wide-open chance on goal if he errs), or to stay between the attackers in the hope of cutting off passes between them (but risking a hard shot from the puck carrier). A game can hang on that split-second decision. As it can on a puck that comes out of a *scrum* from the corner to the front of the goal: does the defender swat it away at once, back to the corner it came from (thus giving up the puck to the attackers again), or does he try to corral it and make a play to come out of his zone (thus risking being checked in front of his goal)? There's no time to think about these choices: the game demands instant reactions.

Mistakes are the game. That's why post-game analyses—coloured circles, arrows that point out where, when, and how mistakes occurred—make good TV; but also why they're kind of pointless. Mistakes will be made; the game cannot be controlled the way analysts sometimes suggest they can be.

But coaching, experience, and good positional play can double or triple that half-second of decision-making time and cut down the number of mistakes.

The game ends 2-1.

In Montreal, the team should be up but they come out looking lost and hapless. In the opening five minutes the puck is coughed up by Bogosian, Stuart, and Byfuglien. Fortunately, the Habs lack finish, so there's no immediate scoring. By mid-game the score is 2-1 and it looks as if most of the Jets would rather be somewhere else. It also looks like the run to the playoffs is over; the Jets' season is washed up. Final score: 3-0.

The loss is bitter but it's not as important as what the loss portends. The Jets just don't have it. They work themselves to a point where they're in contention, then fall apart right at the juncture where they could make a move. They will continue to give everything they have, but it will see them with an (at best) .500 record at season end, somewhere between five and ten points out of the playoffs. They don't have the moxie to "take it to the next level."

The Jets are in eleventh spot, five out of the playoffs, with two teams between them and the final position, requiring a nearly impossible leapfrog.

Jets fans' spirits have flagged at a number of points in the season but this is the lowest, a real downer.

SNAPSHOT: Sport Is Good For Us?

Sports, they say, are good for us; sport, they claim, builds character; put your kids onto teams, they'll be the better for it. But I'm not so sure.

In a rink in St. Boniface one night I'm on the bench when an overweight, greasy-haired bruiser from a beer league team at the bottom of the table takes offence to something my teammate Melly has said or done. At a stoppage in play he skates up behind Melly and cross-checks him viciously in the neck. Melly goes down. Teammates on the ice rush to his rescue; the referees escort the bruiser out of the arena. Melly is out for the season. A case is brought against Bruiser. He gets a life-time suspension.

This is not a unique occurrence in recreational hockey.

I'm coaching a Bantam AA team against "Rangers," a team from a largish area of the city. We're at Dutton Arena, our home ice. A bulky kid who stands over six feet and weighs close to 200 pounds, a kid cut from a AAA team, hammers one of my less able players, a boy who stands maybe five-foot-six and weighs 140 pounds, into the boards—face-first. He goes down and does not move. In a flash I'm on the ice, fortunately accompanied by a physician, the father of one of our players. We both fear the worst for young Tony.

This is not an isolated incident in minor hockey.

I'm not sure I want to recount the number of times I've seen otherwise fairly sensible, ordinary middle-class guys lose it on the hockey rink and do unconscionable things. I don't want to think about boys like Tony, who have been seriously injured by acts of brutality and never returned to the game.

How many NHL pros have done mean and nasty things in the name of winning, temporarily regretted it, and then done almost precisely the same thing only a few games later? I have a list of names here.

"No one wants to hurt another player," is the pious claim after a vicious check that sends an opponent to the hospital, "no one wants to end someone else's career." But that's exactly what happens. Necks are broken, throats are severed, brains are permanently damaged. I have a second list here.

Is this the way to build character?

Men involved in professional sports where there's brutal physical contact know what they are doing when they smash an opponent, and yet they do it anyway. It's their paycheque and their ticket to being somebody, the only way for them to get the money, the fame, and the girl. They know it; we know it.

Contact sport is dangerous and nasty. You put your life on the line every time you go out there. There's an old saw in the locker room: *If you don't want to get hit, go play golf.*

And yet when they injure an opponent so that his body is wracked no less brutally than during the Spanish Inquisition, what they say is, "No one wants to end the other guy's career," adding a lie to a piece of human nastiness equivalent to the Inquisitors. And the leagues they belong to—the NFL and NHL in particular—suspend the perpetrators for a few games, fall back on rule books, wring their hands piously, but let the mayhem continue. So they conspire in the duplicity. And the players, young, impressionable men for the most part, learn the lesson from their elders, the gentlemen in the blue suits in charge: when someone goes down with a serious injury, mouth the correct words but keep on doling out the damage. Appear to be repentant, but wink and continue business as usual, because "it's good for the league."

Cover up, lie, pretend nothing happened.

This does not look like character building to me.

But who am I?

I'm a guy standing on my feet in the Winnipeg Arena in the WHA days screaming, along with 15,000 other Jets fans: "Kill Durocco! Kill Boileau!"

I'm a guy who attends games at the arena or watches them on TV and gets worked up by dodgy officiating and holds a grudge against NHL executives for pulling my team out of my city; I'm a carper and a grumbler who curses aloud at the name of Gary Bête.

Has being a fan of the Jets built character in me or the thousands of other Jets supporters who follow the team and gripe about the NHL or the tactics of some teams or the behaviour of given players on opposition teams?

You tell me.

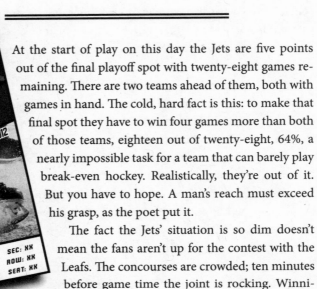

SEC: XX ROW: XX SEAT:XX

HOME GAME 55

JETS VS LEAFS

FEBRUARY 07, 2012

SEC: XX
ROW: XX
SEAT: XX

At the start of play on this day the Jets are five points out of the final playoff spot with twenty-eight games remaining. There are two teams ahead of them, both with games in hand. The cold, hard fact is this: to make that final spot they have to win four games more than both of those teams, eighteen out of twenty-eight, 64%, a nearly impossible task for a team that can barely play break-even hockey. Realistically, they're out of it. But you have to hope. A man's reach must exceed his grasp, as the poet put it.

The fact the Jets' situation is so dim doesn't mean the fans aren't up for the contest with the Leafs. The concourses are crowded; ten minutes before game time the joint is rocking. Winnipeggers are happy to have a team, even if it's a team now about to see its playoff hopes extinguished.

I look around for signs that read, WE STILL BELIEVE. There are none.

The play starts briskly. One thing that can be said: the Jets are keen, even if they're out of it. Kane is back in the lineup after an absence with "concussion-like" symptoms. He looks good: fast, if a bit reckless. No wonder he crashed his head out there. But on some nights, he alone is worth the price of admission.

Before too many minutes have elapsed, the teams settle in at a slower pace: a few energetic rushes, but mostly cautious and defensive play. At the midway point of the period the shots are 5-4. Toronto score on a zinger of a wrist shot by Kessel just at the midway point; but the Jets answer a few minutes later. Score after one: 1-1.

"Not behind," I say to Kristen. "At least."

"Outplayed at the start, but they've evened it up now."

Early in the second, the Jets begin to carry the play. And then on a dash from centre by Wheeler, another of those magical *snapshot* moments, they score to take the lead halfway through the game. But it's still tight out there, a lot of dump-and-chase, a lot of neutral zone play, both teams looking afraid to lose rather than determined to win. Going into the third up by a goal has not been a great winning formula for the Jets, so it's take a deep sigh and expect the worst.

Kristen asks, "What do you think?"

"Oh," I say, "they'll lose. Probably 3-2."

But the Jets carry the play. Toronto played last night and it begins to show. They have difficulty mounting attacks. And the Jets are playing a "road" game; taking no chances in their own end, dumping and chasing, content to work at a slow pace. The minutes tick by. At the halfway point of the period Toronto has managed only two shots. When they pull their goaltender as the game runs down, they manage none at all, flailing around in their own end, losing the puck in the neutral zone, rushing the play up ice and getting nowhere, finishing the game with just eighteen shots and looking anemic—it's not that easy to score in the final seconds with your goaltender out. Jets fans are excited. They cheer the success, go home buoyed up. Maybe there's still hope.

Two games on the road, two games against strong teams that the Jets have had difficulty beating. The first in Washington has them facing the Caps' firepower, much in evidence from the start of the game, the Caps applying pressure, buzzing the Jets goal, making them play frantically in their own end. By the midway point of the game there's no score but the Jets are on the back foot: in the face of Washington's attack they seem not big enough, not strong enough, not determined enough. It looks like they're hoping to win the shootout in a 0-0 game.

The previous game between these two teams also went to the third period with no score, before Ovechkin scored the heartbreaking goal in the dying minutes. Are we about to witness the same result? It's still 0-0 at the end of the second. In the third, Washington's fans are cheering lustily. Their team is very much the aggressor. Hold on to your hats, it looks like this one will go down to the wire. But then

SEC: XX ROW: XX SEAT:XX

AWAY GAME 58

JETS VS CAPITALS

FEBRUARY 09, 2012

SEC: XX
ROW: XX
SEAT: XX

a ludicrous situation: a Caps player slashes a Jets player, the Jets player slashes back; the referees seem content to let play go on; but the Caps player cries out in protest and a penalty is awarded much after the play ends. Once again, inept officiating: the home team is calling the penalties!

Here we go again. A few nights ago in Ottawa, where the Senators played the Bruins, Hassenfratz and Walsh managed to call seven penalties against Ottawa and three against the Bruins, effectively giving the game to Boston. Along the way, they missed a crushing, illegal check along the boards dished out by Milan Lucic. Again Lucic. He sent Buffalo goaltender Miller to the sidelines with a vicious check, and he did not receive a penalty, did not receive a suspension. Is he connected?

These are the things that are galling. Both teams were playing well, the game was being equally contested; then the officials step in and influence the result. It's more than a shame when referees' decisions are the key points in the game; it's a disgrace to the league.

Washington score on a powerplay. Shortly after the first goal, the Jets take a four-minute penalty for drawing blood and the Caps score again. Game over. There's less than five minutes remaining and the Jets have difficulty scoring once in a game, never mind twice in five minutes. We're missing the playoffs for sure. We. Sick at heart, I throw my hands up in disbelief and cry out, "You see!" One solace of being a pessimist is that you find warped satisfaction when things turn out as badly as you predicted. Bittersweet though it is.

But then when all seems lost, the Caps take a penalty, and while they're killing it, they take another. The Jets pull their goaltender to make it a six-on-three advantage for the Jets. From a wild scramble in front of Washington's goal, Kane scores. 2-1. Now we're into pure nerves. Surely they cannot come all the way back—and with less than five minutes remaining? Anxiety piled on anxiety. The ensuing faceoff at centre ice occurs with a minute remaining on the powerplay. Byfuglien shoots the puck in just to get it deep into the Washington zone, but it deflects off the foot of a defender, bounces weirdly, then dips past the goaltender's outstretched foot, and the score is tied! We're not yet out of the playoff race, my heart surges with relief; there's still a chance.

I realize then that I have not totally given up hope; though outwardly convinced all had been lost in Montreal, deep in my gut I have still been harbouring (cherishing) the wish the Jets would make the playoffs. Like all Jets fans I was keeping a candle burning even when all around was darkness. I feel like a child; I know that to be a fan means to be a child: emotions racing this way and that, wishing one day, despairing the next, ever subject to the slightest change in the wind, out of control, disgusted and enraged at one moment, elated and exultant at the next. Hostages to emotion. Is this why we're fans?

The overtime passes with no scoring. The Jets' Little pots the winner in the shootout. Jets win! WTF! What wonderfully turbulent emotions: fear, anxiety, joy. And that almost perfect game: down by two goals, enraged at the officials, comeback in the dying minutes, victory against the run of play in the shootout. Exultation piled onto righteous indignation. You don't get this feeling at the opera!

SNAPSHOT: Sports Fever 6

Late in the game against Washington, a 0-0 tie, Kristen and I are in the TV room watching when the referees call a dumb-ass penalty against the Jets. I get up and leave the room. There are papers to be faxed in the morning that have not been organized and I set about organizing them rather than watch any more of this fiasco. Moments later the Caps score a powerplay goal, a goal gifted them by incompetent officiating: from a nearby room, I hear the crowd noise go up. A few moments later, there's another roar from the Washington crowd: 2-0. I cross back through the TV room, papers in hand. On a powerplay, the Jets score. Kristen calls out, "There!" I'm out of the room again when I hear Kristen shout, "It went in, my God, it went in!" 2-2 draw.

I sort and organize the papers. Then watch the overtime and shootout. The Jets win. Later, I watch the parts of the game I missed on PVR.

The next evening, Kristen says, "You were upset last night, you left the room."

"I thought the game was being played evenly, it had become a good contest, it was fun. Then the referees step in and screw things up. I was disgusted with them."

"It was a bad call," she says. "But I kept watching."

"Yeah, that's the difference between us. The kinds of fan we are."

I take it too personally, she argues, meaning I guess that my expectation is that the Jets should win every game, but that's not it. My expectations right from the start were based on the fact the Jets are not a strong team, that they would do well to play at the .500 level, maybe squeak the last playoff spot. Winning is important, yes, how could it not be? But it's complicated. I want the team to play well, to the level of their abilities. I want them to succeed in that way, and when they piss about on certain nights, it's frustrating. But last night, it was not the Jets that were the problem, it was the referees. God, this team has to work hard enough to grind out victories, they don't need incompetent officiating to make it more difficult.

But I can see what she's getting at: she's a fan too, but it doesn't affect her the way it does me. I'm a certain kind of fan. The Jets' performance matters too much to me. It's a sickness of a kind.

"Why?" she asks. "Why does it matter?"

The answer is, I don't really know. No doubt there are learned studies by psychologists on the subject of *fandom*, but I want to puzzle it out for myself. And what I see is this. For most people regular adult life is pretty ho-hum. Going to work, bringing home money, buying things, all that. It's bland, not very engaging, really, but we pretend it isn't: go into the job, grind along, seemingly happy on the surface but boiling with unrest underneath. Though we never admit that. What we're searching for is that feeling on Christmas morning when you're five and you open that incredible package: WOW! It rarely happens. But in the sports arena we can feel it—pure exultation.

No doubt there are many who would argue that they get great satisfaction from their jobs. But I'm talking *exultation*. Satisfaction is like disappointment. Watered-down emotion. Fans—fans like me—move along the scale from exultation to despair.

Most of us, I think, don't experience that. Though we probably wouldn't admit it. We feel satisfaction with our jobs, with our families, other things. But exultation I might feel very rarely, when I score a goal, even in old-fart hockey. Moments that intense. So we are fans because we want to experience both positions along that continuum, despair all the way to exultation. In fact, the best moments come when despair is *transformed* into exultation, during the perfect game. That's so good. We want to go there, it's what makes us fans.

That's the reason we came to bemoan the famous cyclist: by taking drugs and ensuring he'd always win the Tour, he took away the possibility of our moving along that scale. He took that out of the equation, the central reason we watch sports: we want to see someone overcome the odds, start near the bottom, but struggle to the top. And we groan when we're cheated out of that by Marion Jones, whoever else. We want to go through the transformative process. That's what makes sport feels so good.

The old saw used to be, *If you get up by two goals on the road, you should win.* The Jets have trouble scoring two goals on any night at all. But they start a scrambly affair against Pittsburgh by potting a lucky one only a few minutes in, and follow with a second not long after.

Two-goal lead! Can they hang onto that precious cushion until the end of the period? They can't. The Pens respond within ten minutes, a weak goal, the kind Pavelec has been blockering out all season. He's entitled, he's saved the Jets' butts so many times in the year, he's due a bad goal. Or two, it turns out. The Pens score again by period end and the two-goal margin is gone. Sigh. The Jets cannot play defence.

So at the start of the second period it's 2-2, whole new game. But now the Penguins smell blood, and now they're starting to play like a team near the top of the division, outclassing the Jets in all three zones. By the five-minute mark they've taken the lead. By the midway point of the game it's 4-2. The Jets are sunk.

But Fleury, the Pens goaltender, is not having a good night either. The Jets get another one past him. 4-3. The Jets are back in this contest; anything could happen. It does. The Pens keep up the pressure and soon it's 5-3. Just when the Jets had a chance, the game gets away on them.

As the third period begins the Pens are in command. But in this game anything could happen, it seems. And it does. The Jets score: 5-4. They're back in it again. If only they can play defence and turn the game from *run-and-gun* to a close-checking affair that gives them the opportunity to bide their time and equalize. If only. But hardly a minute elapses before the Pens register a quick countering goal, another weak one. Pavelec is flailing. The coach should have lifted him long ago, if only for his own self-confidence. The score is 6-4.

It's one of those nights. *First team to ten wins!*

The Penguins are determined it will be them. They score a seventh to make it 7-4, but surrender another before putting in the final marker of the night: 8-5.

There were two moments in the game when the Jets came back from two-goal deficits, heroic efforts in a way. They didn't fold, they didn't collapse. But in both instances, they could not hang on long enough to settle the game down and then turn it around. They have too many defensive inadequacies.

And a new motto: *Just When We Had a Chance!*

As the Jets leave the ice, there are grim looks and disconsolate faces. Once again they've blown an opportunity, once again they've put themselves within reach of the brass ring only to fumble it away. They remain in tenth place, five out of the ever-elusive playoff spot. In that dressing room they must be very discouraged. Certainly their fans are.

SNAPSHOT: The Boot

It's early February, a little early for this kind of analysis, but since the Jets seem to have ceded their playoff possibilities, it's maybe fair to say, as the trade deadline approaches, who should they keep? What makes it a fair question, probably, is that this team is not the Winnipeg Jets, per se, it's the Atlanta Thrashers, and maybe the new team needs to seriously clean house, as they did with the coaching staff before moving to Winnipeg. Their performance and record argue it might be a fine idea.

Also, what can be said about changes is that many teams find themselves in the same position as the Jets: with a squad that simply isn't good enough to compete. Or maybe it's fairer to say: with a squad that can *just* compete. The talent pool in the NHL is thin; quality players are not easy to come by. When a team sets out to replace a mediocre skater or two, they're likely to receive back in return—a mediocre skater or two. *Plus ça change, plus c'est la même chose.*

That being said, if the Jets really could acquire legitimate quality players of NHL calibre, this would be the prescription.

Build from the defence out. Keep Pavelec and Mason, they're both competent tenders who deserve better than what they've experienced. Keep Bogosian, who's young and promising; keep Oduya because with the right partner he's effective; keep Byfuglien, who's a force—as much for bad as good most nights—but move him up to forward, where his numerous gaffes won't hurt the team as much. Keep Stuart, who, like the GST guys, is as good at what he does as can be asked. Hainsey is steady, a remarkable +7 on a team that is -21. The rest can go: Enstrom is too weak for the league, although he could be kept purely as a powerplay specialist. Jones is out of his league in the NHL—literally. But Mark Flood can play, and he should be kept. Ditto Arturs Kulda, who did not look out of place when he was up during Hainsey's injury.

And keep Kane: he could be a big talent in the NHL, a power forward, a goal-scorer. And keep Wheeler: since the twenty-game mark, he has shown he cares about his performance and is willing to work at improving it. Keep Ladd, mostly for sentimental reasons, and Wellwood because he's been the Jets' most reliable forward all season. Keep the GST line because they've done what they're on the team to do—work hard, shut down the opponents' top line, be the "energy guys." The rest can be cut—and should be cut. Little, Antropov, Burmistrov, Fehr, Stapleton are all guys who might have done something in the NHL—and still could in other circumstances—but have shown themselves to be talents of AHL quality only. As have all those "other" guys the team has tried: Cormier, Gagnon, Miettinen, et al. Management might be able to package two or three of these guys and get in return one or two legitimate NHLers. They should be looking for guys like Brooks Laich, Tomas Fleischmann, Alexander Steen, guys who are strong and can skate. The key is toughness, not cuteness.

The blueprint should be: bigger, stronger, more willing to pay the price. Think of the Florida Panthers, think of the St. Louis Blues. Young, strong, speedy, but mostly tough. Physically and mentally. Otherwise, this team will "thrash" through another season, looking promising at times, but invariably neither dynamic nor potent enough for this league. Not enough of them really make the cut.

SNAPSHOT: THE CUT

I'm leaning against the boards at the Winnipeg Arena with Al White, taking a breather between skating drills. It's 1965, winter. Al plays for the Winnipeg Rangers in the Manitoba Junior League. We work together during the day in the same office building downtown, josh around, munch sandwiches over lunch, watch the pretty girls who come trooping through our area with correspondence from executives. I'm at the firm to earn money to pay college tuition costs next year; Al is picking up pocket money while he waits for a pro career in hockey to develop.

Al is a good hockey player, a slick forward with nifty hands who skates at a high tempo. He's also the first black hockey player I've ever known. He's a star on the Rangers, scouted often by the cigar-chomping, rye-tippling, notepad-bound brigade that follows junior hockey. Al has great expectations. He could be a high draft pick.

He's invited me out to practise with the Rangers. "You play," he said one day when I'd been telling him about the juvenile team from our area of the city. "Come on out and let Coach have a look."

I'd dodged. I was an okay juvenile player but junior seemed a big step.

"Come on out," Al insisted. "Coach likes to see new talent. There's a couple other guys coming out tonight, you won't be alone."

So I'd thrown my bag over my shoulder, driven to the arena, taken a deep breath, and gone into the Rangers' dressing room. Heart in throat.

The coach is a good guy. He smiles, he gets our names, he throws practice jerseys at us. On the ice there is a routine, skating for five minutes in a group round and round, no pucks, sprinting between blue lines, picking up overall speed so the pace is quite high by the time the five minutes have elapsed. Shooting drills, mostly giving the goaltenders the feel of the puck, no shots near the head, put the first few on the pads or in the catching glove. Routine stuff, but at a brisker pace than I am used to. Leaning on the boards with Al, I'm puffing.

I can't help comparing myself with the others. Al is head and shoulders superior to anyone on the ice. A couple of the other guys are very good: built like fire hydrants, they skate powerfully, make hard shots, and look like they could knock me right through the boards. I'm tall but thin, a growing boy at seventeen; little in the way of bulk.

For drills the coach has us do three-on-twos and then two-on-ones. A defenceman, I'm paired with a stocky, gritty guy who keeps his left arm outstretched as the attack approaches, and holds his stick in his right hand, pointed to three o'clock. My juvenile coach had insisted on the twelve o'clock position. Al and his mates wing up the ice at us. We stop them about half the time, not a great ratio. On the two-on-ones I hold my position and make the shooter shoot, taking the other attacker out of the equation. But I feel slow in my lateral turns, a split-second behind the play.

"You're doin' good," Al says as we lean on the boards, my heart finally slowing.

The last part of the practice is scrimmage. Again I'm with the stocky guy and we do okay, breaking up passing plays in the neutral zone, moving the play up the ice, easing forwards wide so they have to shoot from difficult angles. I get a shot from the point but it's deflected wide of the net. One of the guys rams me into the boards in my end, a kind of initiation. For a few seconds I can't catch my breath.

Afterward the coach sits beside me in the dressing room. "You got size," he says. "Come out to a game. We'll sign a card and see how it goes."

I hardly sleep the night before. During the work day Al keeps his distance, but as we're pulling on our jackets, he gives me a wink. "See ya later."

I sit through the first period, fingers clenching and unclenching my stick. The Rangers are playing the weakest team in the league and lead 2-0 after one period. In the second, the coach taps me on the shoulder and I'm out with Short and Gritty, happy now to have him on my side. We do okay. We stand our ground in front of the net, we clear the zone, head-man the puck, we break up plays crossing our blue line. But when the puck goes into the corners, I feel panicky, I want to get to it and dish it off to someone, I don't want to hang on to it or try to make a stickhandling play. I'm afraid to make a mistake, I'm afraid to *play*.

The coach says nothing directly afterward. Next game Thursday night. I turn up again, play the same way, okay but always panicky when the puck goes into the corners. I'm fearing something bad will happen, rather than trying to make something good happen. This is my Achilles' heel. I'm not good enough. I know it. I've got size and I can skate but something's missing: confidence, skill, poise? I play parts of three games for the Rangers and pack it in. By my own judgement, I don't make the cut.

Al is drafted number one overall by the newly-formed Long Island Ducks of the WHA, a team that never plays a single game. One spring day he says to me, "You shoulda kept coming out, you know. We were just starting to see what you could do out there."

SEC: XX ROW: XX SEAT:XX

HOME GAME 58

JETS VS ISLANDERS

FEBRUARY 14, 2012

SEC: XX
ROW: XX
SEAT: XX

Are we tired of looking at the standings? Of listening to the water-cooler talk about whether or not the Jets should be *buyers* or *sellers* at the trade deadline?

Hockey is only a game played by agile young men, after all; it's popcorn and beer and cheering for the home side and going home with a buzz on just because we witnessed an engaging pro contest amid an animated crowd. Maybe that sounds like a different note than has been sounded earlier. The famous poet once asked, "Do I contradict myself?" And he answered: "I contradict myself." It's the condition of our condition.

On this February night the Jets are at home to the Islanders. And their fans are pumped for the game. Go Jets Go! peals through the MTS Centre. It's Valentine's Day. Below us a girl has a sign saying MY ♥ BELONGS TO THE JETS. Across the way a woman has a pink piece of buffboard: JETS MY VALENTINE.

The game begins with both teams skating hard. The play is open and goes up and down the ice at a quick tempo. Like the Jets, the Islanders are a young squad: fast but not very good in their own end. Both goaltenders are busy. By mid-period the shots favour the Jets 10-5, but there's no score and it looks like another one of the nights when the Jets fire dozens of pucks at the opposition and get few goals. Near the end of the period they put one in. The period ends 1-0, shots 16-10.

In the concourse the consensus is *mediocre period* but everyone is happy the Jets are ahead. A few more goals would help. This has become another mantra with Jets fans: *a few more goals would help.*

In the second period the Islanders begin to come on. They have a two-on-one and then a two-on-none. And then they score before the five-minute mark on a penalty of the "dubious" variety. The Jets sag visibly. The Islanders pour on the pressure for five minutes and the Jets are scrambling in their end. But they survive and the game evens out again. By mid-period, halfway through the game, the Jets have taken twenty-three shots. But have only a single goal. Grumbler behind us says, "They can't put the puck in the net."

On a powerplay, they control the puck and get it to the front of the goal but they can't score one of those garbage goals teams like the Flyers and Bruins thrive on. Their play in front of the opposition net lacks intensity, ferocity; they don't want it badly enough. A few rows over a guy calls out: "What is *wrong* with this team?" At period end the Jets have taken twenty shots but all they have to show for it is one goal.

The game is still very much up for grabs. In the concourses the fans are yakking among themselves and sipping drinks. But an undercurrent of restlessness is there.

The Islanders register a quick goal at the beginning of the third period. Now it's up to the Jets to show what they're made of. Lots of shots, it turns out: some fly wide of the net, others are blocked before they get there, yet others make it. The Islanders goaltender is having a good game. But when the Jets hit the thirty-shot mark and still have only one goal, it's obvious what this team really lacks.

They're awarded a powerplay but flounder around, unable to bring the puck across the Isles blue line. Someone behind calls out, "Skate already, Byfuglien." A second voice chimes in: "Byfuglien, you *bum*." The Jets circle in their own end, try to set up in the opposition zone. The puck is fumbled away and shot down the ice. I hear the first boo directed at the Jets I've heard at the MTS Centre all year. A single, brief burst: *booo*. But it's a harbinger of things to come: the fans are moving from frustrated, and past annoyed to outright enraged; they're about to turn on the home team. A new era is about to begin.

A final powerplay in the dying minutes produces no result and the Isles pot an empty-netter. Final score: 3-1. Shots on goal: 38-25. In a league where the average goals to shots taken is around 8.4%, the Jets have produced this number: 2.6%

As we're leaving the arena, we bump into a guy I played with on the Silver Bullets. He gives me the grim look that fans share after losses like this and shrugs his shoulders. "In the shoot-yourself-in-the-foot department," I say to him, "the Jets are running out of toes."

In the car on the way home, Kristen gives me the same grim look. "They're not going to make the playoffs," she says, "are they?"

"No. They give us hope and then they show us what they really have."

SNAPSHOT: CAP GEEK

I go on to a site called "CapGeek" and find out that the highest-paid Jets are Byfuglien, Hainsey, Ladd, Antropov, all earning over four million for the season. Seven others come in over two million. It's a lot of money, and we all agree that it's far out of line, when nurses and teachers, trained people who make worthwhile contributions to society, fall well below $100,000 in annual salary, while these entertainers earn two and three times as much at the bottom end, and forty times, if you're Byfuglien. It's old fogeyish to carp about such inequity, but there are days when we all must shake our heads over it.

There are those who say, *I don't blame them, if I could command that kind of money, I wouldn't hesitate to grab it* and it's an understandable sentiment that's also socially irresponsible. But that's the world we live in, a world where corporate CEOs earn one hundred million in bonuses per year, a world where movie stars command hundreds of millions per

Hollywood blockbuster, a world of snatch and grab. A world in which we've grown accustomed to think of self first, self second, self third.

There's no point in complaining, because we're the ones paying those salaries, we're the ones filling the arenas and cinemas and sitting on our couches watching the sitcoms and games on HD TV. It's crazy what we pay these people, obscene in some respects, when millions go hungry every day in other parts of the globe. Why do we do it?

Answer 1: from at least Roman times, mankind has needed to witness young men inflicting damage and death on each other in a public arena where cheering and hurling verbal abuse were not only permitted but encouraged. *It's just in the nature of who we are,* is the argument, and while arguments from nature are deeply suspect, often appalling (it's in the nature of things for men to be doctors and women nurses), there's a sufficiently long history of this behaviour for it to warrant a brief passing glance.

Answer 2: we're a sport-mad culture. The NFL, NBA, NHL, and MLB are all licences to print money but only because we're willing to fill those stadiums and pay hundreds of dollars for a ticket to a game. Some among us may also go to the opera, attend a play, eat at a fine restaurant. But a few thousand spectators at the theatre pale by comparison with the 80,000 packed into the new stadium built for the Dallas Cowboys, or the 70,000 at Old Trafford to see Manchester United. Or even the 15,000 to be found at the MTS Centre for a Jets game. These are crazy numbers, numbers that would puzzle someone like Samuel Johnson, author of the first English dictionary, if he were to be brought back from the eighteenth century. For the spectating of sport is a relatively recent occurrence, hardly one hundred years old. So saying we're a sport-mad culture is a bit of a tautology. What finds us at this place in this time of our collective cultural history?

Answer 3: the cultural anthropologist might say that more than half of the fans at sporting contests are men under the age of forty, the age when, historically, men were out in small groups hunting together or part of military brigades, where carnage and killing were part of the cultural bonding that ensured a social group's continuance. And in the absence of that *comitatus*, young men gather now to view sports together and express violence in a socially acceptable way. We have given up blows and blood in favour of insults and cheers. Sport as social safety valve. This theory makes sense, but does not account for the millions of us sitting at home in front of the TV cheerily lustily when the Jets score—or the women among us.

Answer 4: most of us now spend our days at sedentary occupations, working in offices, sitting in front of computer monitors, around boardroom tables, liaising in one way or another, teleconferencing, earning fat-cat salaries and getting fat butts. The social psychologist might see in our flooding to stadiums and arenas the need to release a lot of pent-up emotion that is suppressed in our daily lives. We could find an outlet for those emotions by smacking a tennis ball around a court, or by playing team sports, or by pounding a baseball bat into the grass in the backyard. But overall we're sedentary people: finding time for team sports, putting in the effort arranging squash matches requires a certain energy. And pounding the grass in the backyard might have the neighbours calling up the police. We turn instead to a group activity, ritually donning the gear of our heroes, cheering as one voice for the home team, enacting at the arena a kind of minor madness—but a socially permissible one. It's tribal, but it's okay.

In brief, we're messed up. We need to attend these games for one reason or another; we're happy to pay two dozen young men enormous amounts of money to bash into each other for our pleasure and our social and mental health. We fans, at least; those content to read a novel in front of the fireplace while sipping tea, or sitting on the edges of their seats during the final scenes of *Madame Butterfly* are another matter altogether.

SEC: XX ROW: XX SEAT:XX

AWAY GAME 59
JETS VS WILD
FEBRUARY 16, 2012

SEC: XX
ROW: XX
SEAT: XX

The first of two games in two nights—one away, one at home—the second of which is against the Bruins in Winnipeg, a game the Jets are unlikely to win, given their abysmal record when they play the second of back-to-back contests. But first, the Wild in Minnesota.

This one starts slowly, neither team making mistakes but neither generating much in the way of offence, either. Near the midway mark of the period the shots are an uninspiring 2-2. But then the Wild score on a three-on-one. Yet not much changes. It's ho-hum hockey, not much happening, the Wild checking hard, the Jets shooting but not hitting the goal, lots of stoppages, little flow to the game. Right near the end of the period the Jets tie the score, and the frame ends 1-1, shots 8-6 for the Jets.

The Wild thrive on this kind of hockey—slow, plodding, a game that can be won off a fluke, or a powerplay, or the kind of breakdown on which they scored their goal, a gaffe by Burmistrov at the Jets blue line. He tries so hard, he's such a likeable kid. Maybe when he bulks out, he'll turn into a solid pro.

There are a lot of Jets fans at the Minnesota arena. And signs. One reads WE'RE LOUD AND WE'RE PROUD. Another, held by a young woman is directed at Kane: I WANNA HOLD YOUR STICK. Will the Jets respond to their encouragement?

They come out skating. Unlike the first period, this one opens with the Jets on the fly. They look like a different team—high energy, driving toward the net, intent on making an impression. The Wild try to answer back, but they're not the skaters that the Jets are, and at least in the opening minutes the Jets carry the play. This they score, Kane notching his second of the night only three minutes in. Both teams settle into an up-and-down rhythm, chipping and chasing, looking for an opening that will produce a goal. The midway point of the game passes: 2-1. Now it's a good pro contest, the Jets carrying the play, outshooting the Wild 4-0 just past the midway point of the period. It's the kind of hockey the Jets like: a little open ice to work in, high-tempo action. But it's the Wild who score, on a powerplay, and again against the run of play. The period ends 2-2, the Jets looking better, ahead in shots 19-9.

Though we know it's unrealistic, we're still hoping the Jets can make the playoffs, but it's feeling more and more like Linus of "Peanuts" hoping for the Great Pumpkin.

In the intermission, the hard roll at the bottom of the TV screen shows scores from other games: Tampa Bay in a dogfight with San Jose at 3-3, Buffalo being handily thrashed by Philadelphia, Islanders losing to St. Louis. Just as the play starts at the opening of the third period, the TV shows a young woman with a sign: GIVE US SOME SUGAR, KANE. It's the Wild who come out blazing. They score just past the minute mark. The Jets respond two minutes later: 3-3. But now the Wild are a different team, bottling up the Jets in their own end, forechecking fiercely, firing shot after shot at Mason, in the Winnipeg net. And the Jets are muddled; the shots are piling up, Mason is keeping the Jets in the game; it seems only a matter of time before the Wild score. With five minutes remaining, I say to Kristen. "The Jets will be lucky to get out of this with a point." But they do. And they win in the shootout, Kane scoring again. They've missed this guy.

We're still in the hunt for the final playoff spot. What a wonderful story this is turning out to be. It occurs to me again that a hockey season, linear in nature, progressing inexorably forward from start to finish, the ending unknown, is a terrific narrative, it's a novel with a great cast of characters, compelling plot, distracting sidebars, gripping denouement. What a treat to be part of such a romp; the only thing missing is gypsies!

SEC: XX ROW: XX SEAT:XX

HOME GAME 60

JETS VS BRUINS

FEBRUARY 17, 2012

SEC: XX
ROW: XX
SEAT: XX

The Bruins. Defending Stanley Cup Champions. Atop the Eastern Conference, twelve points ahead of the Jets in the standings. The Bruins: hard-working, tough as boot leather, mean. The Bruins: a few nifty skaters but a team of scrappers and thugs. An unlikable but successful squad. "Do I repeat myself?" the famous poet also asked. "Well, then, I repeat myself."

And the Jets with a wretched record in the second of back-to-back games: 0-9.

But buoyed up by the victory in Minnesota less than twenty-hours ago.

The crowd is excited. An original six team, a contender. Go Jets Go!

As the Bruins come on the ice the booing begins, loud and insistent. And when the game begins the fans are vociferous in ragging first Lucic and then Chara. *Boooo*. There are people who find this barracking of the other team rude, a sign of disrespect for the opponents, unsportsmanlike. They contend it gives the city a bad image, that it makes the city bush-league. Perhaps there's an element of truth to that view; but mostly this crowd response is not a mean attack on players from the other side. It's theatrical and artificial, more about ourselves than the other team. Whatever, it morphs almost immediately into ragging of the Bruins goaltender Tuukka Rask: *Tuu-kaa, Tuu-kaa.*

It doesn't seem to bother the Bruins. They come out playing their hard-hitting game, harassing the Jets defence and crashing the net. These are not players who are going to win the Lady Byng Trophy for sportsmanship. But they execute their style of game successfully, bottling up the Jets and forcing the play in the neutral zone. At the midway point of the first period the shots are 5-1, the Bruins in control. Behind us a guy asserts, "They gotta do a better job of that shit, clearing the zone." And the period ends on the same note: little room for creative play, lots of stoppages, more hits than shots. The score is 0-0 and the shots 13-4.

The Jets did not look good in the first, ragged on the attack and collapsing into their zone too often, leaving the Bruins space to shoot. But very early in the second, Burmistrov scores. The crowd goes wild. This is what we came to see, to live. And the kid takes such pleasure in his goals. Okay, then, when trading deadline comes, keep him. The question is: can the Jets hang on, or will they founder, as they have so often in the past? How long can they hold the lead? About four minutes, it turns out, the Bruins striking back after the Jets miss making it 2-0. "A difference of two goals," I say to Kristen, meaning it might have been 2-0 but instead it's 1-1.

The crowd refuses to be daunted. Go Jets Go rings through the arena; when Chara touches the puck, the booing is louder than earlier. This period is being played at a higher tempo, the shots even, both teams intent on scoring next. As the halfway point of the contest passes, it looks as if whoever scores next will win. For a while, no one does, but then on their eleventh shot of the game, the Jets post a marker and the period ends 2-1, the shots almost even at 9-8.

As we await the start of the final period, the guy behind us says, "Ladd is a bum, he can't do anything." "But Thorburn," his companion says, "I love the guy." It's a common sentiment in the city, where the hard-working underdog is appreciated more than the highly-paid star. And Thorburn is perfect for our city: a potent mixture of fury and talent. "Why is he the captain anyway?" the guy behind says, continuing on the theme of Ladd. There seem to be no such feelings about Kane: one sign reads: KANE IS ABLE.

Before the first minute of the third has passed, the Bruins score. 2-2. Once again the Jets have been caught flat-footed at the start of the third period. Oh-oh, here we go again. Statistics float up: Jets 0-9 in the second of back-to-back games. The Bruins have outscored opponents 76-43 in the final frame and the Jets have been outscored 62-43. They're not going to win this one 2-1. But they do not collapse, even when the Bruins go on the powerplay immediately. They survive, and then they pick up the pace and attack the Bruins goal. Hockey is a game of power but it's also a game of perseverance, taking the brutish hit along the boards and continuing on, battling for position in front of goal. The Jets persevere. And score. What a turn-around! Kill the penalty, then score directly after. Games alter on moments like this, momentum shifting from one side to the other, defeat morphing suddenly into victory. And so it happens. Before two minutes elapse, Little, scorer on the go-ahead goal, puts the Jets ahead 4-2. Is he proving himself worthy of retaining, too?

The Bruins keep coming. If only the Jets can hang onto the two-goal lead, so much safer than one, because if you fritter away a two-goal lead, nerves take over and it's easy to give up another. But now the Jets have taken a page from Boston's book and are running time off the clock in the Bruins end, chasing and dumping, cycling the puck, grinding it out along the boards. This is maybe the best the Jets have played all year: disciplined, poised, answering hit for hit, shot for shot, smart hockey, taking few chances in any of the three zones. Minutes tick by. The Bruins take one penalty, then another. They're a truculent bunch that hates losing and shows it by becoming dirty. Ten minutes remaining turn into three. Fans are shouting *Shoot! Shoot!* as the Jets move the puck around the outside of the Bruins defensive box during the powerplay, but they're playing it cool, whittling time off the clock, taking no chances. The final buzzer goes: 4-2 Jets. Have they played the perfect game this time?

19 February 2012

Team	SP	PTS
New York R	56	79
Boston	56	72
Philadelphia	57	71
Pittsburgh	58	71
New Jersey	57	70
Ottawa	60	68
Florida	57	65
Toronto	59	64
Washington	58	63
Winnipeg	60	62
Tampa Bay	58	58
New York I	58	58
Montreal	59	58
Buffalo	58	55
Carolina	59	55

There's a buzz in the MTS Centre again. The Jets have won two games in succession, the last playoff spot dangles tantalizingly within reach. The team is at the beginning of an eight-game home stand, an eight-game Hope stand. Maybe they can win a handful of games, maybe they can close the gap on the teams ahead of them in the standings, maybe they can….

This is how we go to the games: against the odds, against what reason dictates, against the maths. There is forever the need to dream and to have faith. If the blood pulsing through the fans is tribal, the glue binding them together is religious. And Go Jets Go has the ring of the devotee's chant as much as the clannish bellow.

The match against the Avs is the second of the eight-game home stand. And Colorado is a team on the rocks, foundering and floundering, their record 3-5-2 in the past ten games, after a blazing start to the season. Can the Jets jump on them early?

The game begins at high tempo, both teams skating and throwing bodychecks, intent on scoring that crucial first goal. But despite the pace and intensity, there are few shots on goal, the defences playing well, keeping the attackers along the boards. By mid-period only seven shots have been taken, and the game is oddly unexciting, even though it's being played at high tempo. The Jets are given a four-minute powerplay and look terrible, can manage only three shots on goal. Behind us a guy mutters, "We need more shots." A boy holds up a sign: I Love the Jets More Than My Little Sister. 0-0 after the first.

In the concourse a friend says, "Not much happening out there."

"Yeah. Kinda ho-hum hockey."

"At least they're not behind."

"Maybe," Kristen says, "they'll pick it up in the second. The second used to be the Jets' weakest period, but lately it's their best."

They come out with an edge, carrying the play to the Avs. Only a minute and a bit into the second, the Jets' Kane shovels in a backhand. Almost before the crowd has caught its breath the Jets pot another for the two-goal lead. Now both teams are playing hard, the Jets smelling blood, the Avs trying to close the gap. The play goes back and forth, chances at both ends; at the midway mark of the game the shots are 13-11 for Colorado; just past it they score on a powerplay: 2-1. But it doesn't faze the home side; they respond within a minute: 3-1. The crowd is in a frenzy. For most of the season the Jets have had trouble scoring more than once in a game; against the Bruins they managed four; halfway through this match and they have three. This is reminiscent of the old WHA Jets: never out of it because of their firepower.

Behind us a guy shouts at the Colorado goaltender, "Hey, Varlamov, try taking up golf."

The Avalanche keep coming; the Jets hold them off. By the end of the period the Avs have outshot them 20-8. The coach won't be happy about that. Nor with a late-period penalty at an important juncture of the game.

In the concourse a friend has a goofy statistic: when Evander Kane scores their first goal, the Jets have a record of 7-1. Who keeps track of such stuff?

Can the Jets hang on? For the first time in a long time, it feels like they will; it feels like they're in control of a game, even though they've been outshot. But not outplayed. Despite having to kill off an early powerplay, they score just past the five-minute mark of the third period: 4-1. "When," I ask Kristen, "was the last time the Jets had a three-goal lead?"

"Hmm, that game they gave away in Ottawa?"

There's a flurry of penalties, the Avalanche trying to shift the momentum to their side, the Jets responding with the kind of rambunctious hockey that comes with *swagger*. A boy in the crowd holds up a placard: I HAVE A SIGN. Does he know about the famous Magritte painting? One chorus after another of Go Jets Go! peals around the arena.

I'm watching one player now, wherever the puck is. Sometimes when games hit a certain point where not much is happening, I do this. Tonight it's Randy Jones who's the focus of my attention. I've been tough on him. Since the beginning of the season he's looked out of his depth to me. He's big and he's strong and he falls into the category of not-flashy-but-reliable. But too often he's on the ice when goals are scored; too often he makes mistakes near the net. To me it seems he's anxious when he's out there, concerned more about not making mistakes than making creative plays with the puck—and, as result, making mistakes. I'm probably being too harsh but I'd rather see Mark Flood, who has some offensive flair, or Arturs Kulda, who plays a hard game, physical, tough. For every one good play Jones makes, he makes two bad. The rumor mill has him being traded before the deadline, teams like Chicago looking for depth on their blue line as they approach the playoffs. That would probably be a good thing for the Jets—if they can get a useful forward in return, someone who really can give them "secondary" scoring. Or a second- or third-round draft pick this summer.

With less than five minutes remaining, the Jets score again. Everyone in the crowd, it seems, is on their feet. "When was the last time the Jets had a four-goal lead?" Kristen asks.

"The Fiasco in Philly?"

It ends 5-1. The Jets circle at centre, saluting the fans; the crowd is jubilant.

"They're one point out of the division lead," someone says as we make our way out of the arena. And only one point out of eighth spot, the final playoff position.

Was it me who said the dream was over? Was it me who was prepared to turn my back on the Jets, on the game? Shame on Wayne.

SNAPSHOT: Rink Rats

I'm at Starbucks with my writer pal, Dennis. I've got my caffe latte in one hand and I cross to him at our table carefully, lowering myself into a chair with a grunt.

"That doesn't look good," he says. "What's up?"

"Ah, my SI. I gotta bit of pain in the sacroiliac, sciatic nerve maybe."

"Tefs," he says, "you gotta start acting your age. You gotta give up that game."

"Age," I say, waving away the idea with one hand. "What does that mean?"

I'm thinking of Bruce Chatwin saying that Australian Aboriginals do not divide life into months and years, or even moons, or whatever. Their divisions are *young man*, prior to puberty; *man*, the height of one's powers; and old man, *wise elder*.

The point is I don't feel I'm an old man, and I'm certainly not a young man. I feel, if it comes to that, like I'm about fifty, not sixty-four.

"Act your age," Dennis laughs. "Give up that bloody game."

I laugh too. But I do not say anything.

Dennis shakes his head, sips coffee, and then asks in more serious voice, "Why do you continue to play that crazy game? Why, Tefs, do you do it?"

"Because I love the game," I say, not missing a beat. "I love hockey."

And that's all there is to say.

The dash up the ice, the pancake pass that you float onto a teammate's stick, the poke check that breaks up a two-on-one rush, the slapshot from the top of the circle that bulges the back of the net. The adrenaline rush of the goal, the high-five on the way back to centre ice. We love skating, passing, bumping along the boards, ripping a shot at the net. We love the game, all of us who go out in beer leagues, who show up at 11:00 at night and skate our butts off, and then lie in bed with adrenaline rushing through our veins until 3:00 before we fall asleep, who gather for "shinny" on Friday at noon and Sunday at 8:00 AM, who have a lifetime of nicks on our chins from elbows and lose teeth from deflected shots in front of the goal.

For me, it goes farther than that, farther than the game itself. Writers live solitary lives. We stare at computer screens, typing on keyboards for hours at a time, happy in our studios, checking facts on the Internet, sipping coffee, glancing out the window and dreaming our dreams. There are whole days that pass in my life when I do not interact with a human being for seven or eight hours: Andrew off to college at 8:00, Kristen to work at 9:00. A phone call, maybe, emails, walking down to the post box to mail a letter.

Hockey is not just the game on the ice; for me, it's also the camaraderie of the locker room, the "Here he is!" that greets me as I enter the dressing room, bag over shoulder, the personal put-downs and jibes, the jokes—some off-colour, others dodgy in our increasingly PC world. The ethos of the locker room. I've known it for more than fifty years, as player, as coach. It's a parallel universe for me, and it's a place not only comfortable and safe, but a place where I matter, where I share an hour of vigorous exercise with twenty other guys who love playing a game as much as I do, guys who I might not like that much if I spent a day with them, or who my wife might find sketchy dudes at the least and abhorrent at the worst, if we shared a dinner out, but guys who I think of as *my guys*, guys I share a deep if unspoken bond with, if not a world view.

Hockey is a great game; but for many of us, even at ages when we're riding on the cusp between *man* and *old man,* the locker room feels like our second home, the pong of slightly mouldy equipment, four-sided chatter about the games last night, the grunts of other old farts lacing up skates, we are still—and maybe always will be—rink rats.

Once more into the cauldron of compulsions.

We've checked the standings; we know there's still hope. Slim though it is.

The crowd at the MTS Centre is yet again at octane intensity. Signs on buff board bloom everywhere: ILYA STINKS; PAVELEC RULES. Behind us the guys are restless before the drop of the puck. "Put 'em away early," one says, "that's the key."

That's always the key. But easier said than done.

The Flyers are a good team: big, strong, disciplined. And mean. Like the Bruins, they play thug hockey and they come out hitting the Jets and clogging up the neutral zone, slowing the pace of the game. They're masters at pushing the rules on illegal play to the very edge, obstructing and interfering, but just inside the limits of what is allowable. And the Jets are having a difficult time getting going. As in a number of games recently, they start slowly. By the midway point of the period the shots favour the Flyers by two. But then the Jets score on a powerplay: 1-0, home team ahead. Immediately the crowd begins to rag Ilya Bryzgalov, the Flyers goaltender: *Eel-yaa, Eel-yaa.* More than half the crowd is into it; it's a loud chant. But it seems to inspire the Flyers, who tie the score within three minutes. The period ends 1-1; shots 15-10, Flyers.

"They're being outplayed," I say at the intermission.

"But not outscored."

"Not yet."

In the concourse a guy is wearing a Jets jersey with the number 61. Where the name should be on the back: Leafs Suck. Another guy walking past him shouts, "Nice shirt." Whatever else can be said, the dislike of Toronto's Leafs is widespread.

When we take our seats, Kristen says, "Fifteen shots, that's a lot."

"I got a bad feeling about this game."

At the restart, the Flyers are pushing hard. The Jets take a penalty and the Flyers score: 2-1. The Flyers mount attack after attack. Pavelec is under siege. But then the Flyers take a penalty and the Jets score: 2-2. At the midway point of the contest the shots are 24-14. The Jets are being outplayed; the Flyers are flying.

But it's the Jets who score: 3-2. Tonight they're playing hard in front of the net, fighting for loose pucks, scoring on rebounds. At a break in the action the crowd chants *Eel-ya, Eel-ya*. Most nights two or three thousand are into this hexing of the opponent's goaltender; tonight it's more like 10,000. The roar is deafening. When you look around, you see that most of the fans doing the hex are smiling and laughing: if this is meanness, it's of a nominal sort only, nominal nastiness. There's an aspect of self-parody at work, the fans laughing at themselves as they perform the ritual hex. In fact, there's always an element of theatre to being a fan: the cheering and jeering a chance to release rage and rapture in a way we cannot in our workaday lives where cubicles and desks, computer screens and mobile messages govern our mental landscapes, anesthetizing such raw emotions. But poor Bryzgalov. He's not having a good night; and the ragging is unrelenting. The Flyers, though, are also unrelenting. They tie the score just past the halfway mark of the game: 3-3 at the intermission. Shots 31-20, Flyers.

"Next goal wins," I say.

"Even if it ends up 6-5," Kristen says, laughing.

A guy with a Jets jersey goes by, number 9; on his back HULL-KANE.

In the third, the Flyers continue the onslaught. But they take a penalty.

The Jets move the puck around. "Shoot," someone behind calls out. To the side another voice chimes in, "Get it to the net." The Jets work the puck around the perimeter of the Flyers diamond. "Shooot," the guy behind us shouts again. His voice is loud and intense, an appeal, a command, a plea. But does he actually think Wheeler can hear him? He cannot; his voice is one of thousands in a crowd; it cannot possibly penetrate the distance and the plexiglass barriers between him and the ice surface where the crackling of skates and clacking of sticks blots out everything less booming than the chant of Go Jets Go! So why does he continue to shout?

It occurs to me that in calling out *give it to him, shoot,* we're not actually instructing a given player to make a play but making clear something about ourselves: it's our hopes, anxieties, and fears that are important here. In one respect, we know our calling out is futile, pointless, the players will do what they will do. But we call out anyway, hoping for an act of sympathetic magic—a goal—and half-believing that if we can cajole a goal on the ice, maybe, just maybe we can cajole similar responses in our own lives, where almost everything is out of our control: the careers we choose, the children we raise, the diseases and afflictions that befall us. So our shouting out *Shoot, Buff!* falls into the realm of a plea, then, a plea to the heavens, desperate but deeply felt.

It's no wonder we return home from games exhausted—and exhilarated.

In the event, the Jets score, their third powerplay goal of the game: 4-3. Will it really be the winner? The crowd believes so. As soon as they're done cheering the goal, they start up ragging the goaltender again: *Eel-ya, Eel-ya.* But it's the Flyers who crank up the pressure. By midway of the third the shots are 38-25. The Jets are lucky to be ahead.

The Flyers pressure is relentless. Pavelec makes save after save. The game is turning into a barrage. The shots mount: forty, then forty-five. How long can Pavelec keep the Flyers out? The Jets are given a dubious penalty. *Bull-shit,* the crowd roars, *bull-shit.* Winnipeg fans know the game: they know when the officials screw up. But the Jets survive the penalty and have only a few minutes left to win the game. The seconds tick by; the crowd is on its feet; the fourth victory in a row is within reach. Forty seconds remain, thirty. Then, with ten seconds remaining, the Flyers score: 4-4. The silence in the arena is thick as soup. Ten seconds! This is the worst yet.

In the break awaiting overtime, Kristen points at the shot clock: 45-25.

It's no surprise when the Flyers score at 4:16 of overtime. Fifty-five shots!

The Jets had this one in hand. But the Flyers did not give up. Without Pavelec in the net, the Jets would have lost much earlier. That aside, the Jets should have won. *Shoulda, coulda, maybe, if.* Some nights you're just beat by a better team.

SNAPSHOT: THE REPORTERS

Another Sunday morning, another Toronto Sports Network panel of pundits making guesstimates about the upcoming playoffs. They're talking about the seven Canadian teams. Vancouver is in. Was there ever any doubt? After that, it's pretty much a crapshoot. "Is it overly polite," the host asks, "to say that the Jets—like the Habs—are lucky to be in a playoff possibility?" In Montreal, apparently, there was an ad placed by the Catholic Church saying PRAY FOR 8TH PLACE. There are days when it's a good thing to be living in secular Winnipeg.

Yes, the pundits agree, everyone else is on the bubble. For Winnipeg, as for Montreal, "it's not impossible." *But,* is the implication. *But not very likely.* Which is what I think, too. And that Ottawa is overachieving and may find themselves sliding out of their current seventh position as the heat goes up in the run to April. For that city, making the playoffs will be a bonus. A big one. The team really under pressure, of course, is the Leafs. It's been so long since they won anything—correction, since they *did* anything. And they've spent so much money: $62 million in salaries, as compared to the Jets at $52 million, say, and the Senators at $53 million. The Leafs *should* make the playoffs, one voice says. They should.

And Winnipeg and Ottawa are playing with house money, a voice chimes in.

With house money, I think, which they can't take on the road.

SEC: XX ROW: XX SEAT:XX

HOME GAME 63
JETS VS LIGHTNING
FEBRUARY 23, 2012

SEC: XX
ROW: XX
SEAT: XX

Twenty games to the end of the season. Every one a big one. And the Jets are actually in eighth spot for the first time in a long time, though two of the teams that are contending with them have games in hand: Toronto and Washington. Dare we imagine the home team can do it—eclipse other teams?

Tonight it's the Lightning: Lecavalier, St. Louis, Stamkos—who has forty-two goals.

"We're disappointed to let the point slip away against the Flyers on Tuesday," the coach says going into the game against Tampa Bay, "but I'm not pounding on the players. They know what they have to do. And we've got seven of the eight points on the home stand."

Can the Jets score and get the early lead?

In the opening minute the Lightning pour on the pressure, forcing Pavelec to make a brilliant leg save. Things do not look good. But then the Jets score just past the seven-minute mark. The crowd goes wild. Up on feet cheering, banners waving, the chant of Go Jets Go! When we're seated again, the goombahs start in on hexing the Lightning goaltender: *Gar-ron, Gar-ron.* Tampa Bay has traded away three players in the past few days and it's showing on the ice: they look disorganized: passes go astray, there's confusion in their end about defensive assignments. "The Jets should jump on these guys," I say. And they do. At the fifteen-minute mark the Jets score again, a Philadelphia goal, jam away at the puck in the crease until it crosses the goal line. Ugly. But at period end it's 2-0.

In the concourse Kristen says, "Predict the final score."

"Could be 4-0. But I'm guessing 4-2."

"I'm saying 5-2."

To start the second, the crowd is on their feet cheering Go Jets Go! In the stands a woman has a sign reading: FLEW HERE FROM CALGARY TO SEE REAL HOCKEY. On a powerplay a loud guy several rows behind shouts, "Shoot, Byfuglien." He does—and the puck goes in: 3-0. Only minutes later the Jets have another powerplay. The guy shouts "Shoot,

Byfuglien." He scores: 4-0. It looks as if the ice is tilted toward the Lightning goal. They're having a hard go of it. And the Jets are continuing to press. At the midway mark of the game the shots are 23-10 and the Jets are buzzing. The Lightning coach changes goaltenders. Now it's Dwayne Roloson who's getting the jeers: *Roll-es-son, Roll-es-son.* The Jets seem totally in control. They carry the play, they fire shot after shot at the Lightning goal, they forecheck and hit with force and intensity. At the end of the second period the shots are 26-15, Jets.

The third period is hardly underway when the Jets take a penalty. Tampa Bay is blessed with gifted goal scorers. They buzz the Jets goal. The Jets survive, only to take another penalty, a "phantom" trip in the Lightning end. When it's shown on the scoreboard screen, the fans roar disapproval. The guy behind shouts, "What planet are you on, ref?" The Jets survive. No one is saying anything, but we're all thinking that after his brilliant performance against the Flyers, Pavelec deserves the shutout. Five minutes played and for four of them the Jets have been short-handed. This can't go on. When the Jets are given a third penalty at the ten-minute mark the guy behind roars, "Ref, you retard, learn the game!" The Lightning score: 4-1. The game still seems in hand but now the next goal is crucial. "Put 'em away," a voice calls to our rear. But it's Tampa Bay who are carrying the play now. This is reminiscent of the match against the Flyers, when the opponents took the game away from the Jets in the third period. The Jets are hanging on. They get past the fifteen-minute mark. In the dying minutes Tampa Bay lift their goaltender—and score: 4-2. Then the Jets take a penalty. Now it's six-on-four in the Jets end; shots are fired at the goal, Pavelec is making one save after another, holding off the barrage. The Lightning score with less than ten seconds on the clock: 4-3. What was a cakewalk has turned into a nail-biter. The memory of the loss to the Flyers two nights earlier is fresh—and agonizing.

But this is what we love, isn't it, dancing on the knife-edge? We may say we'd prefer a comfortable but drab 4-0 win, but what really gets our hearts thumping is the drama of the comeback, or hanging on against the odds.

The Jets survive.

Yes, indeed, nothing is easy with these guys.

SNAPSHOT: THRASHERS OR DESERT DOGS?

Well past the halfway mark of the season, it's maybe time to pose a question to Winnipeg fans about their franchise: do they prefer the team they've now got—or the team they might easily have had?

Word has it that in the spring of 2011, David Thomson and Mark Chipman were within minutes of purchasing the Phoenix franchise, of bringing the Coyotes back to Winnipeg, which they left as the old Jets in 1996. The papers had passed through the lawyers' hands, the signatories were in a boardroom in New York, the pens were lined up in a row. And then—at virtually the last possible minute—the word came from Glendale: the city had come up with the $25 million needed to keep the team in Arizona. So it was that close. Jets 2.0 might well have been the re-"transitioned" Coyotes/Jets.

Instead, months later, Winnipeg got the flailing Thrashers. Now Jets 2.0.

We love them, it need hardly be said. Right now we wouldn't trade these guys for anyone. They've captured our hearts; we've walked down the aisle with them. But would we equally—or more so—have loved the transplanted Coyotes?

There are many reasons to think yes. Start with the fact that they're a good team. All through the 2011-2012 season they've been at or above the .500 mark, either well inside the playoff line or just above it. Where the Jets stand at sixty-five points, three above the break-even mark, the Coyotes are at sixty-nine, nine above it. Where the Jets precariously occupy ninth spot in their conference, waiting for three teams below them to catch up a number of games played and knock them backwards, the Coyotes sit in seventh in the more competitive Western Conference. Considering only their playoff prospects, the Coyotes are the more desirable team.

And they're a strong team. They play hard, they're disciplined, they achieve good results. Their goal differential is +6, whereas the Jets' is −18. Overall they are also a young team. They have a number of very fine players, players who measure up to the Jets' stronger guys: Whitney and Vrbata in the forward positions, comparable to Kane and Wheeler; Yandle and Ekman-Larsson, equal to Bogosian and Byfuglien on defence.

Their goaltenders boast the better goals-against average: 2.52 to the Jets' 2.82.

They've got Shane Doan, a big fan favourite back in 1996, who, though near the end of his career, would also be a fan favourite now: a steady, hard-working, straight-up prairie boy, equivalent to Andrew Ladd.

When looked at in the cold light of day, there's not much to choose between the two squads. Had the Coyotes been moved here, it's fair to wager, Winnipeg fans would have instantly embraced them and made them *ours*.

What about matters financial, important to things such as ticket prices and long-term viability? The Jets have considerable cap room, an important fact for teams that are building for the future: about $12 million. The Coyotes have $9 million. Again, not much to choose between. Where the Coyotes are at a real disadvantage is their enormous debt. The terms under which Thomson bought the Thrashers are not easy to ascertain; but the Phoenix franchise would have cost considerably more—whoever takes them on (Quebec City?) will have a huge debt load to deal with, in addition to the market price of the franchise per se. In that respect, Thomson was wise not to saddle himself with the Coyotes.

That's the squads; that's the numbers.

Emotionally, we're committed to the team we have. Go Jets! We've turned a corner in Winnipeg and we're looking down the road, excited about the team today, exhilarated by the prospects in the future. The Thrashers are now the Jets. Forget about the Fiasco in Phoenix. What's done is done, water under the bridge, all that. But just for a whimsical moment it might be kind of fun for Jets fans to muse about what also might have been.

As March approaches, team managers become active in the dealing of players, looking for the February Fix. Those no longer harbouring play-off hopes trade players for prospects and draft picks, building for the future; those poised on the cusp do the opposite: giving up prospects and draft picks to acquire key players. As do teams in solid playoff positions, who look for the proven scorer or solid defenceman or reliable goalie who might take them all the way through on the run to the Cup.

It's a difficult time for players. When the phone rings at home it might be the call from their agent telling them to pack their bags. So they might be jittery for this afternoon game with the trading deadline approaching, a game at the MTS Centre between the Blues and the Jets: piled onto the pressures of the playoff scramble are personal anxieties about players' futures in the pro ranks.

The game starts slowly: disciplined checking from the Blues; restrained attacks. Whatever jitters guys might be feeling seem to have been worked off in the pre-game skate. Maybe most of the players on these two squads are confident their futures are secure.

However that may be, now more than ever the mantra is: *score that first goal.*

Not much happens in the opening stretch: there are no shots at the five-minute mark and the checking is tight. "Great back-checking," a guy to the side says when young Burmistrov skates hard to break up a Blues attack. Yes, keep the youngster; he has promise. Then the Blues score on a gaffe near the Jets goal near the midway mark. On their second shot of the game: 1-0. For a moment the crowd is deflated. In the last few games we've become used to seeing the Jets score first. So there's silence in the arena when the Blues light the red lamp a second time in the last minute of the period: 2-0.

In the intermission I say, "This has 4-2 written all over it."

"Or 5-2," Kristen says.

The second period begins as a mirror of the first: sleepy hockey. This suits the Blues, who are intent on keeping the Winnipeg crowd silent. Fierce checking, attacks forced to the outside, template of the sound road game. But as the period progresses, the Jets pick up the tempo. Now their shots are dangerous, from in close, where the sixteen they managed in the opening period were mostly routine saves for the goaltender. They're making more space for their attacks and winning the battles for pucks in the corners. In the eighth minute they score on their twentieth shot: 2-1.

The crowd goes wild. For almost half the game they've been sitting on their emotional hands; finally they have a chance to cheer. Go Jets Go!

Suddenly on the landing below us is "Dancin' Gabe." Usually he's over to our left, doing his thing in the sections above and behind the penalty boxes. Dancin' Gabe suffers from what his mother believes is autism; he's beloved by Winnipeg fans. Years ago, back in the old NHL days at least, someone (his brother?) brought Gabe to a Jets game. Being who he was, he jumped up when the organ music was playing in a break in the action and began dancing in the aisles. The fans loved him; they cheered. So at every break in the action, Gabe got up to dance, clapping in his innocent way, face alight with joy at the music and the fans' response to him. This went on. Soon Gabe was at every game, wearing a Jets jersey, dancing in the aisles. He was a boy then, perhaps a young man. In a few years, we heard that the Jets had given Gabe a season ticket. He was the unofficial cheerleader, and he remains so now, decades later when he's a middle-aged man, maybe, greying at the temples, not dancing with the same verve, but in attendance at every home game, heavier but face still alight. It's difficult to describe exactly what he means to Winnipeg fans: his innocent joy touches that part of us which is childlike still, reminding us the game is just a game (Gabe is on his feet dancing and clapping whether the score is 7-1 for the Jets or against them); he reminds us that joy is what we seek at the games. He's the unofficial Jets mascot and our emotional alter ego. As the poet once poignantly put it: the child is father to the man.

He makes it easy for fans to jump to their feet: Go Jets Go! As do the Jets when they tally a second goal at the fifteen-minute mark: 2-2. This is a good sign, a comeback from being behind by two goals. But another sign is not so good: the Jets have taken thirty-three shots to score their two goals; St. Louis has taken only ten. "Oh, oh," I say to Kristen, "another Islanders game—thirty-five shots and one goal."

In the third period the Blues put their effort into shutdown hockey: dump and chase, clogging the neutral zone, disciplined work along the boards. The Jets keep up the pace but the Blues are wearing them down. As each minute ticks by it looks less likely that either team will score, though the Jets pound shots at the Blues goal. "It's gonna take forty to score three goals," I say. But regulation time ends at 2-2, even though the Jets have taken forty-one shots.

Overtime solves nothing. The Blues win the shootout.

It wasn't 5-2 and it wasn't 4-2. But the game could have been won. Will the loss of the second point that goes with a win come back to haunt the Jets in April? At the moment they're tied with Washington for the final playoff spot, though they have played two more games than the Caps.

SEC: XX ROW: XX SEAT:XX

HOME GAME 65

JETS VS OILERS

FEBRUARY 27, 2012

SEC: XX
ROW: XX
SEAT: XX

On trade deadline day the Jets send Oduya to Chicago but otherwise stand pat. That's okay, the coach is still learning about his team; they're young, there's a lot to build on, there's a lot of promise right down the roster. And a couple of guys in the minors could develop into strong players. Most importantly, management did not feel pressure to make a move at the deadline—to do *something, anything*—and as a result give away important assets, like Stuart, Mason, Fehr. They're in the scrap for the final playoff spot and that's where their attention should be focused.

On this frigid February night, it's on beating the Oilers, another young squad.

Can they snatch the first goal?

Right from the drop of the puck the Jets seem off their game. Defenders are out of position, passes go astray, their legs seem leaden. The Oilers get first one odd-man rush, then two, the puck dribbling through the Jets crease, their defencemen flailing. This is as bad as they've looked in some time, maybe since the fiasco against the Penguins, when they lost 8-5 and the coach said, when asked what went wrong, "Take your pick: turning pucks over, Ds up the ice, getting caught." Before the game started he voiced his worry about getting into "pond hockey" with the Oilers, a wide-open style that suits Edmonton's young guns but not the Jets. What he's getting is worse: a team looking dazed and rattled, one step behind the young, speedy Oilers.

The first period ends 0-0, the Jets lucky to escape without being behind.

The second period unfolds in a similar way. The Jets seem rattled, just plain out of it. There's no explaining how a squad that looked so on top of things against St. Louis seems, only two days later, to be thrashing about. Pooped. But then again, this is the eighth game they've played right at the edge: tussling for every puck, never ahead by enough to relax, aware that a gaffe that leads to a goal could mean the end of their playoff aspirations. They've been put through the wringer for at least fourteen days and it's starting to show: they're gripping their sticks tightly and at the same time are as limp as rags.

Despite that, they rally towards the middle of the second period and tally with about five minutes remaining before the intermission. Aroused, the Oilers strike back within minutes, but the Jets muster a second goal immediately after and the period ends 2-1. In the concourse we agree with friends that the Jets are lucky to be ahead.

In the opening minute of the third, the Jets take a phantom penalty and within seconds the game is tied, 2-2. Oh, oh. It seemed they might hang on and win this one despite being outplayed. But the Oilers smell blood. Before two minutes elapse, they count a third goal. "This has 5-2 written all over it," I say. The Jets look emotionally drained and physically drained, a team with no energy. There's nothing in the tank. Before the midway mark of the period Edmonton score again: 4-2, making it three goals in less than ten minutes. It's Pittsburgh all over: a weary ship about to sink in choppy waters. When the Jets get a powerplay opportunity, they pass and pass around the perimeter: "Shooot," the guy behind screams; and then begins a new chant in the MTS Centre: "Shoot the puck! Shoot the puck!"

It's the Oilers who score: 5-2, before the Jets close the game out with a late marker, making it 5-3.

"You can't win every game," Kristen says philosophically.

"True. But they're at the point of the season where they can't afford to lose at home to a team like Edmonton."

"They can still be in it if they beat Florida on Thursday."

"True."

"So we can't give up hope."

"No," I agree reluctantly, but the little boy in me is muttering something else.

SNAPSHOT: Medium and Message

I'm watching the Oilers / Jets game on TV. I do this sometimes, go over games that I've attended, looking at the recorded version a day later to review key moments and confirm impressions. What I notice on this occasion—and have noted on others—is that the game comes across differently: the recorded version seems more lively—faster, more spirited. Hits are dished out, players are skating hard, the action is dynamic. Yet at the arena the action seemed slow, not at all compelling. The game was rather ho-hum. What accounts for the disparity?

The play-by-play commentary, for one. In the arena there is no guiding voice accompanying the play, giving it focus and direction. On TV, the commentator's voice is compelling; he's excited about the flow of play, his tone rises and falls dramatically with rushes up the ice and shots on goal. Part of this is salesmanship—commentators are trying to make the game exciting, it's part of their job to enhance the spectacle of the game; hype, call it. And they themselves are genuinely enthusiastic about the action. So they lend the game "value added," an extra dimension of urgency.

Second, the TV itself contributes to this urgency. The arena is a spacious venue with cavernous width and depth where sound dissipates, where things other than the action on the ice are occurring—other fans coming and going with food and drink, commercial announcements, hawkers in the aisles selling popcorn. All of this can dilute the game's gusto. The TV's small screen compresses the action and distills its intensity, just because it narrows the field of view, eliminating the distractions of the *in situ* game and replacing them with one animated voice in a condensed field. Compression equals intensity.

Third, there's the colour guy on the TV broadcast. When the commentator's voice stops, the colour guy fills in, changing the tone, modulation, pitch, and lending the broadcast a secondary rhythm, one that steps up the feeling of drama, the way multiple voices in a theatre production do. Not so long ago the colour guy sat in the booth with the play-by-play commentator. Several years ago he moved down to ice level, occupying a position between the two players' benches, a locale from which the sounds of the game are transmitted: the clacking of sticks, thumping of boards, and the like. All of this raises the dramatic intensity of the TV presentation. As do the "in-game" interviews with players that have become part of the TV broadcasts only recently. These too are done by the colour guy, from his locale at ice level where it's all happening, where everything is excitingly in process.

Great games in the arena are great games—the raucous crowd, the blatting of horns, all that hoopla; and they give you the feeling that you're part of something notable and significant. There is nothing like it. But less-than-great games can feel ho-hum in the arena. Watching on TV—whether at home or in a noisy bar with other fans—you may not get the same feeling of being part of a vital communal moment, as you do in the mix at the arena; but the TV version of a game has its own dramatic intensity, transforming pedestrian encounters into compelling contests.

All the games are important now but this one is crucial: facing off against an important conference rival, the leaders of the division. If ever the Jets need to gain two points, it's on this night, at home with the final playoff spot in the mix. They're in ninth place, two back of the Capitals, who have played two fewer games.

For this contest Florida is without their big scorer, Kris Versteeg, who's been a human Exocet missile against the Jets: six goals and two assists in his last three games versus Winnipeg. Jets fans are happy he's out of the lineup; and equally pleased to see the return of Zach Bogosian, who has been missed the past half-dozen contests. He brings to the roster weight, size, strength, poise, and a laser shot from the point.

In the opening minutes of play he looks game-rusty, fumbling a puck on the Panthers blue line and taking too long to make a pass in his own end, both resulting in turnovers that lead to shots on the Jets goal. It's the Jets who score first, though, off a turnover in the Florida zone near the five-minute mark. The fans have been shouting Go Jets Go! from before the opening faceoff, and the rooting grows louder. When the Jets notch a second two minutes later, the crowd is on its feet.

The play settles, and for the remainder of the period the teams trade scoring chances. There's no choosing between them; and the Jets are lucky Versteeg is not in the lineup. The first period ends 2-0.

At the start of the second, Florida plays much harder, looking to break through and swing the momentum in their favour. But Pavelec is steady and when the midway point of the game passes, the shots are 18-17. The Panthers are outplaying the Jets, winning battles below the goal lines, creating better chances. It seems only a matter of time before they score. But they don't, and the period ends 2-0, the Jets lucky to be ahead.

"Well," Kristen says in the intermission, "what do you think?"

"This has 3-2 written all over it. But I wouldn't hazard a guess for who."

It's clear that Florida will make a big push at the start of the period; everyone is aware of the Jets' poor record in the third. The fans hold their collective breath. The Jets survive the initial onslaught and then score to make it 3-0 at the two-minute mark. The fans are jubilant. No collapse. A three-goal lead. Not even the Jets give away three-goal leads very often. When they tally again before the five-minute mark, the crowd is on its feet. In staid Canada we don't go in for the kind of embracing that occurs on the terraces in European football matches, hugging and kissing, but there's genuine passion in the crowd on this night. And of course, the goombahs start up on the goaltender; the roar of *Joes-say, Joes-say* is deafening. Poor Jose Theodore. The goals haven't really been his fault. But the goombahs have no sentiment or sympathy; they're ruthless. His coach replaces Theodore. The crowd goes ballistic.

"Well," Kristen says when we're seated again, "it's not going to be 3-2."

The Jets keep coming. They score to make it 5-0, and then before the midway point of the period 6-0, Kane notching his twenty-sixth, an impressive achievement. When the crowd gets on its feet, the cheering is sustained for several minutes at an ear-splitting level. I've never heard anything quite so loud. At ice level it must be thrilling and daunting, both at the same time. What did it feel like to be in the Nürnberg rallies in the 1940s?

There are some who say they don't enjoy high-scoring games, lop-sided affairs. I'm not in that camp. Along with the Jets' delirious fans, I've enjoyed every goal. It has been so rare that they've scored five goals in a game, and six without answer ranks is amazing. So, yes, we're delirious, exhausting our lungs with cheering, hands aburn from clapping. A blowout is a rare thing, and this one against a top division rival is beyond satisfying. Ecstatic. It will be difficult to forget many of these goals.

Sport crystallizes moments for us so successfully we hardly take note of them occurring. Consider these three only: Selanne's record-setting goal celebration (much more memorable than the goal itself); Paul Coffey's decisive defensive play that led to Canada winning the 1984 Canada Cup; Bobby Orr's aerial goal in the 1970 Stanley Cup final. These moments not only galvanize a spot of time, they create triggers we build myth around, solidifying our collective belief in the worthiness of sport. This may not be the best game the Jets will ever play, but it's bound to enter our private, psychic "halls of fame."

The game ends 7-0. Not only have the Jets scored an armful of goals, they've also recorded a shutout. There are more kinds of "perfect" games than one, it turns out. And their playoff hopes once again have been revived. Are the Fates just toying with us?

SNAPSHOT: It's a Beautiful Game

I have a friend who moved to Winnipeg from the United States. All his life he had been a basketball fan. But because he was athletic, he gave skating a try. Then hockey. He became good at both. One day we were lacing up before shinny and he said to me, "I used to think basketball was the best team game. But it doesn't hold a candle to hockey. It's beautiful."

A beautiful game, I thought, why yes it is.

The sheer speed is the most immediately evident thing. A pro player can breeze from one end of the rink to the other in less than ten seconds.

It can be breathtaking to see a man grab a puck behind his own net, wheel below the faceoff dot and dash the entire length of the ice in less time than it takes to cough. Only the hundred-metre dash compares.

But raw speed does not begin to evoke the elegance of stickhandling, the way a skilled player takes possession of the puck, maneuvers it slickly from forehand to backhand, seems to offer the disc up to his right and then switch it to his left in one seamless second of time, one graceful motion that can leave a defender bedazzled and spectators awestricken. How did he do that? And moving at such pace!

And body control. The way a dextrous skater speeds at an opponent, then at the last split-second shifts to one side, gliding past, dangling the puck off one hand before moving it in one expert motion first toward the goaltender and then, with the slightest tilt of the stick away—and up into the netting of the goal. All without for one second losing balance or control of the puck.

Consider these refinements:

The saucer pass flicked from the faceoff dot to the front of the goal, where a teammate tips the puck behind the goaltender; the 180-degree pirouette just inside the opponents' line that frees the attacker from the checker for the nanosecond it takes to lay a pass across ice to an oncoming teammate; the wrist shot from the top of the faceoff circle that finds its way over the goaltender's shoulder and under the crossbar for a goal; the keeper's lightning glove going out to snatch away a goal.

Hockey can be magic: the timing in the basic deke; the elegance of the toe-drag executed at speed; the orchestration of passes involving two driving attackers and a trailing teammate; the first-post pass; the unanticipated snapshot; the save when the keeper is on his back and seemingly out of it. Each can be a wonder, each can be worth the price of admission on a given night. As thrilling, as unique as the great tenor hitting the climactic note in "Nessun dorma." It takes away your breath; you're left standing agape. Such skill at such speed. Surely this is what is meant by the human divine.

The last game of the eight-game Hope stand at MTS Centre that has seen the Jets garner ten of the possible fourteen points. They have the third-best home record in the NHL. And they'll need it as the season comes down to the finish line and the final playoff spot is up for grabs, a spot the Buffalo Sabres have their eye on, too.

Before the action starts the colour guy from NBC, who's positioned at ice level between the two benches, says, "It's so loud down here you can't think." The play begins at a furious pace, testifying to the crucial nature of the contest. Both teams are skating fast and checking hard below the goal lines, producing chances—but not great chances. The chant of the fans—Go Jets Go!—is almost continuous. And the home team is forcing the play, using their speed. But by the midway mark of the period there's no score, and the game settles into a rhythm, rush and counterattack, both teams having opportunities to score but neither cashing in. Then the Jets break through with about five minutes remaining in the frame: 1-0.

"Whoa," I say to Kristen in the break. "Barn-burner. This could go either way."

"A two-goal cushion would be nice."

The play in the second period is even, fast, rugged. It's an exciting game, it's what we yearned for all those years after the Jets left Winnipeg for Phoenix: top-level hockey, the highest degree of excitement, thrills and spills, the contest on the line, blood pumping with hope, heart in throat from apprehension. By game-end we'll be ecstatic or despairing, and where we'll end up hangs in the balance while forty-odd young men dash up and down the ice. In the final minute of the period Buffalo score: 1-1.

"Arghh," Kristen says. "I have a bad feeling."

"The two-goal cushion would have been nice."

"You think they'll blow it?"

"No. It looks like 3-1 to me. But a nail-biter."

In the third the colour guy says, "This game is being played at a breathless pace." Almost literally, it seems; he's gasping from his commentating position in an effort to make himself heard above the crowd noise. The puck goes up and down the ice; a turnover leads to a Buffalo three-on-two attack, but the shot is missed and the Jets turn the rebound into a breakaway by Wheeler, who scores a dazzling marker. Goal! The crowd goes ballistic. It's 2-1 Jets. The goombahs immediately start in on the Sabres goaltender: *Mill-ler, Mill-ler.* The colour guy says, "This reminds me of old Chicago Stadium—unbelievable noise."

Now the Sabres play with desperation: forcing the neutral zone, forechecking like their hair's on fire. But it's a risky tactic and just past the midway mark the Jets score again: 3-1. It looks like a victory. And for the first time, for me, it feels as if the Jets really are in a battle for a playoff position. Up to now, as the team has slowly ascended the standings from tenth to ninth to eighth, I've been thinking, *Yes, but,* and *the other teams have games in hand.* I've been holding back. We've been let down so many times that we're used to holding back that final measure of belief, the residue of conviction that transforms spectator to fan. The team's startling resilience over the past games has me thinking now that this season is epic, rather than tragicomic. Suddenly I'm ready to shout with the delirious mob at the arena: We can do it!

We're in eighth place, one up on the Caps.

SEC: XX ROW: XX SEAT:XX

AWAY GAME 68
JETS VS
CANUCKS
MARCH 08, 2012

SEC: XX
ROW: XX
SEAT: XX

Vancouver is not the best place for the first game on the road after the eight-game Hope stand. Among the league's elite teams, the Canucks are strong, skilful, and speedy. In many ways these two teams are mirror images: they skate fast, move the puck quickly, and check hard. They play hockey at the highest level, entertaining sport, without the thug factor.

So it's no surprise this game begins at a high tempo. The Canucks carry the play, but the puck goes up and down. When the Jets take a penalty, the Canucks manage eight shots on goal, half a game's worth for certain teams on some nights. The Jets hang on, Pavelec once again solid between the goalposts. The period ends 0-0 but the shots favour the Canucks 20-11.

"Yikes," I say, "this does not look good."

Andrew says, "Take out the eight shots on the powerplay, and the differential is not that gruesome: 12-11."

I'm not the only one doing the calculus of win and lose.

On a penalty kill at the start of the second Vancouver score shorthanded when a Jets' clearing pass is inadvertently tipped by a referee's skate onto the stick of a Canucks checker. Stupid and heartbreaking at once. But what can you do?

The Jets tie the score fifteen minutes later, following furious action in both ends, the game being played with speed and skill. The Canucks really are a pleasure to watch: they weave through the neutral zone, change speeds as they enter the Jets end of the ice, cycle with flair and check vigorously. The Jets answer their mastery with their own skill and pace. At the end of the second, the score is 1-1, the shots in the period 12-9. It's a real contest. The next goal could easily win it.

"Great hockey," I say. Earlier in the season the Jets had difficulty playing at an elevated level for a full sixty minutes. They seem to have turned the corner on that shortcoming. They don't collapse, they're not a soft touch. It's a shame, really, that games like this cannot be appreciated just for themselves alone, without their meaning to the standings and the playoff picture overshadowing the beauty and skill being demonstrated on the ice. How did we get to this point?

It's the Jets who get the go-ahead goal. Hearts across Winnipeg flutter. Can they hang on?

They cannot. Less than three minutes later the Canucks tie the score. The play goes up and down: one team has a good chance; the counterattack produces an equal opportunity at the opposite end. A great save at the Canucks goal is followed by a shot off the crossbar of the Jets net. The midway mark of the period passes; the play is even, the shots too. If only, I'm thinking, the Jets can hang on until the buzzer at the end of sixty minutes; we'll take the single point. But Vancouver scores with about five minutes remaining. Though the Jets lift their goaltender and press the Canucks goal in the dying seconds, the result is 3-2. With so much at stake, a painful loss. But a good game: highly entertaining, thrilling the way professional sport should be. If only the result could have gone the other way.

Now, Jets fans feel, winning in Calgary on Friday has become vital.

SEC: XX ROW: XX SEAT:XX

AWAY GAME 69
JETS VS FLAMES
MARCH 09, 2012

SEC: XX
ROW: XX
SEAT: XX

Some games in a season are critical. Though in November the colour guy on TSN said the Jets were then playing in a "must win" contest, he was exaggerating for TV drama. But this game truly does fall into that category. Win and the Jets still have a shot at the playoffs; lose and they're out of it. Of course, the argument can be made that even if they lose there's still a mathematical chance, but that's talk only, hype to keep fans interested. With fifteen games remaining, tonight it's do or die.

So when the Jets fall behind to Calgary 2-0 early in the first period, a kind of despondency settles over Jets fans. Yes, it's early in the game; yes, teams can come back from two-goal deficits. But not the Jets. And not when they're on the road playing the second of back-to-back games. So when the score goes to 3-0, despair looms; there's not much to say, other than: it's been a good run. The Jets have made it interesting. Almost at mid-March, they've sustained their fans' interest through most of a full season. They've shown spirit and they've shown grit. Their resilience has been admirable. The coaches have got the very best out of a marginal team. All credit to them, then, but they've fallen short. They're in Next Year Country; and we are too.

They're not the first team to go there. Carolina fans packed it in emotionally a month or so ago. Columbus has never been in it. Montreal, Edmonton. Even the Leafs had to give up the ghost last week. It's in the nature of things in big-league sport for teams to be eliminated somewhere along the way in every season. The Blue Jays almost never make it past July before they're out of it. The Raptors are never in it.

The Jets show a flicker of life—before the end of the first period, closing the count to 3-2. Oh, no. The Fates are toying with us, sending us once again into the realm of *if only*. The teams go to dressing rooms for the intermission. Diehard fans are still feeling: if only they can get the next one. Folly, probably, but there it is: we're in the kingdom of those things you claim you'll never do again and then find yourself back doing once more, a kind of compulsion to repeat—hate what it's doing to you but cannot stop doing it. We're so needy, so driven, so weak.

And in this game? Calgary score near the end of the second period: 4-2. Only a truly heroic effort can salvage the season.

The hope the Fates dangled before us, it turns out, is as brief a flicker as that of the fish on the end of your line giving one last desperate kick before being hauled into the boat, finished.

"Arrgghh," I say.

Andrew grunts. "They go soft."

"They were in that one, they let it get away."

"Yep. Happens too often."

"*Expliquez-moi.*"

"No can do, Chief."

In the third the Flames close down the game, playing chip and chase, bottling up the neutral zone, minimizing the Jets' chances. Just past the midway point they score again: 5-2. Game over; season over.

In a way it's a relief. For the past two months at least it's been a roller-coaster ride of emotions: one day believing the Jets are out of it; followed by a home stand that revives belief. Up and down. We fans have become dishrags. It's exhausting, and having all that come to an end is a release. Thank god that's over. Our normal lives, normal concerns can take their place in our lives again. We can catch a breath and ask, What's the opera these days? What about the new exhibit at the art gallery? Maybe it's time to call the couple we've been putting off going out to dinner with because we've had to catch the Jets on TV. The burden of being a fan *is* a burden.

In a week or so we can make our final assessments of the season. There are, when you step back from the vortex of the hockey season sucking you down, more important things than living and dying every day with a pro hockey team. It's just a game, after all. *Basta*, the Italians say: enough.

SNAPSHOT: JUST A GAME 2

There's no point in saying, *It's just a game,* because it's not just a game to the players—and it's not just a game to fans, it's bigger than a game, something primal.

Our hearts are in this, in some respects more so than the players themselves, the coaches, the management. Those of us waving banners and screaming our heads off in the stands care as you care only when you're a child.

During a cycling trip in Italy years ago we stopped for lunch at a pizzeria one afternoon. We ordered and were soon joined at a nearby table by a family of four. The youngest was a boy of perhaps five. They ordered too. Our pizza came and soon so did the plates of three members of the family. For some reason, that of the little boy did not arrive. "My pizza," he wailed, "where is my pizza, mama?" She tried to console him. But, child that he was, he was inconsolable. Minutes ticked by, the family looked around every time the waitress crossed the room but still the boy's pizza did not come. "My pizza," the boy wailed, "where is my pizza, mama?" The father stood up and went to check with the kitchen. "My pizza, mama!" We looked at each other. You could feel his misery; it was palpable; we wanted to offer him some of ours. His anguish was too much.

There was no point in saying *It's just a little delay,* there was no point in using reason. This was not a matter of rational argument but of emotional despair. The little boy was suffering at a depth beyond the reach of reason and good sense.

That little boy lingers in all of us. Perhaps especially in fans.

You can say it's just a game, you can point out to me that tomorrow's another day—I mouth the words myself and half-believe them: "it's just a game played by young men," "there are more important things in life than the Jets"—but there's a little boy inside feeling something right in the pit of his gut, a thing more raw, a little boy who's ecstatic at each win and inconsolable at each loss.

Don't tell me you're any different.

Having lost those two critical road games, can the Jets still make the playoffs? They're not mathematically out of it, whatever that means. If Washington, the team directly above them in the standings, loses five out of six, if the Jets win five out of six. If, maybe. The algebra of *if only* is endless—and tantalizing. Less likely things have happened in sport, but the painful fact is the Jets are no longer in control of their own destiny. With thirteen games remaining, they now need the help of other teams to beat the teams they're contending with, a dodgy proposition at best.

They need some kind of intervention.

"Pray for 8th Place." In a time before we started keeping time we bowed down to idols, our minds riveted by them. But then they lost their power over us—happily, I think. The images that go with them—the virgin, the cross—rivet our minds now little more than the blue, red, and white jerseys of the Jets, which, maybe, are the new iconography, at least on game nights when we brandish posters, wave banners, chant Go Jets Go!

It's not that the fans' banners are as powerful as the images and idols of old, not by a long shot. But we've given up on the idols; we create in their place a new iconography, we fans at least, that constitutes its own closed system—as we wave and chant rhythmically, we celebrate ourselves, and our cry of Go Jets Go! is not *Sieg Heil*, it does not seek to change others or enslave them to our belief, it's self-referential only, look at us, look at how much we care (but only in a playful sort of way), and when we return home from the arena to families and jobs, we're happy citizens of meaningless Fanland.

But while we're at the arena, it's cheer cheer cheer.

The players believe they can do it. Or at least the players say they can do it. Whether or not this position is for public consumption, while behind closed doors the players and coaches concede the playoffs have slipped away from them this season, is impossible to determine. Probably they do believe it: they're young athletes, not graduates of MIT who comprehend statistical probabilities and permutations and combinations. They have to believe it. Otherwise, why play? Why not "mail in" the remaining games, as the saying has it?

Certainly the fans are in belief mode. Almost continuously from the team's appearance on the ice, Go Jets Go! rings through the arena. Well, this contest against Dallas may be the last hurrah. After tonight, aspirations for the playoffs may be pipe dreams only.

The Jets start fast. *Push, push, push* is their mantra. Their coach has said, "I'm hoping we can play with some zip and excitement tonight; I hope we have some jump to our game." And they know the Stars are playing the second of back-to-back games. The Jets are intent, registering a goal early. The crowd rises as one. The game settles into a familiar pattern: fast rushes up the ice, shots from the outside, fierce forechecking. No penalties. It's exhilarating stuff: great entertainment for "neutrals." There's a lot on the line and both teams are giving it their all.

The Jets have started fast before and then run into a wall in the second period, when their opponents recover from the initial onslaught. This game seems different; at the intermission it seems the Jets are in control—though a quick goal (or two) can easily change that. So there's a sigh of relief when they score early again: 2-0. Loud cheers from the crowd; jubilation at ice level. *We can do it!* Before very little time elapses the Jets score again. 3-0. And then before the midway point of the game, yet another goal: 4-0. No one could have anticipated this. Dallas has been experiencing a great run: no losses in the past twelve games. But the Jets are relentless; and they have luck with them: the Stars hit the goalpost; the Jets go down the ice and score. Andrew Ladd: his season total is now twenty-four, wow; how did that happen? At the end of the second period the score is 5-1.

Some wag once quipped: the first place you lose out in sporting competitions is in your head; only after do you lose out on the ice. And these boys seem not to have given up, not to have lost in their heads.

In the third the Jets show surprising composure. Earlier in the season they had a habit of squandering leads in final periods, letting games slip away by abandoning defence and succumbing to fire-wagon hockey. In this game they chip and chase, they forecheck, they cycle the puck in the Stars end, stay out of penalty box. Though the Stars score late in the period, the result is never in doubt: 5-2. As the players circle at centre ice, saluting the fans, the cheering crescendoes into a roar.

Once again, the home team has given us cause to believe. The roller-coaster ride is not yet over. Our hopes buoyed, we check the standings. Back in tenth spot, five points out of the final playoff position with 12 games. But still a chance they could make the playoffs: with continued good play, with luck, with help from other teams in knocking off contenders like Washington, Buffalo, and Florida. A lot of *ifs*, so to speak, but *ifs, maybes,* and *dreams* constitute the DNA of fans.

14 March 2012

Team	GP	PTS
New York R	69	96
Pittsburgh	68	89
Philadelphia	69	87
New Jersey	70	85
Boston	69	83
Ottawa	71	82
Florida	69	79
Washington	70	78
Buffalo	71	75
Winnipeg	70	73
Tampa Bay	69	71
Toronto	70	68
Carolina	70	67
New York I	70	67
Montreal	71	67

SEC: XX ROW: XX SEAT:XX

HOME GAME 71

JETS VS CAPITALS

MARCH 16, 2012

SEC: XX
ROW: XX
SEAT: XX

So we go back one more time, whether in person at the arena or sitting in front of the TV. Part of us wants to believe; and part of us fears to believe. Part wishes the season were over, its heartaches behind us; part of us craves for the season to go on. Craves more—more what? Pleasure? Pain? Emotional stimulation under whatever rubric? Just let us watch, just let us cheer, just let our hearts be engaged. It's an addiction, we hardly know what we crave; we only know we want more.

And of course tonight's game is "critical." Haven't they all been since about mid-February? Lose this one and we're out of it; win this one and we might still grab that last playoff position. Seen from a distance, we're playing a mug's game. The odds of winning game after game, while other teams above us are losing just enough for us to replace them, what are those odds? The odds of falling out of contention are much higher. If our "investment" in the fate of the team were occurring in the stock market, we'd be "shorting" the Jets—betting against them. But that's part of the allure—beating the odds at the craps table. The sure thing is not what we live for; our blood pulses with the long-shot bet, victory secured against the odds—like getting a team back in the NHL itself was a feat that defied the odds. We beat the odds once before; we'll beat them again.

So Go Jets Go!

On this night against Washington, they start fast, as do the Capitals, both sides pressing for the early goal. Everyone knows the first goal is critical; everyone knows that when the Jets score first at home they almost always win. Once the initial flurry of attacks is over, the game settles, both teams checking intensely, keeping the shots on goal low. The Jets score just past the midway point of the period; within seconds the Caps answer and then begin to carry the play. The period ends 1-1. The Jets are fortunate the score is 1-1. "They've gotta hit the reset button now," says the colour guy. But the Caps open the second period pressing. It

249

doesn't look good for the home side. They hang in there, though, and by mid-period they're carrying the play. They hit a post—drat; they hit a second post—*damnation*; a third—*this is too much.*

"Maybe not their night," I say.

"It has to be their night," Kristen says, "they have to beat Washington." They score with less than five minutes remaining in the period and this time hang on to the conclusion of the frame, though right at period end they take a penalty.

"Gotta kill that off," I mutter, "if they hope to win."

But they don't. The Caps score at the beginning of the third: 2-2. Now it's all up for grabs. The action is intense. If Washington win, they go six points up on the Jets in the scrap for the final playoff spot; if the Jets win, the margin sinks to two.

The Jets leaders are working hard: Ladd forechecking with zeal, Wheeler carrying the puck resolutely, Byfuglien and Bogosian using their weight effectively.

"Big Buff would be good in the scrum," Andrew says. "Got a gigantic butt."

"He's playing all five positions tonight."

Andrew chuckles. "Yeah, that takes good coaching."

The teams trade powerplay chances. Then at the midway mark of the period the Jets' Byfuglien crashes his way to the Caps goal and muscles the puck in the net from a scramble in front. "More will than skill on that one," the colour guys remarks.

But it's the margin of victory—despite a penalty to the Jets in the final minute that turns into a six-on-four for the Caps, and furious action around the Jets goal.

Once again the crowd is ecstatic. The noise in the MTS Centre grows louder with every game it seems: ear-splitting, riotous. And once more our yearning blazes: if we can beat Carolina on Sunday, if Washington stumble in Chicago and Philadelphia. There seems no limit to the hopes astir in our breasts.

Eleven games remaining in the season. Into the home stretch. Jets fans can consider themselves lucky: the team has hung in there. The roller-coaster ride—one day they're out of it, the next they're back in it—has been exhausting but it has also been exhilarating. Consuming. Would we have had it any other way? With only a few weeks to go, interest in the team's fate has never been higher. Doubters can misgive; neutrals can observe; dreamers can dream. Wherever you stand, there's reason to go to games, to turn on TVs: we're engaged, we throb to the beat of our team's dance.

Win this one, we intone, *beat Carolina, close the gap on the Caps.*

Both teams are up to the challenge, skating and checking hard, scuffling below the goal-lines for possession, taking the puck to the net. There's more than a little feistiness in Carolina's game: they take one and then two penalties, but the Jets fail to score on the powerplay, despite their enviable record in that department. It's the Canes who get the breakthrough goal near the midway point of the period—painfully, it's a short-handed goal. Not a good omen; everyone knows the team that scores first usually goes on to win. But the Jets rally and tally four minutes later, allaying those apprehensions momentarily, and the period ends 1-1.

At the break I ask, "Do you think they'll win?" My suspicion is they will, despite being outplayed in the opening frame.

"I'm not going to say," Kristen responds.

After the skate the team held on Sunday morning, Jets forward Blake Wheeler said: "Good teams come out and win these games." He was right. It's easy to get up emotionally to play Washington, who are above them in the standings; the real test of a team's character comes against teams below them in the standings, as is Carolina. I dare to have faith that he's right, that the Jets will pull together and triumph. But I've been wrong many times before.

In the second period it's the Jets' turn to be sent to the penalty box. Carolina score on their first powerplay opportunity: 2-1. Then the Jets have to kill off a major penalty of five minutes; they do. And it seems to give them life. Now they're making a better fist of it. They score at the game's midway point: 2-2. And then again late in the period to take their first lead of the game: 3-2. The fans are wild.

I'm guardedly hopeful. In the early part of the season the Jets had a terrible time hanging on to leads in third periods. As they also struggled on the powerplay and lost time and again on the road. In the past twenty or thirty games they've improved in two of three of those categories, no longer regularly collapsing in third periods.

I have to concede the team has gelled in the second half of the season, the coaches have achieved something valuable, the players are better professionals now.

Compartmentalize. Get past the five-minute mark. Then the ten.

Can you wish a victory? Can you will your team to win? Fifteen thousand fans in the MTS Centre believe so. Thousands more in front of TVs. And the Jets do get past the five-minute mark, and then ten.

Just past the midway point of the period, disaster strikes. Andrew Ladd, last man back. is trying to dump the puck from Carolina's blue line deep into their zone; he muffs the attempt; the puck is chipped past him and he's caught flat-footed while the Canes' Staal is released on a breakaway and scores. Ladd was guilty of these dreadful blunders earlier in the season—gaffes made from trying too hard—but seemed to have ironed them out of his game. But this one may prove to be expensive. This one may prove to be the Jets' undoing—and not just in this game.

In an earlier era Ladd would have found himself consigned to the far end of the bench where the backup goaltender sits, made to fester unused in humiliation to the end of the game. But this is a different era; and Claude Noel is not that kind of coach. He puts his captain back on the ice, providing him the opportunity to redeem himself.

Ladd's an interesting study. His two Stanley Cup rings must speak loudly in the dressing room; his teammates must both admire and respect him. But they're also a bit of a curse, those two Cup rings. They tempt him to bad judgement, to flawed decisions, to take the team on his back and try to do too much as a individual—and these things can hurt a team. For Ladd himself his success at a young age puts him on something of a cleft stick.

He and his teammates try to respond. But Carolina has the momentum and they continue to carry the play, attacking and forcing the Jets back on their heels. With five minutes remaining in the period we're silently hoping the Jets can get at least one point out of this game, maybe steal two in the overtime or shootout. But Carolina score with less than two minutes to go and the Jets' fate is sealed: 4-3 loss. For the fans a bitter pill to swallow. Now the home team is three points out of the final playoff spot—but with only ten games remaining. Virtually impossible. More to be down about than up.

In the Jets dressing room twenty young men will be silent and subdued. Their captain will be harbouring grim thoughts about himself as a leader and a man.

SNAPSHOT: Man Up

An afternoon in 1977 at Bison Gardens at the University of Manitoba. A game has been arranged between professors from the Department of English and the grad students. Though technically I'm both, teaching classes and working on my doctoral degree, I've been put with the students to even things up.

Things need equalizing. Most of the guys gathered in the dressing rooms are not veteran hockey players, though quite a number are—or once were—good athletes, guys who played collegiate basketball (David) or were baseball pitchers of note in their hometown (Dennis). Along with most others on the ice, they are now rickety skaters, prepared to make a rink-length dash with the puck, but not certain how to bring themselves to a halt after shooting. Our goaltender is such a poor skater that he has been allowed to man the net in steel-toed boots. Only two of us have played the game at a high level: Robert, who like me is both graduate student and lecturer, and me. So the game should be a hoot, the contest should be a laugh. But the competitive waters have been muddied.

The professors have brought in a ringer.

Perhaps to counter my reputed skills, they have parachuted in the brother-in-law of the head of the department, a guy who has no connection to the university or the Department of English. But a good player. He and Robert make a formidable duo. Both can skate, both are fit, both are intense. They have each other to make passes to and rely on for defensive backup; I have me.

The game has one other remarkable feature. The renowned poet, Alfred Purdy, writer-in-residence at the university, is in attendance. Along with scattered wives, girlfriends, and curious members of the Department of English, he is in the stands as the game gets underway.

It is a hoot. David has agreed to play goal. A big man, tall, carrying a few too many pounds, in his pads and goalie mask, he's Golem. Dennis, wearing a knit blue sweater rather than a hockey jersey, is as tenacious as Ritzo Ratso. A rickety skater, he goes to the corners in his own end with zeal, fighting doggedly for the puck with our one Central American student, Mauricio, who also teeters on his blades but is equally fierce in pursuit of the puck. He emerges from below the goal line and flutters the puck at me. I could shoot and score but I try to set him up in front of the net. The puck dribbles off into the corner and changes hands. Robert scoops it up. Now my real work begins. I cut him off before he gets up a head of steam but he passes the puck across to the ringer on the far side of the ice. I have to go after him now.

He dashes down the ice; I am half a stride behind and flick my stick at his as he shoots. His shot is not as hard as it might be but it still goes in: 3-2. The "professors" are ahead. Now instead of working the puck into their end and trying to set up one of my teammates, I feel I must even the score. Questioned, I would not quite know why I feel this way but I do. Hockey brings out the macho in me. Man up! In Robert, too, it turns out. When I rush up the ice, he barges into me near the centre red line, attempting to throw me off stride and win the puck. He's my equal in height and sturdily built, a mesomorph with big shoulders and powerful legs. Though not as strong a skater as me. I brush past him, I glance across the ice to see if any of my teammates is in position to score, I shoot hard along the ice through David's feet and tie the game.

A pattern emerges. I'm dogged by one or the other of the professors' two strong players and find myself dashing from one end of the ice to the other, hot in pursuit of them. None of my teammates has the skating legs to help much, though occasionally they break up a rush or thwart a scoring chance. Our steel-booted goaltender is a good athlete. He stops shot after shot. But the game is soon sapping my energy and wind. I'm having to play defender, forechecker, setup man, and scorer. I'm becoming frustrated. We fall behind by a second goal. As I charge back up the ice, intent on scoring, Robert cuts me off at centre and we collide along the boards. I elbow him; he elbows me back. Angry words. In a moment we're slashing each other with sticks, faces aflame, and in another moment we're tussling against the boards, punches seem possible. Fortunately there's a referee present. He blasts on his whistle. He sends us to respective penalty boxes. We exchange heated words.

My heart thunders in my chest. My arms shake.

The penalties wind down. I'm in a funk.

I feel shitty. Shitty the game was spoiled by the connivance of the professors and equally shitty that I gave in to the lowest of impulses, macho crap I thought I had put behind me at twenty. When I look over at Robert, I can see he's feeling the same: here we are, two supposed intellectuals, at the university to study the words of poets and thinkers, to hone the cultured skills of writing and speaking, and we get into a back-alley fracas in a meaningless game of shinny. This contradiction runs deep in us: we love sport but its passions have a way of bringing out the worst in us. Yet more evidence that sport does not build character—if more evidence were required. I hang my head. Though my blood is up, my spirits are down. I harbour dark thoughts about myself as a man. I pray for the game to end—and soon enough it does.

When the renowned poet writes a poem about the game, he has his own take: the professors, as he sees it, overcome their younger, more athletic students. Robert emerges as hero. The ringer is not deemed worthy of mention; neither am I.

SEC: XX ROW: XX SEAT:XX

AWAY GAME 73
JETS VS PENGUINS
MARCH 20, 2012

SEC: XX
ROW: XX
SEAT: XX

"Oh," I say, studying the reports on Monday night's games before the puck drops in Pittsburgh, "Washington beat Detroit last night. Too bad." Meaning it looks as if the Jets draw closer and closer to elimination from the playoffs. They're five points out with ten games remaining.

"It's all over," Kristen says. "I'm watching tonight just to watch."

It's hard not to agree. It's hard not to acknowledge that the Jets' playoff run is over. When the Penguins score barely two minutes into the game it seems a death-knell has been struck. The Jets respond, though, tying the score almost right after, and then going ahead 2-1. Is there really still hope? Can they leapfrog both Buffalo and Washington?

The colour guy is in there boosting: "This is more like it," he says.

Is he perhaps right? Can the improbable run continue?

It can't. By period end the Penguins have tied the game: 2-2. Only the most diehard supporters can continue to believe that winning this game is possible, that anything except defeat and its consequences is likely. Still, that's why they play the games: the outcome is in doubt, a turnaround is possible. Anything is possible.

The second period is hardly underway when the Penguins score again. *Geez Louise,* why do the Jets always get sucked into playing fire-wagon hockey by teams that are sure to beat them at it? They counter again within two minutes: 3-3. Okay, hold on now for a ten-minute stretch, settle the game. But it's not possible against the high-powered Pens. By the midway point of the game it's 5-3. The Jets draw to within one again: 5-4. The colour guy says, "This is amazing, the Jets keep coming back, they could do this, they could win." But the words are hardly out of his mouth when they give up another goal: 6-4. That's how the period ends.

In the days of the WHA the old Jets did this, played "river hockey." *First team to ten wins!* But those teams were superior to their opponents:

letting Hull, Nilsson, and Hedberg loose meant letting terrific firepower run rampant, meant the other team was certain to lose against the Jets. This current team can only manage the feat occasionally—and certainly not against the Penguins, who boast the equivalent of the "Hot Line" in Crosby, Malkin, and Neal. For the Jets, things look very dim indeed.

The colour guy says, "It's still possible, there's still reason to believe."

But the little boy in me is saying, I don't want to hear any more about belief. There is no hope. Just let this be over. I don't want to hear anyone saying there's still a mathematical chance, that they still believe we can do it. Let's just accept we're out of the playoffs, let's just accept it's over. It's too painful hanging on like this, too painful keeping the candle burning. The players aren't good enough; the coach isn't smart enough. There's no reason to believe, that's the truth. We have to get used to there being no hope.

The Penguins score near the opening of the third period to make it 7-4. There truly is no hope. The last time these teams played, the final score was 8-5 for the Pens and the Jets coach was disgusted with his squad's performance. "I find it's being disrespectful to each other, to the goaltenders, everything," he said of his team's performance on that night. Things are headed in that direction again. When the final horn sounds it's 8-4. The Jets slink off to their dressing room, whipped dogs. They have nine games remaining and they will put in the best showing they can—they're professionals, after all—but it's all academic, as they say, the Jets' season is over.

SNAPSHOT: Losing

Sport is about losing. Well, all of life is, really. Looked at from the largest perspective, we get it and then we lose it.

But without spinning into maudlin...

More than 10,000 people started last year's Boston Marathon. Only one was the overall winner—though prizes were awarded in a number of categories and, of course, in the kinder, gentler world of the new millennium, everyone who participated could be deemed a "winner." One mustn't be too hard.

In my neck of the wood, literary prizes are awarded every year. From all the books published, a handful are nominated for various prizes: maybe five, maybe fewer. Those not nominated are—this is being harsh—losers. When the winners are announced three to five more nominees are made losers. Well, that is a tough way of looking at things.

Thirty teams begin the NHL season, each one resolved on winning the Stanley Cup. Sixteen make the playoffs, making the remaining fourteen losers; at the end of four rounds of competition, one team emerges as the ultimate winner; only one team really "wins." Last season the Vancouver Canucks went all the way to the seventh game of the Cup final before Boston prevailed over them. Boston became the winners; the Canucks—if you look at it in the harshest light—losers.

So sport is about losing. And more important, about how to deal with loss, with that nearly inevitable day when someone else is the winner and you are not. Players must get used to it; so must management; and so, finally, must fans, bitter though it is to accept. How many junior players—from many different national teams—have we witnessed weeping tears upon losing the final of the World Championship? They're just boys, we say, in time they will harden into adulthood and its myriad strategies of acceptance. Strategies we all have evolved for our fragile egos: next September, we tell ourselves, brings promise of a better team; next season brings, as well as eighty-two games, the chance that we can go all the way. Meantime, we lick our wounds; consider ourselves blessed that we made it to the first round of the playoffs (if we're the Senators), or nearly made it to the playoffs (if we're the Jets); revel in memories of the tremendous games we've attended, the stupendous goals we've been fortunate to have witnessed. It was a great run. The team played well most nights, and exceeded most fans' expectations. We're back in hockey's big league and our team is not out of place there. Hurrah.

It's been a remarkable winter in Winnipeg: temperatures well above average through the entire run from November; snow gone from yards and boulevards by mid-March. Winnipeggers are amazed. As they are astonished that the Jets are still in the hunt for the final playoff spot. Virtually dead but still alive, mathematically.

With nine games remaining in the schedule they're five points behind Buffalo and Washington, who jointly occupy eighth spot. Five points. The Jets seem to have been five points out since forever—scrapping and scrambling to close the margin—and from time to time doing just that. But time is against them now. With so few games to go, they have to win three more games than both Buffalo and Washington in order to pull off the feat: in a rule-of-thumb way it works out to winning seven of their last nine games.

Impossible, you say?

Highly unlikely, Jets fans respond. But stranger things have happened before.

The Jets players know it too. *Win this one,* must be their mantra. Let the out-of-town results take care of themselves. *Win this one today.*

Kristen says, "I'm hoping for a good game. Only that." Do I believe her?

The Capitals played last night, forcing a game in Philadelphia into overtime. "The Caps," the colour guy says, "will be good in the opening ten minutes, it's like the fourth period for them." True, I think, but likely too they'll start to fade in the final period.

It's a robust game, both teams pressing hard for the opening goal. For Jets fans it's nail-biting stuff: *get that first one.* The puck goes up and down, the minutes tick off the clock. The mid-point of the period passes. The shots are even. Then the Caps score off a Byfuglien gaffe with less than four minutes left in the first: 1-0. The writing is on the wall. In the break, Kristen says, "It's a good game." Not even two minutes elapse in the second period and Washington score on a powerplay. Then by the six-minute mark they tally again: 3-0. By now we don't even feel deflated: the letdowns have been so frequent in the past month that this one seemed inevitable. We're numb from hoping and having hope defeated. Time to pack up emotional commitment; to resign ourselves to Next Year Country.

It's a sensible decision, but the Jets won't let it happen. Not two minutes go by before one of the AHL call-ups backhands a shot into the Caps goal. And hardly a minute later, the Jets score again, making it 3-2. Brian Little, his twenty-second of the season. Twenty-two! Maybe I've misjudged him. Whatever, the Jets bench is going crazy; the Washington fans are stone silent. Now the intensity level of the game is at fever pitch: the Jets intent on getting the equalizer, the Caps hanging on with desperation. The period ends 3-2, Jets having outshot Caps 15-14.

"Well, how about that?" I say in the intermission, thinking, The Caps may well get leg-weary in the third, the Jets might steal this one yet. They come out storming, pressing the Caps in their end, mounting attack after attack, firing shots at the Caps goal. By the seven-minute mark of the third period the shots favour the Jets 10-0, and the Caps are hanging on by their teeth. With less than five minutes remaining the shots are 13-0. But the Caps are still hanging on. Then another of the AHL call-ups puts the puck into the Washington goal: 3-3 with less than four minutes remaining. The Jets storm the Caps end, but regulation time ends in a draw.

"Unbelievable," I say to Kristen.

"Down 3-0 on the road, and then to come back—when has that ever happened?"

"Never."

"Not that I can recall."

Never has the Jets' resilience been more in evidence. It would have been both easy and understandable for the Jets' young squad to pack it in when the score was 3-0. But as on numerous occasions throughout the season, they did not. The coach did not scream at them; they did not hang their heads; they did not just go through the motions of playing the game out. I've been pleased by many things in their season, but in the past two months this is the one that stands out: the coach does not lose his composure; and that poise transfers to his players, who dig in and with resolve and self-belief, both, give it their best shot. It will be the lasting impression of this first season for the new Winnipeg Jets. And a vital foundation stone for the team to build on in the future. You can acquire expensive free agents in the off-season; you can trade for key personnel; you can select a stunning youngster in the draft. But one thing you cannot just acquire is the quiet resolve that Claude Noel has instilled in his young team over the course of this season. It augurs well for the years upcoming.

Just two minutes into the overtime, Jets' Stapleton scores on a play set up by Byfuglien and the Jets skate off with a remarkable 4-3 victory. They're still four points out of the final playoff position, the task is no less daunting, but Jets fans can leave this game whistling a happy tune: *never give up, never give in.*

SNAPSHOT: That Was My Plus!

An arena in north Winnipeg on a Wednesday afternoon where twenty or so old farts are playing a game of shinny on a winter afternoon in 2009. Our side, the "whites," is up or down a goal or two, it doesn't really matter, that is not what will be memorable about this day.

What is memorable about these games is not the final score; those days are past—as are the days of beating yourself up because a nifty, faster forward deked past you at the blue line and went in to score. What's memorable is the look on the face of the guy who rarely scores when he puts one in, the cry of *you bastard* when you put one by the goaltender; the jeers from the guys on *your* bench when you dipsy-doodle and pot a nifty goal: *get outta town!*

The puck is dumped into our end, and I wheel and chase it behind our net. I pause behind our net with the puck. No one is forechecking so I pass across to Darryl R, who's waiting in the far corner and we start up the ice. The puck comes back to me at the red line. I'm skating at two-thirds speed, looking to make a play but also in need of making a change on the fly. As I come to the far blue line, I pass it cross ice to a forward who cuts into the other end, going wide on the defenceman there, a forward who then rips a slapshot into the top corner of the net. I'm on my way to the bench and glance quickly in that direction, confirming that the goal was scored. The door at the bench swings open and Thomas S jumps out to replace me. Laughing, I call to him, "That was my plus!" He's almost at centre ice before he turns back and skates toward the bench. Pointing his stick at me he yells back, "And you need every damn one of those you can get!" The guys on the bench beside me roar with laughter. I take a slug of water. Watch the play on the ice as it develops. Unaccountably I find myself whistling quietly under my breath.

Eight games to go; four points to make up. The Jets season has come down to numbers and calculations: if the Wild can beat the Sabres; if the Bruins can beat the Caps; if the Jets can prevail over the Predators. Numbers and possibilities: *if, maybe.* According to my rude calculations, the Jets can afford to lose only two more games before they're out of it, an unlikely possibility but not a devastating one: it's not the Slough of Despond. They've made a good run of it. It's the end of March, they're still in the hunt, we've been treated to great games. Sure, it would be fantastic to the go to the MTS Centre for a couple of Stanley Cup contests, the city throbbing with energy, the cheering, the arena rocking, the sheer entertainment of it. What a great story that would make! Maybe.

Tonight the team is in Nashville to play the Predators, a solid if uninspiring outfit that puts more emphasis on defence than offence but that has marshalled an enviable record playing that way. And it's the second of back-to-backs for the Jets, so a victory is unlikely—but no more unlikely than the comeback in Washington last night. What the hell! Go Jets Go!

The game means a lot to the Predators too. They're trying to hold onto fourth place in the Western Conference, which guarantees home-ice advantage during the first round of the playoffs. So the game is tightly played in the opening ten minutes, neither team wanting to fall behind. "What do you think of the Jets' chances?" I ask.

"If they get through the opening period without giving up a goal," Kristen says, "Nashville may become anxious. They've lost two in a row."

"That's their only chance?"

"Their best chance."

Nashville carry the play. The farther the teams go into the period the more the Jets look tired. Pavelec makes two, three, four critical saves. Where would they be without this guy? The frame ends 0-0.

When we look at the NHL scoreboard, there's little but bad news: Buffalo lead Minnesota. Buffalo is one of the teams the Jets must leapfrog to get into eighth spot. Being a fan, the little boy in me feels, amid all this drama, has never felt more like punishment.

Just into the second period, Nashville score. This does not look good. Now the Predators play fierce defence, "radiology hockey": *anesthetize the other guys.* They record a second goal. During a break for TV commercials, two Atlanta Thrashers fans at the game throw their Thrashers jerseys on the ice. "In protest," the colour guy says. "Never seen that before," Kristen says. They're upset. Fans everywhere behave the same; diehard fans of the Thrashers must feel as betrayed and despairing as we did in 1996 when our team was "re-franchised" to Phoenix. Do we have any sympathy for them? Not much, it seems. It's not something I've heard anyone comment on. Maybe it was a topic on talk radio programs in the spring and fall. Almost a whole year has passed since then. Perhaps we're being cruel and callous, blocking our ears to the pain of others, hardening our hearts. They're our Jets now. As the poet said: *drive your cart over the bones of the dead.*

Again the Jets look tired as the period comes to a close.

But they do not give in. At the beginning of the third they show spirit, carrying the puck to the Nashville goal. Both Byfuglien and Wheeler use their size to force the issue down low. Just at the ten-minute mark, the Jets score: 2-1. There's still hope; the Jets could tie this, go into overtime, steal the points. But Nashville stiffen their backs. Without star players, they're a good team: well-coached; they're disciplined in the neutral zone and hold their positions in their own end; it's difficult for the Jets to mount much in the way of attacks. When they pull Pavelec for an extra attacker, the Predators score into the empty net.

Of the two games the Jets could afford to lose at the start of play on this night, they've lost one. When they lose for a third time, it's lights out. But for now, they're on their way home to play two games at the MTS Centre. Does hope spring eternal?

26 March 2012

Team	GP	PTS
New York R	75	101
Pittsburgh	75	100
Philadelphia	76	96
Boston	75	91
New Jersey	76	90
Ottawa	77	88
Florida	75	87
Washington	76	84
Buffalo	76	84
Winnipeg	75	77
Tampa Bay	75	77
Toronto	76	75
Carolina	76	75
New York I	75	73
Montreal	76	71

SEC: XX ROW: XX SEAT:XX

Here is where Jets fans might wail: *if only they'd won that game in Toronto; if only they hadn't lost that one in the dying minutes to Washington; if Philadelphia hadn't scored with nine seconds to go and then won in overtime back there about ten games ago.* At those times you couldn't help thinking, This is going to come back to bite them. At this juncture it's easy to look back with recrimination at the games the team gave away in Pittsburgh and Buffalo and Calgary and… When the playoff hopes are disappearing down a dark tunnel, blame and bitterness beckon.

But the Jets also pulled a few games out of the fire, the miraculous victory in Washington just days ago only the most recent. They've tied games late; they've stolen points against better teams; they've also had their share of winning against the odds. Fans forget that. On the whole, probably, they've lost more of these "if-only" games than they've won; that's something to improve on next year; winning "cliffhangers" is what better teams do consistently over a season.

Whatever the case, it's Ottawa tonight, and it's last-gasp time. As the game starts someone in the stands holds up a sign: DON'T STOP BELIEVING.

It's a high-energy opening. Both teams like this style, skate-skate, shoot-shoot. Let the chips fall where they may. High tempo, high energy, high entertainment. At one point the teams play for almost seven minutes without a whistle. Right at the end of the period the Sens score: 1-0. In the intermission I say, "Jets must score the next goal." But it's the Sens who put the puck in the net: 2-0 with less than two minutes played in the period. Sigh. Not again. But the Jets respond immediately to make it 2-1 before the five-minute mark, and then they start to carry the play. The action is furious. The Jets score: 2-2. Ottawa reply: 3-2. It's a wide-open game, which suits the Senators, and which the Jets can play, but it's hair-raising stuff. At period end the shots on goal are 30-21 Jets, the score tied at 3-3. The colour guy at ice level tells us that the players on the bench are gasping after every shift. It's wild hockey, to be sure: no holds barred. Even if the Jets lose, their fans have been entertained at the highest level. That should be enough. But will it be?

The play is somewhat tentative at the start of the third. A lot is at stake. In the past weeks the Senators have slid down the table and, for the first time all year, are in danger of not making the playoffs. The Jets have their backs against the wall. A gaffe in the Jets end leads to an Ottawa goal: 4-3. The Senators try to play shutdown hockey, and for five minutes or so it works: the Jets have difficulty penetrating their zone. It looks as if the game is over. After yet another thwarted attack, I say, "The season is over, only twelve minutes to go." But the Jets continue to be resilient; they throw caution to the wind and storm Ottawa's goal: ten shots, fifteen. They've now taken forty-five shots on goal. With less than three minutes remaining, they finally put one past the Sens goaltender: 4-4. The crowd is on their feet: banners wave, feet stomp, the cheering is thunderous. Once again the team has shown its resilience; once again they've bounced back. Maybe they can get to the overtime; maybe they can steal two points. In the stands faces are aflame, hearts thump wildly.

It feels like a Cup game.

It feels as if the team is going to do it. The Jets have beaten the odds. Jesus, who are these boys? They continue to bless us with miraculous play. But the puck has hardly been dropped and Ottawa score; only twenty-four seconds have passed. Heads drop. Though not the heads of the Jets. They press on fiercely, lift the goaltender for an extra attacker; Byfuglien goes to the front of the Sens goal and creates mayhem; the Jets get one, then two scoring chances. All for naught. The Sens put in an empty-netter.

It's come right down to the wire. A game where there was barely time to catch a breath or think about anything except what was happening right at the moment; a game that was stunningly watchable, a game you couldn't keep your eyes off of.

In a way the game epitomizes the Jets' season: a stumbly start with lots of high-tempo play but little scoring and few results; a second phase where the Jets grabbed fate by the scruff of the neck and played as well as any team in the league; a final phase where they fought bravely, almost made it to the playoffs but fell that little bit short. Upsetting to see them go down, yes; missing the playoffs a bitter pill for the fans to swallow; but high entertainment, excellent play, and great drama. Almost operatic in the way the season at first seemed doomed; then gave heart-elating hope; only to see that hope dashed in the final movement.

In the stands at game-end a boy is holding his rucked-up Jets jersey to his face, twisting the fabric in his fists and biting the logo in anguish.

SNAPSHOT: Logo Loyalty

Our loyalty is to that logo: not the players, not the team, not the management, not the coaches, but to the colours blue, white, and red, the facsimile jet. It's the logo that holds us and nothing else. Jets.

We "love" individual Jets; the adulation for Selanne, gone fifteen years, shows that. But good players move on. They become free agents and their agents tell them, "The Jets are paying you a million a year, they may go as high as 1.5, but one of the big clubs will come up with 2.5 over three years." What twenty-two-year-old can look that kind of money in the eye? He says, "I'll think about it," meaning to put off the agent, he's loyal to the city, after all, the fans, but the more he thinks about it, the more he comes back to the fact that a pro hockey player's career is short, and 7.5 million is a lot of money. So he signs with the other club, regrettably; he may even become misty-eyed at a press conference; but he goes, he moves on.

Coaches too. Assistants. Managers. Sometimes it's not the allure of money but the opportunity to live closer to family, to work for one of the big clubs in a big city. Whatever. We may like the coach, we may admire him, but we know how these things work. We cannot place our loyalty with the coach. At the final buzzer, it's the logo that holds our loyalty. *Go Jets!*

Prediction: within a year, two at most, management will alter the new logo, and not just to sell more merchandise, or to "de-militarize" the look of the Air Force jet. They will work their way back toward the previous Jets logo, they may even bring back the old logo. Because our ties are located there, back as far as 1972, that's where we consign our loyalty.

Our. There I go again. I'm constantly bedevilled by the split between observer and participant, fan and reporter, being inside and outside. It's the fate of the writer, inevitably, to draw on the energy of the crowd, to sense a belonging with the fans, to claim *we*, but at the same time to stand on the sideline, watching and commenting on the action and the fans, seeing them as *they*. It's an inner division more disquieting than *uncertainty*, it's a kind of weakness, a failure of identity.

Yes, *we*. And what are *we*, finally, this aggregation of lawyers and cops and teachers and farmers, aging businessmen, students, salespersons, seniors, little boys with Jets jerseys rucked up their mouths in anguish? What we are is a brigade that marches to the beat of the same drummer, a unified kinship that enters the arena as individuals and fast becomes one entity. And here's what we can do for our beloved team: cheer their names, jeer the opposition, decry the refs, scream for the Jets to play on, hope to raise their will to win—on the strength of our rabid support to rouse them on to victory.

After the deeply discouraging loss to Ottawa, the Jets may find it difficult to summon the energy to put in a good game tonight. Like their fans, their emotions will be at low ebb. Their playoff hopes dashed, they will be tempted to go through the motions to the end of the season. I'm secretly hoping they will put in a strong effort, an effort that says to their fans, the city, and themselves as well: *we belong here, we can play, we can do this.*

They're playing the Rangers, a solid outfit: big, strong, disciplined in all three zones. Workman-like if not flashy, with little of the verve of Detroit or Vancouver. Not very entertaining, but likely to prevail in the end. In the previous meetings between the two teams the Rangers have bottled up the neutral zone and checked well along the boards and below the goal lines, wearing the Jets down and scoring opportunistic goals on powerplays and turnovers.

This game looks much similar. Played at a slower pace than is typical of the Jets, it unfolds with the Rangers in charge—bodychecking, occasional dashes up the ice, shots from the perimeter. The Rangers, the colour guy tells us, are the hardest team in the league to score on in the first period. It's grinding hockey and at the twenty-minute mark the score stands 0-0, shots 11-4 Jets.

Ho hum. But just into the second period the Jets tally. Maybe they've got that spark I was hoping for. It seems they do; at the five-minute mark they score again to make it 2-0. The fans at the MTS Centre rise to their feet. That must be heartening to the players. It's been a bad week. But then, true to form, the Jets give up a goal while on a powerplay: the dreaded short-handed goal that is always such a downer. Then, also true to form, the Rangers score on a powerplay of their own to tie the game before the end of the period: 2-2.

At the break, Kristen asks, "What do you think?" But before I can answer she adds, "4-2?"

"Maybe 5-2. The momentum has swung."

"It was that short-handed goal," Andrew chimes in, "they just suck the life out of you."

"The reverse goal."

"The anti-goal," Kristen says, "the ungoal."

"And the Jets will start the third killing a double minor penalty."

It was for high sticking, Ladd lifting the stick of a taller Rangers forward into his face. Not a penalty, actually, but called one by the referees for the night, Watson and Dwyer. The Jets kill the penalties at the start of the third, but it saps all their reserves and the Rangers score only seconds after the expiration of the penalty time.

Arghh. It was so clear on the replays that an infraction had not occurred. In the intermission it was roundly agreed by the TV guys that the referees had blown it. As they had the night previously in another city, counting a goal that was not a goal, and the night prior to that in yet another locale, missing a major penalty.

What to say about that without it sounding like mere grousing? This: we've reached the point where technology has outstripped authority in sports, and it's proving embarrassing. It's not the only place where the digital reality is provoking questions about modern life. Right now there's a case before the US Supreme Court concerning the use of GPS systems to monitor movements of suspected criminals; does the state have the right to follow a citizen's every move by the use of this technology and undermine the once-sacred right to personal privacy? Our lives today are hedged by such technology: CCT cameras, wiretapping, GPS. In the world of sport there now exist sophisticated HD cameras that show us in razor-sharp detail whether or not on-ice officials have made the right call. Back twenty and thirty years ago we simply took the word of the officials when they made a call: we respected their authority. But now we can all see on these replays when they have made errors. And nightly in the NHL, it seems, referees are making critical mistakes: counting goals that are not; not counting goals that are; awarding penalties that are not infractions; not making calls when they're warranted. They look like fools. And their decisions are influencing—*ruining*—games. Technology has undermined Authority. It's time for the NHL to step boldly into the twentieth-first century. Appointing slippery Shanny "Commissioner of Suspensions" seemed a promising move in that direction—but it's been a disaster: no consistency. And more than anything in the league, the officiating looks outmoded: a Model-T Ford rattling along the Autobahn.

In the event, the Rangers go on to score another powerplay goal near the ten-minute mark. The Jets do not give up. They battle to the end, storming the Rangers goal, and to their credit almost scoring when they lift their goaltender. It ends 4-2.

Whatever glimmer of hope for post-season play flickered going into this game has been extinguished. Five games remaining to the end of the season, four on the road, one final contest at the MTS Centre. Can we say with the famous playwright, "Our revels now have ended"

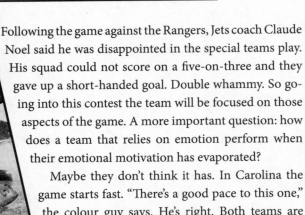

Following the game against the Rangers, Jets coach Claude Noel said he was disappointed in the special teams play. His squad could not score on a five-on-three and they gave up a short-handed goal. Double whammy. So going into this contest the team will be focused on those aspects of the game. A more important question: how does a team that relies on emotion perform when their emotional motivation has evaporated?

Maybe they don't think it has. In Carolina the game starts fast. "There's a good pace to this one," the colour guy says. He's right. Both teams are playing as if something is at stake. Though nothing is. Nothing but pride. The Jets score early. Then toward the midway mark of the period, Carolina respond: 1-1. It's an evenly played contest. But then the Jets give up a short-handed goal, their eighth of the season. *Disheartening* doesn't quite suggest how much of a downer this must be to the team and coach. The period ends 2-1.

Early in the second Carolina score again. Everything that has characterized the Jets' season is coming to the fore in this game—their high energy, weakness below the goal-line in their own end, poor powerplay, propensity to give up short-handed goals. At 3-1 the game looks to be over; the Jets have a terrible road record. They continue to play doggedly, though, and at the midway point of the game close the gap to 3-2. The period ends with the Jets coming on, re-energized, it seems, by the goal.

As the season winds down, it's clearer and clearer that this team has been a great pleasure to watch: speedy and adroit, with just enough grit to hang in against the bigger and better teams. They may have been more successful had they been thugs or bruisers, but they've suited Winnipeg well: entertained us hugely, made watching them a treat, regenerated our Winnipride.

Through the opening five minutes of the third, the Jets carry the play. They hit a goalpost—for the third time on this night. Bad luck seems to be dogging them. The minutes tick past: eight minutes remaining, seven, six. Carolina is hanging on. With less than five minutes remaining, and on a powerplay, the Jets score: 3-3. Silence falls over the Carolina arena. Can the Jets hang on, steal a single point on a night when it seemed they were going down to their fourth consecutive loss?

They hang on. Once again they've proven their resilience. Remarkable, I think. A credit to the team—and *chapeau* to Claude Noel. Another remarkable comeback. But not quite as remarkable as potting the winner just a minute into the overtime, Ladd fighting in front of the net and getting his twenty-fifth. A memorable achievement in what was a meaningless game, testament to the team's character. Four games to the end of the season, the next on Saturday against Tampa.

In Tampa Bay the Lightning and Jets play a good game for two periods, Tampa winning in overtime, the final score 3-2.

But that's not what is notable about this contest. Once again what's notable is the horrible officiating in the third period, when the two donkeys in charge, Ian Walsh and Chris Rooney, ruin a nicely balanced contest by awarding Tampa two overlapping five-on-three advantages, and then just when the second of these has expired, yet another minor penalty to the Jets: four consecutive and overlapping penalties, the final one of which produces the tying goal.

It cannot be, can it, that officials actually conspire to determine the outcomes of games? It cannot be, can it, that they—or the NHL powers-that-be—want one team to win and the other to lose? On a night like this, it certainly seems so. It's either that or the guys who the NHL hires are incompetents of such magnitude that it simply defies reason they're employed in a position involving good judgement. Time and again they make bad calls and show themselves to be fools. Players who made so many errors would be sent to the minors; coaches who demonstrated themselves to be asses would be replaced. But

SEC: XX ROW: XX SEAT:XX

AWAY GAME:79

JETS VS
LIGHTNING

MARCH 31, 2012

SEC: XX
ROW: XX
SEAT: XX

guys like Walsh and Rooney carry on, game after bungling game, piling stupidity onto bad judgement with no consequences from the league. They're immune to either public criticism or official censure. It's a dreadful failure at the league level, yet another reason to view Bête Noire and his toadies with rank suspicion: *rank* being the operative word. If this had occurred in a soccer match in Columbia or El Salvador, Walsh and Rooney would have been lucky to have escaped with their lives, a fate, come to think of it, not unworthy of their performance on this occasion.

Let's be clear about what happened in this game. The score at the end of the second stood 2-1 Jets. The result hung in the balance, the game was both interesting and exciting, the teams playing hard. There were lots of good plays but it was by no means a perfectly played game: miscues in both ends, giveaways, turnovers. Still, the teams were determining the outcome. Then Walsh and Rooney decided they wanted to have a hand in the game's result. They gave Winnipeg four consecutive minor penalties, three of them overlapping; in effect, Tampa had a five-on-three advantage back-to-back, an advantage lasting a total of five minutes and thirty-two seconds. If the referees had been designing to give a goal to Tampa they could not have done a better job. And Tampa did tally, making the score 2-2. In total Tampa Bay were given eight powerplays to the Jets' three; four of those eight, it should be emphasized again, within a five-minute stretch, creating two overlapping five-on-three advantages. Does that not seem unconscionable? The game itself was, of course, ruined, not because the Jets lost, but because as an evenly contested match between equal opponents, it deteriorated into a tangle of penalties and short-handed moments from which the game, as a game, could not recover. It became instead a waiting game, where the issue was: when would Tampa eventually score? (It seemed, incidentally, that Walsh and Rooney were prepared to award Tampa powerplay advantages *until* they scored, as if that were their real objective.) It wasn't, one hopes; they are not, we trust, in the pockets of organized crime as officials in the NBA and the Bundesliga have been shown to be; nor were they pawns in a conspiracy against the Jets; merely incompetent donkeys.

The league will do nothing about their inept performance. But let's give them a resounding catcall: Hee-haw, to two donkeys named Walsh and Rooney!

In the meantime, the Jets' season is waning and so are we.

SNAPSHOT: Waning

I don't really notice when it starts to happen. Somewhere past the thirties, mid-forties, maybe. I wake up at 5:30 AM following a game with a pain in my left knee. Shift around in bed. It doesn't quite go away but it diminishes enough for the drop back into sleep. Then the next time I play it's there again in the early morning hours, more insistent; I roll over a few times, do not find the position that brings sleep; I have to get up, take a Tylenol. During the day, the pain returns, a nagging bite when I climb stairs and lower myself onto the seat of the car. I reach down, massage behind the knee, stretch it this way and that when I get home. It goes away.

Up to that time, there have been injuries but not nagging pain. Sometimes I lose an edge and crash into the boards, an ankle twists and hobbles me for a week; someone takes a slapshot and it hits the toe of the skate, the nail of the big toe throbs inside the boot and when I examine it later, it's turning black, throbs through the night. With the blackened toe I don't play for a few days; with the twisted ankle it's almost a week. These things happen during my late thirties and early forties.

Professional players have this happen every day. They go down to block a shot and take it in the rib cage; they fall into the boards and jam a shoulder; they crash into the net on a headlong rush and twist a wrist. They limp back to the bench; they are last seen trotting down the corridor to be examined by the trainer in the dressing room. Their lives are one painful incident after another. I do not live that way, but my hockey life nibbles around these edges, the outback of anguish.

Somewhere in the forties, things change. Another guy and I hook skates behind the net and I go down hard on one hip. My first thought is not what happened to my body but what happened to the puck. When I'm skating back to the bench, I feel a sharp stab in the hip bone, an electric current of pain that persists through the game and on into the evening. That night in bed it's difficult to find a position to sleep.

Injuries are one thing. This kind of pain is another. It goes away after a few days but a warning bell has been sounded. The warning bell is named Age. The sound it makes is to the tune of a song I'm hearing more and more: *old guy, old fart.*

I've had headaches in the past after playing, big boomers sometimes that wake me in the middle of the night, blinking my eyes, and persist despite Tylenol. The next day I'm groggy. It happens again; and again. I'm sent to a neurologist. He asks, "How often do you get these headaches?" I tell him, "Only after hockey." He raises his eyebrows. "The solution is simple," he says, "stop playing hockey." I laugh. He laughs. "All right," he says, "you won't quit playing hockey. We'll call it *athlete's migraine*. Here's a prescription."

It's for Cafergot, and it does the job; it takes the headaches away.

But what's happening through the forties is not headaches. It's bone pain, it's muscle pain. When I lost an edge and crashed into the boards in my thirties, I got up and continued to play; it hurt a bit but it went away. A sore knee, yes, a bit of pain in the back, maybe. It did not slow me down. It did not keep me from sleeping. It did not send me to the chiropractor. By the time I hit the fifties, these things had changed. I was learning about pain. I was learning to suffer. By the mid-fifties I was living with pain. I discovered what it meant to regularly visit the chiropractor.

Now pain has taken over. I now know the chiropractor on a first-name basis. Now a bottle of anti-inflammatory sits beside the Tylenol.

In the intermission of a game a retired pro is being interviewed. He played with the Philadelphia Flyers who won the Cup several times in the seventies. His collarbone has been broken four times. All his fingers have been dislocated. Both ankles have been fractured. One knee has been operated on twice, the other once. Both shoulders have been separated; on one rotator cuff surgery was performed but it didn't quite work. This in addition to cracked ribs, broken nose, ruptured spleen, fractured wrists. He was a big guy who went to the front of the net to create havoc and screen the goaltender. He took abuse. He has several Cup rings. The interviewer asks, "Do you regret having played?" He says: "It's a shame that at fifty I cannot go out and play a round of golf."

It's a cautionary tale. What he's experienced is more violent than what my pals and I experience, more brutal, more part of the daily round of a life lived where you put your body on the line.

Playing is still fun, but pain is winning out. Every time I come home from the rink, there are tingling electric currents, nerves have been lit on fire in the lower back, in the hips, down the legs. I have a troubled night's sleep. Sometimes I have to get up and walk around downstairs to ease the pain. In the morning, a visit to the chiropractor. The anti-inflammatories have changed names but they've become a part of daily life: Naproxen, Vioxx, Celebrex. Now when I weigh the balance between pleasure in the one-hour game and the two days of discomfort that follow, I waver about the joy I have always felt playing hockey. Is it still worth the price I'm paying?

Now I'm more concerned about not getting hurt than I am about scoring goals. Do we call that irony? The game is still fun, but … I used to come home and be greeted by Andrew at the door with: "How'd it go?" He's a rugby guy. I ask him the same every time he comes home from the pitch. I used to say, "Good, it went good. I scored a goal." Now I say, "Good, it went good, I didn't fall and get hurt."

The famous cyclist quipped that riding the Tour de France was 3000 kilometres of pointless suffering. He was right; sport means not just enjoying what the body can do—it means grinding the body down, breaking the bones, stretching the tendons, abrading the muscles, tearing the flesh, ripping the cartilage. Pointless suffering. The famous cyclist made that statement when he was in his mid-thirties. In his mid-sixties he'll know more than about suffering, he'll know about pain, he'll know that going out to play requires each time an act of will to put   the   body on the line one more time and the knowledge that the day is coming when even that will not be enough.

Going into Florida with three games remaining, the Jets have been officially eliminated from playoff contention. The comeback win in Carolina was emotionally draining; as was the stupidity in Tampa Bay occasioned by the referees. Jets fans are prepared to see the home team play out the string—play well, do themselves and the city credit, finish with strength and dignity. It's the Winnipeg way.

The Panthers are still scrapping for a playoff spot, so the action starts at high tempo, both teams intent on scoring first. Florida break through just past the eight-minute mark; and then two minutes later on a powerplay, making the score 2-0. Their fans are boisterous. That play-off spot seems assured. The game settles into tight play, the puck going up and down, but not too many chances on offer. The Jets are skating at good tempo but lack finish in the Florida end, but maybe that's Florida holding them in check. When the Panthers pot yet another goal in the first minute of the second period, the game seems over: 3-0. Behind the Jets bench, Claude Noel is seething, his team is being outmuscled and outplayed. Halfway through the contest the shots are 20-6 for Florida and the shots are indicative of the play.

But against the run of play the Jets score on a two-on-one, Evander Kane notching his thirtieth of the year, a genuine accomplishment for one so young (twenty). The Jets begin to apply pressure. To the game's halfway mark the ice had seemed tilted toward the Jets goal; it's now Florida that struggle to get control of the puck in their zone and mount attacks. The Jets light the lamp again, making the score 3-2, and before period end mount attack after attack. It's now the Florida coach who has a troubled look on his face. His team is fortunate to escape the period ahead.

Can the Jets mount another incredible comeback? At the beginning of the year they were sunk if they fell behind by more than one goal. Through most of the season they could not hold on to leads in the third period—much less come back from deficits in the third—their record a dismal 2-22-3 in that category. But they score early in the third, and then remarkably again on a powerplay before five minutes elapse: 4-3. The Panthers' arena is stone silent; a game that was in the bag has suddenly been stolen—or given—away. And now the Jets are trying to play "kitty-bar-the-door": bottling up the neutral zone, forechecking fiercely, keeping attacks to the outside. The Panthers are desperate and determined but the Jets are intent on holding the lead. Minutes on the clock tick by: ten remaining, eight, six. With less than four minutes remaining Florida score.

The game goes into overtime.

"It's been a successful road trip whatever happens now," the colour guy says. "In three games Jets have won one and tied one, and now they've garnered a point in this one." Yes, it's heartening. And it makes their fans think once again, If only they had won those two games at home just days ago against Rangers and Senators; they'd still be in the playoff hunt.

If, maybe.

Ladd tallies the winner in overtime, his grit in front of goal once again evident. This guy really is the captain. Jets win 5-4. Another remarkable comeback.

Resilience, thy name is Jets.

I feel badly for ever doubting them. *Mea culpa*.

SNAPSHOT: On My Knees

In the town of Rocamadour in the Dordogne region of southern France a stairway of more than 100 stone steps climbs from the town centre to the door of a chapel perched on the side of a mountain. The stone steps are well worn, by millions of pilgrims who have climbed them—many on their knees. Kings and queens, it is said, have performed the feat, among them, Richard Coeur de Leon. On the day we cycle through Rocamadour we climb those steps. About halfway up I decide to see what it must have felt like to be a pilgrim. I go down on my knees on a stone step. It hurts. I lift one knee to the step above and lever myself onto it. That really hurts! I pause, head bowed. Then do the same again, onto a third step. It REALLY hurts! I pause again, head bowed, not in prayer, but in excruciating pain. I don't think I can climb more than a dozen steps without passing out. And I begin to suspect the fabled kings and queens had retainers who slipped cushions onto the steps for the nobility to kneel on. But people were tougher back then. Maybe I malign the royalty wrongly. Whatever the case, after only seven steps one late-twentieth-century jock's legs are numb from hip to ankle; knees stinging for hours afterward.

Laceration is part of Christianity. It cleanses the soul, they say, demonstrating the unworthiness of the body compared to the soul. In addition to that, there's a crossover in the experience of intense pain where the pain transforms into ecstasy, excruciating joy. So there are gains from this pain.

With that in mind I offer up the following: in my days of playing hockey I've behaved badly on occasion—thrown my stick into the bench in disgust; stuck out a knee and nearly injured another skater; barged a weaker opponent over to gain possession of the puck—things that cause me to blush when I recall them; also in this book I've been a little unfair at times; I've descended into the "argument a*d hominem,*" disparaging individuals personally—Scott Hartnell, Gary Bettman, others. Do I feel guilty? Yes. Sort of. My behaviour on ice and the comments I've made have from time to time not been in the best tradition of liberal fair-mindedness. But, then, isn't that the prerogative of the writer?

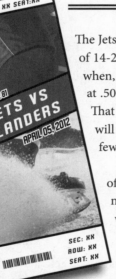

SEC: XX ROW: XX SEAT:XX

AWAY, GAME 81
JETS VS ISLANDERS
APRIL 05, 2012

SEC: XX
ROW: XX
SEAT: XX

The Jets' final game on the road finds them with a record of 14-21-5. This will be an area to improve next season, when, doubtless, the coaches will hope they can play at .500 while compiling another sterling home record. That will be one key to gaining a playoff position, as will a better powerplay, on the one hand, and taking fewer penalties themselves, on the other.

The Islanders have similar ambitions. On the look of this game, they hope to achieve better results next year by playing the passive neutral zone trap, working to stymie the opposition the way their crosstown rivals, the Devils, do. Though in this game they score first, and then again almost immediately, both goals coming before the ten-minute mark: 2-0. The Jets look disorganized and rattled, and the Isles sense it; this is one notable feature of NHL life these days—teams that have opponents on their heels are sharks on the scent of blood—they close in for the kill. But the Jets get a goal quickly—and then another almost immediately: 2-2. Then the period settles into a less volatile contest, and ends that way.

Penalties at the beginning of the second—one truly of the "phantom" variety—eventually wear down the Jets. The Isles score by the midway point of the game, but the Jets stiffen their backs and resist further damage. It's an evenly played contest: hard skating, some good scoring chances, an abundance of turnovers. It's obvious why both teams finished out of the playoff picture; they have many weaknesses on the defensive side of the game. Still, entertaining hockey, the result in the balance. Toward the end of the period the Jets are sagging. The road trip is catching up with them. When the buzzer for the intermission sounds, they've marshalled only four shots to the Isles' eleven.

The Jets' play in third periods has been a study this year. So often they have started games fast only to see leads slip away in second halves. But recently they've become "comeback kids," mounting a number of strong third periods and stealing games it looked as if they'd lost—against Washington and Florida notably in the past few weeks. So it's no surprise when, despite their weary legs, they register a tying marker just before the ten-minute mark of the period: 3-3. Can they hang on—or even steal the game? No, is the immediate answer. The Isles regain the lead only four minutes later on a penalty shot that should never have been called—Byfuglien is still a marked man, it appears. But the big man is so enraged, he single-handedly forces a tying goal only moments later. That point for the tie hovers again, with only seven minutes remaining. The teams play hard. In the final minute Evander Kane coughs up the puck in the Jets end and the Isles win, 5-4.

It's disappointing—the way the whole season on the road has been—but there's much to be positive about too. Though there was nothing at stake for them, the Jets pulled themselves together for this final four-game road trip and managed to do themselves credit by losing only the one game, winning two, and grabbing a point in the fourth. Something to build on for next season.

SEC: XX ROW: XX SEAT:XX

HOME GAME 82

JETS VS LIGHTNING

APRIL 07, 2012

SEC: XX
ROW: XX
SEAT: XX

As they enter the MTS Centre on the final day of the season, the Jets are about to finish exactly where I guessed they might months ago when we started *On the Fly*: just at .500, and out of the playoffs by a game or two. They lost those opening three matches of the campaign, and as might have been predicted, those early losses have come back to haunt them in its closing days. That was then; this is now.

The Jets find themselves in an odd position. Playing against Tampa, who stand only one point behind them, they will move three points ahead if they win, or slip one behind if they lose. These two positions will be important when the amateur draft is held in a few months. For the Jets, a win puts them in tenth position in the Eastern Conference and will see them pick tenth; a loss drops them to eleventh, and that will have them pick ninth. So, a win is a loss; and a loss is a win. For the players, this is not a matter of importance, as it might be for management. The players are in it tonight for pride, not future draft picks.

The fans are another matter. Well before the teams come on the ice the cry of Go Jets Go! is thunderous. Posters are everywhere in the stands: THANKS JETS; LOVE OUR JETS; CANADA'S BEST CROWD. The colour guy shouts above the cheering, "The fans here have embraced the team in an amazing way." After a few moments he adds, "The team was a seven but the fans loved them as if they were a ten."

The opening minutes of the game feature strong skating and chances at both ends, but not the usual fiery tempo from the Jets. Are they experiencing a little post-road-trip hangover? They take a couple of penalties, and though Tampa do not score, they seize momentum from the advantages, putting the Jets on the back heel for most of the period and scoring late: 1-0. The Jets have had only three shots on goal.

That story continues as the second period opens. Tampa get an early one: 2-0. The Jets fans are unrelenting—Go Jets Go! The TV camera pans the crowd; it seems almost everyone in the lower bowl of the MTS Centre is wearing a Jets jersey. And on their feet clapping and chanting. It's a madhouse. When the Jets score at the midway mark of the game, the colour guy says, "I can't hear myself think." The Jets press the Tampa zone; shots for the period are 15-6 but the score remains 2-1 for Tampa.

Is a comeback possible?

"Likely," I say. "It's in the DNA now."

"At home anyway," Kristen says.

"Don't hold your breath," Andrew adds.

But it's Tampa who get the next goal: 3-1. Momentary deflation gives way to renewed cheering. Go Jets Go! The crowd will not accept defeat.

And the team rises to their call, scoring just over a minute later: 3-2. Now the goombahs take up the hex cheer on Dwayne Roloson, Tampa's goaltender: *Roll-ly, Roll-ly*. The camera pans the crowd; everyone chanting the hex is smiling and laughing, laughing at ourselves for being such meanies, even while we're being meanies. Oooh, look at us, aren't we bad!

Down one goal with fifteen minutes to go means the perfect game is in play: comeback from two goals down, snatch victory from the maw of defeat. The Jets know it; so do their fans. The puck goes up and down the ice. Breathtaking saves at each end. With four minutes remaining, the Jets take a penalty. Even if they kill it off, there will be only two minutes left in which to score. They kill the penalty; with seconds left, they pull the goaltender for the extra attacker. The crowd is on its feet, clapping and cheering. With less than a minute to go, the Jets score. Mayhem in the MTS Centre. The colour guy shouts above the crowd noise, "It sounds like the roof is going to come off the building."

It's the perfect game. Come from behind 3-1 to tie 3-3 in the dying seconds.

"Fairy-tale end to a remarkable season," Kristen says.

"How about that," Andrew says.

I cannot agree more. "Fitting."

Or nearly the perfect game. It goes into overtime and Tampa win. But that's as nothing to Jets fans. On the final night of the season they were treated to superb entertainment: great open-ice hockey, splendid goaltending, a fabulous comeback, a crowd that never gave up on the team and cheered deliriously to the final moment.

A mirror in most respects of the team's season. High-voltage hockey that had us on the edges of our seats in anticipation and wonder. What more could we have asked for?

SNAPSHOT: Passion, please

There's an element of the opera to a hockey season. Passions are right up front. We hate that guy from Philadelphia, he's as villainous as the one in Boston. We love the rookie sensation—don't you dare say a word against him! Everything is at one extreme of the emotional scale or the other: *boo*, Chara; *yay*, Burmistrov! Kill the refs! It all happens at a searing pace—this is not baseball or cricket. It's up and down, it's all or nothing. Just like the opera. No shades of grey. Hockey wears the arousing blacks and reds of *commedia dell'arte* and the grand operas.

We get the sense that great forces are influencing the action; the colossal passion of the scrap that becomes a brawl mirroring the operatic duel. The white-hot heat of rage at the ref—or the thug on the Flyers—sets our breasts aflame, as does the betrayal on stage by the mustachioed villain. It's so deliciously, so exquisitely overblown.

The players are in uniforms and sides are easy to choose: these guys are good; those jerks are bad. How can you tell? The good guys are wearing the home-coloured jerseys. They're our heroes. We tell them that, we tell each other that by putting on their jerseys ourselves when we come to the arena: LADD, BURMISTROV, KANE stencilled on our backs. We might as well be tattooed! If you're at all unsure, listen to the crowd around you—*hiss* for the bad guys; *yahoo* for the good. It's all love or hate; it's all the highs and lows of classical tragedy; it's all joy or despair.

Oh, great gods of hockey, send us more games!

SNAPSHOT: Sports Fever 7

We will go back. Despite the losses at the tail end of the season, despite the shattering of the dream, despite the disappointing slide into eleventh place at the close. It was audacious to hope for the improbable finish to the season, a fan's fantasy. But who could blame us? The return of a team to the city was unlikely and shocking; the sprint into sixth place during December was the stuff of dreams; the Jets continued hanging on through January, February, March, as unlikely a turn of events as those runs made by Edmonton and Calgary from eighth place to the Cup finals a decade ago were both exhilarating and heartbreaking.

We will have a question or two. The fans, we know, will retain enthusiasm—but will the players? Or will they experience sophomore burnout? They were put through the wringer this season at the MTS Centre, playing in front of a fervent but demanding crowd that never did give them "a night off," but always, *always* demanded more: Go Jets Go! As heartening as that chant no doubt was for the players, it might also have been wearing. In a way, the crowd held the whip-hand over the team with their passion, and they did not relent, they never let up. Can the team play at that level of energy in a second year? A third?

We will wonder, too, if management will do anything in the off-season to improve the team. They played hard, they gave it their all, they entertained and they made it close. Close—but as the old saw has it, no cigar. Will management have the courage of conviction to make the moves needed to improve the team? Or will they play "wait-and-see," relying on the progress of draft choices and the seasoning of promising minor-leaguers in the AHL to strengthen the squad? And if they take the "stand-pat" line, how far into season number two will fans be prepared to go along with this conservative ploy?

A second full season, is my guess. We will still be counting our blessings that we have a team at all; we will remain enamoured of the star players and effusive about those who try hard, putting in the blue-collar effort we so prize in our city. We will cherish the jerseys and treasure the tickets. We will be prepared to dream again, to fill the arena, to dance with Gabe, to shout Go Jets Go!

We're Winnipeggers—we'll be back.

7 April 2012 Final Standings

Team	SP	PTS
New York R	82	109
Pittsburgh	82	108
Philadelphia	82	103
Boston	82	102
New Jersey	82	102
Florida	82	94
Ottawa	82	92
Washington	82	92
Buffalo	82	89
Tampa Bay	82	84
Winnipeg	82	83
Carolina	82	82
Toronto	82	80
New York I	82	79
Montreal	82	78

Acknowledgements

The unidentified quotations are by: S.T. Coleridge (43); Robert Kroetsch (58); Jeanette Winterson (68); F. Scott Fitzgerald (99); W.B. Yeats (101); Ralph Waldo Emerson (130); Arthur Schopenhauer (133); Friedrich Nietzsche (146); Ernest Hemingway (186); Robert Browning (198); Walt Whitman (208); Walt Whitman (214); William Wordsworth (231); William Blake (263); Lance Armstrong (277).

Quotations from players, coaches, and commentators have been reproduced with as much accuracy as humanly possible from TSN, CBC, the *Winnipeg Free Press*, *The Winnipeg Sun*, *The Globe and Mail*, and the *National Post*.

Thanks to Jamis Paulson and Sharon Caseburg at Turnstone for their enthusiasm and commitment to this project, written on the fly and completed under some duress.

Thanks also to all the people cited in the book for generously allowing me to use their names. Many more, whose actual names do not appear, easily could have. I owe all my hockey pals and associates over many decades a great debt for what they have taught me about the game—and about life.

Without the daily support and encouragement of my wife, Kristen, and son, Andrew, this book could not have been written.

And many thanks to Darin Amies, who knows why.